Recovery Resilience Program Facilitator's Guide

A manual for those working with addicted populations (from lay counsellors to psychiatrists) for delivering the evidence-based Recovery Resilience Program (RRP). The RRP is a person-centered, strength and resiliency-based relapse prevention and recovery-oriented intervention that works in synergy with other models, especially 12-step programs. It presents practices that enhance "recovery resilience" – an individual's capacity to effectively apply coping and self-regulation skills in dealing with cravings, triggers, stress, and high-risk situations without reverting to substance use. The program helps individuals to enhance and use their recovery capital at any stage of recovery, and ultimately reach recovery and life goals. It effortlessly integrates with other evidence-based relapse programs, from the original cognitive-behavioral approaches to the newer mindfulness-based and metacognitive approaches. Written by clinicians who have worked with addicts and their families for many decades, the program is easy to implement and very little preparation is necessary, with handouts and PowerPoints included in each session.

Guy du Plessis (1972–2025) was a researcher and instructor at the I-System Institute for Transdisciplinary Studies, Utah State University, and adjunct professor at the Institute for Advanced Psychotherapy, Loyola University Chicago. He studied psychology at the University of South Africa and philosophy at the University of Cape Town and certified in psychodynamic psychotherapy. He worked for over 25 years as an addiction treatment provider and academic researcher. He is the author and co-author of 7 books, two of which are published by Cambridge University Press, also published in several journals and edited volumes, including *'International Journal of Applied Philosophy'* and *'Addiction,'* his research aimed at applying various philosophical perspectives to addiction studies, with the aim of integrating life-affirming philosophical outlooks into existing recovery-oriented interventions, and highlighting life-negating views that are obstructions to recovery and the good life.

Derrik R. Tollefson is the Mind–Body Bridging Professor of Social Work and director of the I-System Institute at Utah State University. He holds a PhD in social work from the University of Utah and is a licensed clinical social worker in Utah.

Robert Weathers is an addiction educator and certified recovery coach and holds a PhD in clinical psychology. Over the course of his career, he has provided thousands of hours of therapeutic counseling to clients and has committed nearly 50 years to training graduate-level clinicians at several Southern California universities.

Kevin G. Webb is a licensed clinical social worker and an Assistant Professional Practice Professor and Associate Director of the I-System Institute for Transdisciplinary Studies at Utah State University.

Recovery Resilience Program Facilitator's Guide

An I-System Model Application for Addiction Recovery and Relapse Prevention

Guy du Plessis
Utah State University, Logan

Derrik R. Tollefson
Utah State University, Logan

Robert Weathers
Addictions Recovery Coach, California

Kevin G. Webb
Utah State University, Logan

CAMBRIDGE
UNIVERSITY PRESS

CAMBRIDGE
UNIVERSITY PRESS

Shaftesbury Road, Cambridge CB2 8EA, United Kingdom

One Liberty Plaza, 20th Floor, New York, NY 10006, USA

477 Williamstown Road, Port Melbourne, VIC 3207, Australia

314–321, 3rd Floor, Plot 3, Splendor Forum, Jasola District Centre, New Delhi – 110025, India

Cambridge University Press is part of Cambridge University Press & Assessment, a department of the University of Cambridge.

We share the University's mission to contribute to society through the pursuit of education, learning and research at the highest international levels of excellence.

www.cambridge.org
Information on this title: www.cambridge.org/9781009378741

DOI: 10.1017/9781009378734

When citing this work, please include a reference to the DOI 10.1017/9781009378734

First published 2026

Cover image: Stone hiking trail on Pico de Arieiro at sunrise (Madeira Island)
borchee / E+ / Getty Images

A catalogue record for this publication is available from the British Library

A Cataloging-in-Publication data record for this book is available from the Library of Congress

ISBN 978-1-009-37874-1 Paperback

To Guy Du Plessis (1972–2025) –
A brilliant colleague and deeply missed friend.

Contents

Preface

For individuals in an addiction recovery process, relapse is an ever-looming possibility (Marlatt, 1985a; Gire, 2002; West, 2005; Ahmed & Pickards, 2019 ; West et al., 2019a). Individuals working on so profound a behavior change as sustained recovery from addiction are confronted again and again with powerful cravings and compulsive thoughts regarding the behaviors they are attempting to change (Brewer, 2017). It is crucial to understand here that, though these addictive behaviors are indeed counterproductive in the long term, they at one point served as highly effective, and even understandable, short-term behavioral coping strategies, for example, reducing acute and/or chronic distress (Lewis, 2015; Winhall, 2021).

Considering this, it should be no surprise that research has revealed a direct correlation between relapse to substance use after rehabilitation and deficits in skills for coping effectively with challenging and stressful situations (Brewer et al., 1998; Irvin et al., 1999; Fleury et al., 2016; Beaulieu et al., 2021). In other words, without effective alternatives to reducing distress, individuals are virtually guaranteed to return to their previous strategies, despite the longer-term negative consequences of the latter. Put simply, in the absence of adequate coping skills, addicted individuals will turn to psychoactive substances as a coping mechanism insofar as alcohol or other drugs, again, provide immediate and quite effective short-term stress relief and comfort. Researchers and experienced clinicians both conclude that one of the primary reasons psychoactive substances remain an appealing option, even for the individual sincerely seeking recovery from them, is owing to the immediate relief these substances provide (West, 2005; Lewis, 2015; Winhall, 2021; Heaton et al., 2023). In short, for many individuals suffering from addictive behaviors, substance use has become their predominant response to coping with life's challenges (Litt et al., 2003; Maté, 2011).

Therefore, a key component in preventing relapse requires that the recovering individual learn and repeatedly practice new skills for coping with both anticipated and potentially unforeseen challenges. Clinical research indicates that employing reliably accessible and effective coping skills is a crucial predictor for successful and sustained recovery from substance use disorders (Marlatt, 1985b, 1988; Witkiewitz & Marlatt, 2007; Heaton et al., 2023). For this very important reason, relapse prevention books or programs must focus on teaching such coping skills (e.g., Bowen et al., 2021).

As implied above, simply becoming acquainted with these coping skills, that is, conceptual understanding, does in no way guarantee sustained recovery. One also needs to repeatedly practice these skills by means of what many professionals and paraprofessionals in the recovery world call, for simplicity's sake, working one's personal *recovery program*. The gap between cognitive understanding and behavioral implementation is evidenced, at least indirectly, by the observation that addiction treatment and relapse prevention programs continue to have high rates of relapse, despite many individuals in treatment having been exposed to a plethora of skills, along with their often-high levels of intrinsic motivation for successful recovery (Xie et al., 2005; Fleury et al., 2016; Beaulieu et al., 2021).

One, central focus of this *Recovery Resilience Program Facilitator's Guide* is to highlight that there is a psychological process that can significantly *hinder* individuals in recovery from *effectively applying* their acquired skills and recovery programs (Block et al., 2016; Ho & Nakamura, 2017; Du Plessis et al., 2021, 2024). The American vernacular expression pertains here: "They've got a hitch in their get-along." That is to say, something continues to undermine even the most well-intended individuals' capacity to stay sober. The *Recovery Resilience Program* outlined in this manual teaches clients how to first recognize this "hitch," or *hindrance*, by presenting clear and concrete practices, which if put into action with consistent effort, aid that individual in learning to reduce the adverse effects of such hindrances, thus enabling them to more optimally apply the entire range of recovery-oriented skills and tools they have at their disposal.

Aim of the Program

The Recovery Resilience Program is informed by Mind-Body Bridging (MBB), a psychological intervention derived from the I-System Model, which was developed by psychoanalyst and psychiatrist Stanley H. Block, and his wife and collaborator, Carolyn Bryant Block (Block, 1987; Block & Block, 2002, 2007; Block et al., 2020). MBB has successfully been used in the treatment of several mood and behavioral disorders and has been recognized as evidence-based for the treatment of addiction (Nakamura et al., 2015; Block et al., 2016; Block & Du Plessis, 2018).

The I-System Model is guided by the premise that we all possess an innate capacity for resilience, well-being, and flourishing.[1] Psychodynamic therapists Jack Danielian and Patricia Giannotti (2017, p. 3) in their book, *Uncovering the Resilient Core*, note: "From the very beginning of life, the mind (like the body) is in a continuing process of working to actualize itself. The process is inherent." Yet, the I-System Model highlights that there is a psychological process that can often obstruct and hinder this innate resilience and our natural capacity for flourishing. The practices outlined in this program focus primarily on teaching clients how to identify and manage such hindrance as it manifests in their activities of daily living. Clinical experience highlights that, by identifying and managing this hindrance, which we refer to as "befriending" it, clients can access their innate resilience (Nakamura et al., 2015). This increases their ability to apply coping skills, work a recovery program, and live the "good life."[2]

The *Recovery Resilience Program* presented in this manual is informed by a specific view of addiction. There is a diverse range of views and definitions of addiction, but most addiction specialists and researchers agree on some key features (West, 2005; Du Plessis, 2018, 2023; Pickard & Ahmed, 2019; West et al., 2019a, 2019b).[3] While our definition of addiction is indeed consistent, in most ways, with conventional perspectives in the field, we do stress one distinctive feature, one that has particular relevance to the program outlined in this manual.[4] We define addiction fundamentally as a *disposition* to use psychoactive substances that is characterized by

1 For a further discussion of flourishing, see Diener et al. (2010) and VanderWeele (2017).

2 We view the good life from a similar perspective as Aristotle's notion of *eudaimonia*, which he thought to be an excellent, flourishing, and happy life. See Kenny (1978).

3 How a society views and understands addiction has great significance for addicted individuals seeking treatment. Although our explanation of addiction has become more sophisticated, there are still serious shortcomings in our understanding of it (see West et al., 2019a, 2019b, 2024; Du Plessis, 2023).

4 See Pickard & Ahmed (2019).

impaired control and harm.[5] Thus, the definition of addiction we apply in this manual views it from a dispositional perspective – having to do with proneness or tendency to engage in certain predictable behaviors that are typically context-dependent (e.g., in the presence of increased stress, triggers, or high-risk situations). Addict researcher and pioneer in the field of addiction studies, Robert West and colleagues define "disposition" in the context of cravings as "a latent characteristic that becomes expressed under certain conditions" (West et al., 2019a, p. 168). This dispositional perspective highlights that individuals can vary in degrees of effective self-control depending on the immediate context or situation.[6] Accordingly, the Recovery Resilience Program incorporates a resiliency-focused and strength-based approach and highlights that individuals in recovery can have the capacity to *influence* this *disposition*, either (1) by having trained awareness of factors that can make this disposition (toward addictive behaviors) more likely, or (2) by having access to resources, support, and practices that can make this disposition less likely to be acted upon. In summary, the Recovery Resilience Program can be understood as a person-centered, strength-based, and resiliency-focused relapse prevention and recovery-oriented intervention, as it emphasizes an individual's inherent strengths, and encourages those in recovery to view themselves as capable of resilience in the face of adversity.[7]

The program outlined in this manual will assist clients in developing a *Recovery Resilience Practice* that will facilitate their addiction recovery process by enhancing their capacity to effectively work a recovery and relapse prevention program. The practices presented in this manual enhance "*recovery resilience*" – a term we coined to refer to an individual's capacity to effectively apply coping and self-regulation skills in dealing with cravings, triggers, stress, and high-risk situations without reverting to substance use (Du Plessis et al., 2024).

The concept of *recovery resilience* is framed within the context of *recovery capital*, a phrase used in recovery communities to refer to the sum of all

5 The notion of disposition is a central construct in Basic Formal Ontology (BFO); see Smith & Ceusters (2010) and Arp et al. (2015).

6 See West et al. (2019a, 2024) that highlight the notion of disposition as part of a comprehensive understanding of addiction.

7 With its foundation in social work, the strengths-based approach focuses on an individual's self-determination and strength. See Hill (2008).

internal and external resources that a person has available to initiate and maintain their ongoing recovery process (Cloud & Granfield, 2004). William White defines recovery capital as "conceptually linked to natural recovery, solution-focused therapy, strengths-based case management, recovery management, resilience and protective factors, and the ideas of hardiness, wellness, and global health" (White & Cloud, 2008, p. 23). The notion of recovery capital reflects a move away from the typical emphasis on pathology and/or pathologizing towards a resilience- and strengths-based approach to addiction recovery. The Recovery Resilience Program is designed to be aligned with this more positively oriented, strengths-based approach to addiction recovery interventions and treatment. White defines three types of recovery capital: personal recovery capital – which includes an individual's physical and human capital; family/social recovery capital – these resources relate to intimate relationships with friends and family, relationships with people in recovery, and supportive partners; and cultural capital – these resources resonate with individuals' cultural and faith-based beliefs (Foote et al., 2014; White & Cloud, 2008).[8]

The construct of recovery capital is central within *recovery-oriented* approaches to treating substance use disorders and situated within the larger framework of *recovery-oriented systems of care* (ROSC). All these approaches value community-based services and supports that are person-centered and build on the strengths and resiliencies of individuals, families, and communities to help addicted individuals achieve abstinence and improved health, wellness, and quality of life. The Recovery Resilience Program is intentionally designed to methodologically and theoretically work in synergy within the frameworks of recovery-oriented interventions and ROSC by framing itself as supporting these interventions and support systems, as well as, and importantly, peer-support communities, especially 12-step communities. The manual works from the assumption that the reader has experience in delivering recovery-oriented interventions, and 12-step programs, as well as being familiar with the clinical jargon of those approaches. For this reason, we have avoided providing explanations for recovery-oriented terminology, which would make it cumbersome to read and follow the instructions, especially since our aim is simplicity and ease of use, and that it is specifically

8 A significant component of strengthening personal recovery capital is in developing psychological flexibility. See Kashdan & Rottenberg (2010).

designed to function within and support recovery-oriented interventions and all accompanying support systems. Moreover, this program is not conducive to harm reduction approaches or programs that are not situated with ROSC, as our program is strengths- and resilience-based only insofar as it is situated within well-established support systems.[9]

In short, a Recovery Resilience Practice aims to strengthen a client's internal resources, by removing what hinders their capacity to draw upon or use all aspects of their recovery capital, which will help prevent relapse and promote long-term recovery and flourishing.

How to Use the Manual

The Recovery Resilience Program outlined in this manual is designed to serve as an adjunct to relapse prevention programs and the recovery-oriented practices of individuals in addiction recovery. It is ideally suited for individuals who have undergone initial inpatient or intensive outpatient treatment and continue to be highly motivated for sustained recovery post treatment. Additionally, our Recovery Resilience Program may also serve as a helpful adjunct to harm reduction programs that work in synergy with recovery-oriented interventions, yet it must be noted that this program has not yet been applied in harm reduction settings.[10]

The Recovery Resilience Practice that clients will develop by completing this program is not meant to replace any of their existing recovery practices but instead is designed to positively augment their unique recovery pathway and help them access their recovery capital. A Recovery Resilience Practice is compatible with most recovery pathways, and its compatibility with 12-step resources is emphasized, as many clients will already be engaged in a 12-step fellowship and/or be participating in a 12-step-oriented treatment program.[11] In short, a Recovery Resilience Practice is designed to support and enhance a

9 See Du Plessis (2019a) for a philosophical analysis of conceptual challenges in harm reduction approaches.

10 For a discussion on harm reduction approaches see Marlatt & Witkiewitz (2002).

11 See Kelly et al. (2020) for the results of a Cochrane review related to the efficacy of 12-step programs.

client's existing recovery practices and support systems, as well as the interventions typically presented in recovery-oriented treatment programs. The manual is specifically designed for ease of use and implementation, especially within inpatient or outpatient programs. Very little preparation is needed, as PowerPoint presentations for each session, as well as printable pdf files that contain all client exercise templates, can be downloaded from the book's page on the Cambridge University Press website (www.cambridge.org/9781009378741). (In the Appendix we provide client exercise templates which may be photocopied.) This program is designed to seamlessly integrate into treatment environments, as the authors of this manual have many decades of experience working "in the trenches" of inpatient and outpatient programs – and are well aware of the heavy client load addiction treatment professionals often have and the limited time they typically have available for group and lecture preparation.

This manual outlines six sessions that facilitators may present in an individual or group setting. The manual provides clients with a structured approach to learning practices that can be completed within a concentrated timeframe; we recommend a minimum of 3–4 weeks. Together, these practices, when practiced regularly, constitute a personal Recovery Resilience Practice. Each session in the manual serves as a building block for the next, introducing a sequence of exercises that teach, through direct experience, aspects of a Recovery Resilience Practice as well as providing the underlying rationale for each of these practices.

There are two scales at the end of each session, the Flourishing Scale (Diener et al., 2010) and the Recovery Resilience Practice Scale, to help both clients and facilitators monitor and document their Recovery Resilience Practice development and improvement, including their self-identified experience of enhanced subjective well-being and flourishing.[12]

It is important to note that the sample dialogue provided and instructions are suggestive only. Facilitators are not required to present material verbatim or follow instructions exactly. We encourage facilitators to present material and exercises based on the needs of the client or group and to present the material at a level that is conducive to the client's or group's understanding

12 See Diener et al. (2010).

and stage of recovery. The program is scalable and can be adapted to a client's or group's specific needs.

Considering that the Recovery Program is an adjunct intervention designed to support existing recovery-oriented interventions and a client's existing recovery practice, this manual does not aim for comprehensiveness regarding relapse prevention or recovery suggestions. Although its primary focus is relapse prevention, it is not designed to be a self-contained relapse prevention program or addict treatment approach, and it is essential that it is presented as part of a comprehensive relapse-prevention program – and should in no way be seen as a replacement to well-researched relapse prevention practices. It is up to the discretion of the clinician in what capacity they want to incorporate it into a client's recovery program. Hence the aim here is not to present all the practices typically associated with relapse prevention, but instead to articulate how a Recovery Resilience Practice might usefully *augment* other existing practices.

In short, we believe the approach outlined in the manual will serve clinicians well in providing an *additional perspective* and *practices* to those they already may be implementing.

Outline of the Manual

The manual is comprised of two main sections. The first, in the Introduction chapter, provides theoretical background, and the second outlines the six sessions of the Recovery Resilience Program. The Introduction chapter has two parts. In the first part, we provide a brief overview of relapse prevention theory and practice. A major objective of any relapse prevention program is to assist clients in *developing effective strategies* for managing high-risk situations, cravings, and difficult emotions (Heaton et al., 2023). We conclude this part by highlighting some common *strategies* used in relapse prevention.[13] The aim here is to provide a background context for the manual in terms of how a Recovery Resilience Practice can helpfully augment other, commonly

13 See Marlatt & Donovan (2005) for a more comprehensive discussion.

utilized relapse prevention strategies. The discussion is merely introductory, and it is beyond the scope of the manual to be comprehensive. Considering that the Recovery Resilience Program is an adjunct to relapse prevention programs we assume that facilitators of this program already have familiarity and experience in presenting comprehensive relapse prevention programs.

While there are a wide variety of relapse prevention programs currently available, we will primarily focus on 'relapse prevention' as originally articulated by Alan Marlatt's pioneering theoretical work, and the cognitive-behavioral intervention strategies inherent to his model (Marlatt & George, 1984; Marlatt & Gordon, 1985; Marlatt & Donovan, 2005; Marlatt & Witkiewitz, 2005; Liese & Beck, 2022; Daley & Marlatt, 2006; Bowen et al., 2021). We acknowledge that several of the constructs we apply are derived from Marlatt's original articulation of relapse prevention. We will clarify how the Recovery Resilience Program expands beyond this cognitive-behavioral approach and how it works complementarily within a cognitive-behavioral framework (Marlatt & Witkiewitz, 2005), as well as third-wave cognitive behavioral approaches to relapse prevention (Fletcher & Hayes, 2005; Bowen et al., 2021).

Following the discussion on relapse prevention theory and practice, we provide a brief introduction and overview of the *I-System Model* and *Mind-Body Bridging*, which is the theory and methodology from which the Recovery Resilience Program is derived (Block & Block, 2007; Block et al., 2020; Nakamura et al., 2015; Du Plessis et al., 2024). Here the aim is not to provide a comprehensive articulation of theory, but only what is relevant for the program outlined in this manual. We conclude this part by highlighting how a Recovery Resilience Practice can *enhance* the common *strategies* used in relapse prevention, as discussed in the first part. This is in line with the focus of the Recovery Resilience Program which serves as an *adjunct* to existing recovery practices and *enhances recovery resilience* or simply put, enhances the capacity to effectively draw on recovery capital.

While we aim for academic rigor and clarity this manual is not intended as a theoretical or academic text and instead attempts to convey all theory and practices presented in such a way that they might be optimally accessible to psychologists, social workers, and addiction counsellors. Therefore, we aim to maintain a balance between adequately articulating the theory in a clinically accurate and relevant way and presenting the methodology in accessible language, avoiding unnecessary jargon whenever possible. For this reason, some readers may believe that some aspects of addiction and its treatment, as well as relapse prevention theory, are presented in an oversimplified or even uncritical way. And they might be justified in this view if that was our chief aim here. Instead, however, we own up to it being beyond the scope of the current, primarily clinical manual to engage in more complex, conceptual debates. Because we aim to keep this manual user-friendly for purposes of clinical utility some complex issues are necessarily presented in simple and direct ways using language that is familiar to addiction treatment providers.

Finally, this manual is designed to be self-standing with all the necessary client handouts and can be used as a companion clinical manual to the *Building Recovery Resilience*: *Addiction Recovery and Relapse Prevention Workbook*, also published by Cambridge University Press (Du Plessis et al., 2024). For this reason, the exercises and accompanying templates, as well as the numbering thereof, are the same in both the workbook and clinical manual. If used as a companion manual clients can complete all exercises in the workbook.

In summary, the Recovery Resilience Program helps individuals enhance and use their recovery capital at any stage of recovery, and ultimately reach their recovery and life goals. It effortlessly integrates with other evidence-based relapse programs, from the original cognitive-behavioral approaches to the newer mindfulness-based and metacognitive approaches. Written by clinicians who have worked with addicts and their families for many decades, the program is easy to implement, requiring very little preparation. This manual, like the program it presents, aims to lighten the load for both client and treatment professional.

Acknowledgments

The authors would like to acknowledge and express their gratitude to Dr. Stanley H. Block and Carolyn Bryant Block, the developers of the I-System Model and Mind–Body Bridging, for their input in the writing and conceptualization of this manual.

Introduction

1 A Brief Overview of Relapse Prevention Theory and Practice

Introduction

In the following section we provide a very brief discussion of relapse prevention. Our aim here is not to be comprehensive but merely provide a context for the program outlined in the manual. We also do not aim to provide the most updated views and techniques of relapse prevention, but to highlight the basic elements of the cognitive-behavioral approach to relapse prevention.[1]

Individuals suffering from substance use disorders (SUDs) are at risk of relapsing after ceasing alcohol or drug use, even following a successful treatment episode (Kabisa et al., 2021). This can often lead to a prolonged cycle of relapse, or re-entering treatment, and recovery. Consequently, there is a focus on clinical strategies aimed at reducing relapse likelihood and managing relapses effectively to minimize negative impacts in cases where individuals return to substance use post recovery (Daley & Marlatt, 2006; Bowen et al., 2021; Mhaidat et al., 2023).

The term "relapse prevention" (RP) emerged in the late 1970s, defining a theoretical model and encompassing various cognitive-behavioral intervention strategies. These strategies were designed to prevent the transition from a lapse to a full relapse in individuals with alcohol dependence (Marlatt &

1 For a more comprehensive discussion see Marlatt & Witkiewitz (2005), Witkiewitz & Marlatt (2007), and Bowen et al. (2021).

George, 1984; Marlatt & Gordon, 1985). Alan Marlatt and his team formulated this model based on research identifying triggers for alcohol lapses after behavioral interventions (Chaney et al., 1978; Marlatt & George, 1984; Marlatt & Gordon, 1985).

The primary objective of RP is to tackle the issue of relapse and to develop methods for either preventing its occurrence or managing it effectively. RP, grounded in cognitive-behavioral principles, aims to pinpoint high-risk scenarios where an individual is susceptible to relapsing, and to employ cognitive and behavioral coping techniques to avert future relapses under similar circumstances. RP can be described as a tertiary prevention strategy with two key goals: (1) to avert an initial lapse and sustain either abstinence or the objectives of harm reduction treatments, and (2) to manage lapses, should they occur, in a way that prevents a further relapse. The overarching aim is to equip individuals with the necessary skills to forestall a full relapse, irrespective of the circumstances or potential risk factors involved (Marlatt & Donovan, 2005; Marlatt & Witkiewitz, 2005; Liese & Beck, 2022; Daley & Marlatt, 2006; Bowen et al., 2021).

RP integrates cognitive intervention techniques with behavioral skills training to help individuals maintain behavioral changes. RP strategies are often integrated into individual and group treatments. Additionally, RP programs are part of various treatment settings, including rehabilitation, partial hospitalization, intensive outpatient programs, and aim to teach clients coping skills and early intervention techniques for lapses or relapses. Research and reviews have demonstrated RP's effectiveness in enhancing recovery and reducing relapse rates (Yazıcı & Bardakçı, 2023).

Lapse and Relapse

The definition of relapse in the context of Substance Use Disorders (SUDs) remains a contentious issue. Einstein (1994) highlights the ambiguity in defining the point at which a return to substance use constitutes a relapse and the implications this definition has for coping, adaptation, and treatment. Over the years, various definitions and interpretations of relapse have been proposed (Litman et al., 1983; Miller et al., 1996; Marlatt & Witkiewitz, 2002; Moe et al., 2022; Mellinger et al., 2024). Marlatt differentiates between a lapse, described as the initial instance of substance use after a period of abstinence, and relapse, which he defines as continued use following the initial lapse and a setback in changing a target behavior (Marlatt & Gordon, 1985).

Studies suggest that a lapse doesn't always lead to a full relapse, as seen in opiate users (Gossop et al., 1989). Milby et al. (2004) found in cocaine users that those in treatment with added abstinence-contingent housing and work were less likely to relapse chronically after an acute lapse. This suggests that a lapse can be a critical juncture: Is the acute return to substance use interrupted before it devolves into a more full-blown, or chronic, relapse?

Given the variation in relapse rates depending on the definition used and the complexity of understanding relapse, it's clear that relapse is better conceptualized as both an outcome and a process involving prior events and predictors interfering with behavior change. Thus, a dynamic assessment model capturing the nuances of relapse over time is advocated (Daley & Marlatt, 2006; Bowen et al., 2021). Identifying and addressing both immediate and distal variables is crucial in preventing a lapse from escalating into a full relapse (Miller, 1996).

Examples of immediate variables affecting vulnerability to an acute lapse include internal and environmental triggers. The former, internal triggers might include: post-traumatic anxiety and/or depression, feelings of personal shame, and/or perceptions of hopelessness. The latter, environmental triggers might include: interpersonal conflict, work-related stress, and/or financial pressures. Examples of distal variables include the implementation, or relative lack thereof, of healthful lifestyle changes in support of physical and psychological well-being. Such recovery-oriented practices may be seen to provide important resources for sustained, successful sobriety. They might include: physical exercise; wholesome diet; adequate sleep; stimulating reading; rewarding social interaction; creative self-expression (e.g., in art or music); and prayer or meditation. A relative lack of such practice-based resources may be seen as distal variables negatively impacting sustained recovery (Daley & Marlatt, 2006; Bowen et al., 2021).

While longitudinal studies consistently show that substance abuse treatment significantly reduces substance use, research also indicates that relapse and subsequent readmission are common after treatment discharge, particularly in cases where addiction coexists with psychiatric disorders (Andreu et al.,

2024). Furthermore, the presence of co-occurring psychiatric disorders is associated with heightened substance use severity, the need for more intensive care, reduced participation in treatment, and poorer outcomes (Grella, 2003). A significant portion of relapses occur within the first year of treatment, with the majority happening within the initial 90 days. However, the risk of relapse remains, even after extended periods of abstinence (Daley & Marlatt, 2006; Bowen et al., 2021).

Studies have shown that individuals undergoing addiction recovery often follow diverse paths, including community use of substances; active treatment; committed abstinence; incarceration owing to substance-related offenses; and in some cases, severe illness or death as a function of substance use (Hser et al., 2001). It appears that undergoing multiple care episodes over several years is a common pattern (Dennis et al., 2005), and that these episodes may cumulatively contribute to the recovery process (Hser et al., 1997). Scott et al. (2005) emphasize the need for a deeper understanding of the factors influencing transitions in the recovery cycle. These approaches involve re-evaluating the chronic and cyclical nature of addiction and considering long-term recovery management models to potentially shorten the recovery cycle. They also entail redefining relapse not as a failure but as an expectable part of the overall treatment process. Related here, individuals who remain in treatment for longer durations have been shown to consistently experience better outcomes (Fleury et al., 2016; Beaulieu et al., 2021).

Determinants of Relapse

Next, we delve into the determinants of relapse through the lens of the Marlatt cognitive-behavioral therapy model for relapse (Daley & Marlatt, 2006; Bowen et al., 2021). Marlatt's cognitive-behavioral relapse model fundamentally hinges on identifying high-risk situations, defined as any circumstance or thought that elevates the risk of re-engaging in substance use, whether in an acute lapse or more chronic relapse (Marlatt & Donovan, 2005; Marlatt & Witkiewitz, 2005; Daley & Marlatt, 2006; Bowen et al., 2021). Marlatt and his colleagues developed a taxonomy for categorizing relapse episodes, featuring three hierarchical levels (Marlatt, 1996a, 1996b).

The first tier of Marlatt and colleagues' relapse taxonomy (Marlatt, 1996a, 1996b; Witkiewitz & Marlatt, 2007) differentiates between internal (intrapersonal) and external (interpersonal/environmental) triggers for relapse. The second tier categorizes these into eight subgroups: five intrapersonal – managing negative emotional states, coping with negative physical-psychological conditions, enhancing positive emotional states, testing self-control, and succumbing to temptations and impulses; and three interpersonal/environmental – handling interpersonal conflict, navigating social pressure, and boosting positive emotional states. The third tier offers a finer analysis of five out of the eight second-level categories, for instance, dividing coping with negative emotional states into managing frustration/anger and other negative emotions (Marlatt & Donovan, 2005).

Since its initial introduction, various critiques (Edwards, 1987; Donovan, 1996; Kadden, 1996; Maisto et al., 1996) have been directed at this classification system, and its usage by clinicians has not always aligned with its original design. Nonetheless, the identification of inter- and intrapersonal relapse determinants within this taxonomy has been proven both reliable and clinically valuable (Zywiak et al., 1996; Larimer et al., 1999). Moreover, twenty years after its initial conceptualization Marlatt and colleagues (see Marlatt & Witkiewitz, 2005) reconceptualized the relapse process and describe a dynamic model where they view the determinants of relapse as multidimensional and dynamic, which highlights the complexity (often unpredictable and chaotic) of the relapse process.[2] They highlight that in every scenario, a person must navigate the complexity of weighing various cues and potential outcomes. The individual response can be understood as a self-organizing system, which integrates distal risk factors (such as duration of dependence, familial background, social networks, and concurrent psychological conditions), cognitive processes (e.g., self-efficacy, outcome expectancies, craving, motivation), and cognitive and behavioral coping skills. It is beyond the scope of this introductory section to articulate this in more detail (see Daley & Marlatt, 2006; Bowen et al., 2021).

Next, we provide a summary highlighting various factors, intrapersonal and interpersonal, and their impact on relapse as understood in this cognitive-behavioral framework.[3]

2 Nonlinear dynamical systems, such as models based on chaos and/or catastrophe theory, have been used in the prediction and explanation of substance abuse (see Ehlers, 1992; Warren et al., 2003).

3 See Marlatt & Donovan (2005) for a more comprehensive discussion.

Negative Emotional States

Marlatt & Gordon (1985) identified negative affect as a significant predictor of relapse. Different emotional states such as anxiety, depression, and anger contribute variably to relapse, but the ability to regulate these emotions is crucial (Baker et al., 2003). Moos & Moos (2005) found that high emotional arousal, particularly that which is perceived as negative or unpleasant, during early recovery can be especially counterproductive to maintaining sobriety.

Positive Emotional States

Earlier research underestimated the role of positive emotions in relapse. Studies now show that positive emotions, especially in social contexts, can relate to relapse (Clarke et al., 2020).

Coping

Effective coping skills are essential in high-risk situations to prevent relapse. Active coping strategies are more effective than avoidant ones (Maisto et al., 2006). For example, proactive stress inoculation by means of mindfulness or other similar strategies has been shown to reduce relapse risk more effectively than ignoring bona fide internal or external stressors (Witkiewitz et al., 2005).

Motivation

Motivation could relate to the relapse process in two distinct ways, the motivation for positive behavior change and the motivation to engage in the problematic behavior. The ambivalence toward change is often highly related to both self-efficacy and outcome expectancies (Marlatt & Witkiewitz, 2005).

Outcome Expectancies

Expectations of substance effects play a significant role in substance use and relapse (Wiers et al., 2002). Both negative and positive expectancies influence relapse. To further clarify, negative expectancies predict an unpleasant or counterproductive outcome of substance abuse. Whereas positive expectancies focus on pleasant outcomes, if primarily in the short term. Thus, negative expectancies operate as protective factors against substance use and relapse, while positive expectancies increase risk of substance use and relapse (Gwaltney et al., 2005).

Self-Efficacy

Belief in one's ability to control substance use is a reliable predictor of outcomes post treatment (Moos & Moos, 2006). Brown et al. (2002) demonstrated that increased self-efficacy following RP intervention relates to improved outcomes.

Craving

The role of craving in relapse is complex and not fully understood, with mixed findings in research. Patients, clinicians, and researchers often describe craving as a formidable adversary in the recovery and persistence of addictive disorders. Mindfulness and acceptance techniques are emerging as effective strategies to manage cravings (Witkiewitz et al., 2005; Carroll & Lustyk, 2018).[4]

Interpersonal Precipitants

Interpersonal processes and social support play a significant role in relapse, with both positive and negative aspects influencing outcomes (Witkiewitz & Marlatt, 2007). Conjoint treatments involving significant others show strong empirical support (Douaihy et al., 2007).

Relapse Prevention Strategies

The approach a therapist takes in RP interventions is shaped by the specific characteristics and challenges of each client. Various techniques are tailored

4 See Bowen et al. (2021) and Witkiewitz et al. (2013a).

to distinct problems, but some key elements of RP are universally applicable. RP is informed on the biopsychosocial model which recognizes that behavior is influenced by a blend of biological (genetic, cellular, neuronal, physiological), psychological (cognitive processes, learning history, and affect self-regulation), and social (interpersonal relationships, social support, economic/vocational viability) factors (Bowen et al., 2021).[5]

The primary aim in RP is to pinpoint and discuss situations posing a high risk for lapses and relapses. This often involves educating clients about the process of lapsing and reviewing past episodes (Kargin & Hicdurmaz, 2020). The therapist and client work together to identify potential triggers, assessing whether these are emotional, social, or physical in nature. While some clients may readily recognize their triggers and high-risk situations, others may need more intensive discussions to uncover these triggers (Bowen et al., 2021).

Once high-risk situations are identified, it is crucial to analyze each one in concrete, specific detail, focusing on the associated triggers and possible coping strategies. Clients are taught to understand cravings as a strong desire to use substances and urges as the intention to use them. It's common for clients to experience strong cravings without the intention to use, or both cravings and a strong intention to use, which increases the risk of relapse (Bowen et al., 2014). Awareness of situations that trigger cravings and learning to cope effectively can significantly lower relapse risk (Bowen et al., 2021). Recognizing and validating the client's experiences and acknowledging that substance use is often a temporary coping mechanism for challenging emotions or situations are also vital (Melemis, 2015). A major objective of RP is to *develop effective strategies* for managing high-risk situations, cravings, and difficult emotions (Heaton et al., 2023).

Next, we will highlight some common *strategies* used in relapse prevention.[6] The aim of RP is *assisting clients in developing these strategies* in preventing relapse. It must be noted that this is not an exhaustive list of RP strategies.[7]

5 It must be noted that although the biopsychosocial model is a useful heuristic, there are still considerable positivistic, ontological, and epistemological underpinnings and assumptions, namely, the abstractionist use of decontextualism, reductionism, and determinism, which hinder an authentic and comprehensive conceptual framework (see Du Plessis, 2023).

6 See Marlatt & Donovan (2005) for a more comprehensive discussion.

7 The following discussion is based on the strategies highlighted by Douaihy et al. (2007) and informed by Bowen et al. (2021).

Comprehend Relapse as a Process and Identify Early Warning Signs

Educating clients about addiction as a cyclical condition involving numerous transitions between relapse and recovery is crucial (Gorski, 2009; Melemis, 2015). This perspective allows clients to view relapse not just as an event but as a process that unfolds in a specific context, with early warning signs often preceding a lapse or relapse. Changes in attitudes, emotions, cognition, and behavior can gradually emerge days or even weeks before the resumption of substance use (Bowen et al., 2021).

Warning signs, which can range from subtle and more internal to overt and more externally observable, act as links in a "relapse chain" (Daley & Marlatt, 2006). Such signs may include behavioral changes such as increased dishonesty, decreased community involvement, heightened irritability, and actions undermining recovery. Additional, overt signs may be a reduced engagement in treatment or self-help groups; more internal, covert signs often include an escalation of cravings for the addictive substance.

Gorski (1995) emphasizes the importance of reviewing the client's relapse history and using tools such as a relapse calendar to identify risk factors, warning signs, and significant life events that could lead to relapse. Gorski (1995) recommends a thorough review process, including analyzing the most recent recovery attempts, identifying personal warning signs, and using sentence completion tasks to recognize potential recovery threats. This process culminates in creating a final warning sign list and a recovery plan targeting these signs with cognitive, behavioral, and emotional strategies.

Identify High-Risk Situations and Develop Cognitive and Behavioral Responses

To prevent a single lapse from escalating into a full relapse, clients must recognize and effectively manage high-risk situations, which encompass both interpersonal/environmental and intrapersonal factors. The success in preventing relapse is more dependent on coping skills rather than the high-risk situations themselves (Menon & Kandasamy, 2018). Evaluating a client's coping mechanisms is essential. Those who avoid initial relapse tend to use behavioral strategies to steer clear of high-risk situations and seek social support to sustain abstinence (Zaidi, 2020). Over time, especially after prolonged periods of abstinence, there is often an observable shift towards personally implementing cognitive and behavioral coping strategies. Such strategies include the recovering individual personally reflecting on the negative repercussions of past substance use as well as the benefits of continued abstinence (Brown et al., 2002). Enhancing the variety and adaptability of coping skills can be instrumental in maintaining sobriety (Csiernick & Troller, 2002).

In addition to imparting specific RP skills for handling high-risk scenarios, clinicians should integrate comprehensive RP self-control strategies (Macaro, 2002). These should not only focus on analyzing initial lapses but also include skills training methods such as behavioral rehearsal, covert modeling, and assertiveness training (Daley & Marlatt, 2006). Cognitive reframing techniques such as coping imagery for early warning signs are also vital, alongside lifestyle balancing strategies such as meditation, mindfulness, and exercise (Bowen et al., 2014; Witkiewitz et al., 2014). Equipping clients with an emergency plan to effectively interrupt lapses and relapses at an early stage minimizes the impact of setbacks (Daley & Marlatt, 2006). A common pathway towards relapse involves a series of minor decisions, termed "apparently irrelevant decisions," each inching closer to high-risk situations or relapse. Identifying and addressing these decisions is a critical part of the recovery process for clients (Daley & Marlatt, 2006).

Enhance Communication Skills, Interpersonal Relationships, and Social Networks

Addressing substance abuse issues without simultaneously supporting clients in improving their relationships may leave them vulnerable and unsupported (Zaidi, 2020). Involving families in the treatment process increases the likelihood of their support for the client's recovery (Nattala et al., 2010). Training in communication skills is crucial for clients and their partners to effectively manage conflicts and stressors in their relationships and lives (Monti et al., 2001). These skills are known to diminish the risk of relapse (Rahbarian & Doosti, 2016).

Improving problem-solving skills and nurturing caring behaviors are observed to positively influence relationships, thereby aiding in substance use recovery.

(Breslin et al., 2002; Menon & Kandasamy, 2018). Clients should be encouraged to participate in self-help support groups and to carefully select individuals to include in, or exclude from, their recovery support network (Mueller et al., 2007). Behavioral rehearsals can be used to prepare clients for making specific requests for support and to address any ambivalence they might feel about seeking help. These rehearsals also equip clients to handle negative responses from others more effectively (Douaihy et al., 2007).

Creating a comprehensive action plan is essential. This plan should cover strategies to identify and manage early warning signs, cues, and high-risk situations; techniques to interrupt a lapse and intervene in the event of a relapse; and methods for analyzing substance use and its context, treating each instance as a learning opportunity (Bowen et al., 2021). Additionally, the plan should involve preparing clients to confront both direct and indirect social and peer pressures to use substances (DiClemente et al., 2011). This comprehensive approach is integral to the overall recovery action plan.

Manage Negative Emotional States

Managing negative emotional states is pivotal in addiction recovery, with depressed mood being a frequently cited relapse trigger among clients with alcohol addiction (Breslin et al., 2002; Witkiewitz et al., 2013b). Other detrimental emotional states leading to relapse include anxiety, tension, anger, and boredom (Smolkin, 2018).

The AA and NA guideline HALT emphasizes the need to recognize and prevent negative emotions – not becoming too Hungry, Angry, Lonely, or Tired. One of the authors (Weathers) of the current book has expanded the more familiar HALT acronym to HAALT-BB: Hungry, Angry, Anxious, Lonely, Tired, Bored, or "Blue" (the latter connoting a sad or depressed emotional state). Clinical feedback suggests the practical utility of this slightly more inclusive list, for example, in post-relapse review of what factors may have precipitated addictive behaviors.

Clinicians should guide clients in learning stress management techniques and cultivating a more balanced lifestyle (Walsh, 2011). Educating clients about the impact of negative emotional states on recovery and helping them identify triggering situations and self-statements prepares them to use their cognitive-behavioral coping skills effectively (Bowen et al., 2021). It should also be noted that clients showing significant mood or anxiety symptoms may require evaluation for mood or anxiety disorders (Bradizza et al., 2006; Bowen et al., 2021).

Identify and Manage Craving and Precursory Cues

Understanding cravings is crucial, with reward cravings (positive reinforcement) linked to the desire for alcohol or other drugs' hedonic effects and relief from cravings (negative reinforcement) associated with avoiding withdrawal symptoms (McCarthy et al., 2010).

In addition to internal stimuli, external, environmental cues may also trigger cravings, leading to cognitive and physiological changes in the direction of heightened vulnerability to acute lapse or more chronic relapse. AA, NA, and CA recommend avoiding "places, people, and things" linked to substance use to minimize exposure to triggering, external or environmental cues. Cue Exposure (CE) therapy reduces clients' reactions to these cues (CE focuses on enhancing coping skills and confidence in resisting urges to use, using techniques such as systematic relaxation, visual imagery, behavioral alternatives, and cognitive strategies. Monitoring and recording cues and their associated cravings can increase client awareness and preparedness (Havermans & Jansen, 2003).

Identify and Challenge Cognitive Distortions

Teaching clients to recognize and address their cognitive distortions and counterproductive thinking patterns, such as catastrophizing, jumping to conclusions, and overgeneralizing, is beneficial for recovery and relapse prevention (Bowen et al., 2021; Sripada, 2022).

Clients can learn to use counter-thoughts to challenge these thinking errors. AA and NA slogans like "this too will pass," "let go and let God," and "one day at a time" can be instrumental in helping clients navigate through urges to use, thereby altering their thought processes and reinforcing their commitment to recovery (Winner, 2021).

Challenging cognitive distortions can also assist in preventing *akrasia*, a common feature of addiction. Akrasia refers to acting against one's better judgment, leading to conduct that individuals recognize as detrimental and had once vowed to forsake, with addiction often regarded as a severe manifestation of akrasia (Heather, 2020; Du Plessis, 2022).

2 Theoretical Foundations of the Recovery Resilience Program

Introduction

This section provides a brief overview of the I-System Model (ISM) and Mind–Body Bridging (MBB), the primary theory and methodology that informs the Recovery Resilience Program. It is beyond the scope of this introductory section to provide a comprehensive articulation of the ISM and MBB, so we will focus on aspects that have clinical relevance for the Recovery Resilience Program.

The ISM is the theoretical foundation for the psychological intervention called Mind–Body Bridging, which was originally developed in the late 1990s by Stanley H. Block and his wife and collaborator, Carolyn Block (Block, 1987; Block & Block, 2002; Block & Block, 2007; Block et al., 2020). MBB has successfully been used in the treatment of several mood and behavioral disorders and has been recognized as evidence-based for the treatment of addiction (Nakamura et al., 2015; Block & Du Plessis, 2018; Block et al., 2016).

It is theorized that MBB has transdiagnostic efficacy because its practices focus on addressing an underlying transdiagnostic psychological process (referred to as I-System Functioning) present in several emotional and behavioral disorders (Ho & Nakamura, 2017). Historically, mental health issues have been classified within formal taxonomies, such as the DSM and ICD, which categorize disorders based on specific psychiatric symptoms and signs (Kendler, 2009). These systems have been influential globally, shaping the understanding, assessment, and management of mental disorders. However, the limitations of these diagnostic models, particularly in addressing the complexity of mental health, have led to a growing consensus on their diminishing clinical utility. In response, there is an increasing shift towards a transdiagnostic approach that transcends traditional diagnostic boundaries. This approach, nascent but rapidly developing, offers new insights into mental health by focusing on underlying processes and theories, potentially transforming ideas about the onset, maintenance, and treatment of mental disorders. This paradigm shift indicates a move away from rigid categorizations to a more holistic understanding of mental health (Kendler, 2009). Transdiagnostic interventions can be seen as those that apply the same underlying treatment principles across mental health disorders without tailoring the protocol to specific diagnoses (Greeson et al., 2014). The emerging literature on transdiagnostic processes has illustrated the benefits of focusing on common psychological processes that underlie clinical syndromes rather than focusing on discrete diagnostic entities (McEvoy et al., 2009).

Research conducted on MBB has shown efficacy in the treatment of several conditions. For example, in studies with veterans, MBB practice improved sleep by reducing sleep disturbance via reducing/improving PTSD symptoms, increasing mindfulness, reducing depression, fatigue, pain, and composite sleep/general co-occurring symptoms (Nakamura et al., 2011, 2017; Lipschitz et al., 2016). MBB has proven to be an effective intervention in managing insomnia in active-duty military personnel (Lipschitz et al., 2016). A study on cancer survivors showed that MBB reduced sleep disturbance symptoms and depression symptoms while improving overall levels of mindfulness, self-compassion, well-being, and attenuated waking salivary alpha-amylase levels, suggesting positive influences on sympathetic neurological activity in cancer survivors with sleep disturbance (Lipschitz et al., 2013). Another study found that MBB was associated with increased oxytocin levels, a neuropeptide hormone associated with calmness and well-being (Lipschitz et al., 2015). Research on domestic violence perpetrators indicated that MBB reduced recidivism and increased treatment compliance (Tollefson et al., 2009; Tollefson & Phillips, 2015). A narrative case study explored the impact of MBB on university students' professional identities, and the findings demonstrated that it helped students develop their professional identity regarding self-confidence, self-awareness, social relationships, and professional future (Lutovac et al., 2024).[8]

8 Ho & Nakamura (2017) present an affect-object generative inference and regulation model that proposes a neuroscience foundation for the theory and practice of MBB. Their hypothesis is that a "hallmark of mind-body well-being can be characterized as a low-frequency anti-correlation between 1) the cognitive control system including the dorsal anterior/middle cingulate cortex, [executive functioning/top-down processing] and 2) the affect-object thought generation system including the ventromedial prefrontal cortex and posterior cingulate cortex [default states/bottom-up processing]" (Ho & Nakamura, 2017, p. 137). Their model suggests that MBB can enhance mind-body well-being by affecting these systems.

In the context of addiction treatment, a study found that MBB significantly reduced drug/alcohol cravings, trauma-related thinking, and disturbed sleep while increasing mindfulness, self-compassion, and well-being (Nakamura et al., 2015). This study was instrumental in the listing of the Mind–Body Bridging Substance Abuse Program (MBBSAP) on the National Registry of Evidence-Based Programs and Practices (NREPP) website, care of the Substance Abuse and Mental Health Services Administration (SAMHSA), a subsidiary of the U.S. Department of Health and Human Services (Block & Du Plessis, 2018). The MBBSAP was rated effective for improving spiritual health; reducing general substance use; reducing sleep and wake disorders and symptoms; and reducing trauma- and stress-related disorders and symptoms (Block & Du Plessis, 2018).[9]

In the following section, we will briefly outline the therapeutic focus of MBB. It must be noted that while many publications discuss and outline MBB methodology, the theoretical foundations of ISM have not been comprehensively articulated in publications. Our articulation of it in this manual should not be seen as definitive, and there are certain aspects of the model that we chose not to discuss as it was not directly relevant to the focus of this manual. Moreover, considering the broad range of theoretical perspectives we draw from, we acknowledge that our interpretation and application of them may be less than adequate for those readers more familiar with those theories. Our aim is here to provide an explanatory theoretical perspective for the foundational suppositions of the ISM and MBB that have been shown to have clinical utility. Lastly, we also acknowledge that other perspectives may have more explanatory value than the ones we have presented here.

Therapeutic Focus of Mind–Body Bridging

The therapeutic aim of MBB is to develop awareness and understanding of the adverse effects of I-System activity and develop practices that reduce its adverse effects. MBB practices are based on the premise that *I-System Functioning*, which is the result of I-System activity, underlies many emotional and behavioral disorders and diminished individual resilience (Block & Block, 2007). According to Greeson et al. (2014, p. 534), "most

9 See Nakamura et al. (2015).

psychological disorders involve a fundamental problem with inflexibility, lack of insight, or narrowed perspective." These inflexible psycho-behavioral processes span cognitive rigidities such as rumination and worry and patterns of behavioral perseveration (e.g., addiction, compulsions). With reduced I-System activity, an individual becomes more psychologically flexible and consequently better equipped to handle life events in resilient and optimal ways, which is referred to as a *Natural Functioning state*. In this state, an individual is naturally more resourceful, creative, psychologically flexible, and resilient than they are when I-System activity is present.

MBB methodology includes psychosocial skills and coping strategies that increase psychological *resilience*. The concept of resilience refers to "the ability of individuals to adapt successfully in the face of acute stress, trauma, or chronic adversity, maintaining or rapidly regaining psychological well-being and physiological homeostasis" (Feder et al., 2010, p. 35). The notion of coping refers to specific processes in which a person engages expressly to deal with stress. Studies have identified active coping strategies and cognitive reappraisal as some of the central psychosocial factors that promote successful adaptation to stress (Feder et al., 2010). MBB psychosocial skills and coping strategies include cognitive reappraisal techniques that allow individuals to re-evaluate or reframe adverse experiences with a growth mindset.

From a psychodynamic perspective, the therapeutic focus of MBB could be understood as removing the hindrance to the innate resilience of the "true self" or "real self." According to the ISM, resilience spontaneously emerges in a state of Natural Functioning. Karen Horney (1950) described alienation from the "real self" as the origin of most psychic distress and described the real self as "the 'original' force toward individual growth and fulfillment" (p. 158). According to Horney (1950), this true self is an "intrinsic potentiality" or "central inner force, common to all human beings" (p. 17) that is the core source of development. Similarly, Donald Winnicott contended that much of psychopathology is a "result of an inflation of the false self and a corresponding underdevelopment of a true self" (in Ryan & Deci, 2017, p. 59). From this perspective, MBB practices focus on restoring the "motivational force or tendency" of the true or real self and thereby unleashing its inherent resilience and "health-promoting force" (Ryan & Deci, 2017, p. 62).

In a recent publication, *Cognitive Behavior Therapies: A Guidebook for Practitioners*, (Vernon & Doyle, 2017), MBB methodology has been compared with therapeutic approaches such as acceptance and commitment therapy (Hayes, 2003), dialectical behavior therapy (Linehan & Kehrer (1993), mindfulness-based cognitive therapy, and other mindfulness-based interventions that are commonly referred to as the third wave of cognitive-behavior therapies. Mindfulness-based interventions is a general term for mind–body interventions that focus on the power of "mental training" in regulating mental and physical health conditions. The category of mindfulness-based interventions includes mindfulness-based stress reduction (Kabat-Zinn, 2003) and mindfulness-based cognitive therapy (Segal et al., 2002). Although MBB methodology shares similarities with many of these interventions, there are methodological differences.

For example, in acceptance and commitment therapy (ACT), they apply the technique of "cognitive defusion." The process's original name within ACT was "deliteralization" (Hayes et al., 1999). Fletcher & Hayes (2005) analyzed the notion of mindfulness, central both to Buddhism and to a new wave of empirically supported mindfulness-based cognitive-behavioral therapies (Linehan & Kehrer, 1993; Segal et al., 2002; Hayes et al., 2012). They concluded that mindfulness represents the confluence of four interrelated psychological processes: acceptance of one's experience as it is, increased contact with the present moment, a sense of self-as-context or "transcendent sense of self" (Fletcher & Hayes, 2005, p. 321), and cognitive defusion.

While MBB methodology shares these aspects of mindfulness practice, it adds a metacognitive practice by labeling or naming specific metacognitive processes that underly psychological distress. The aim here is not merely to observe the thought (or Storylines in MBB parlance) but to gain awareness and familiarity with a *particular style of metacognitive thinking* (I-System activity). We will explore this in more depth in the following section.

Metacognition

From a metacognitive perspective, I-System Functioning represents a *particular style* of sustained and inflexible responses to thoughts, emotions, and threats that is responsible for prolonging and intensifying suffering and that leads to non-optimal behavior. Metacognition is a term used to refer to a specific category of thinking and cognition. Metacognition influences the focus of our attention, shapes our appraisals, and influences the types of strategies that we use to regulate thoughts and feelings. It has a crucial influence on our beliefs and thoughts and normal and abnormal emotional and conscious experiences (Wells, 2005).

The ISM adopts a similar view as the Self-Regulatory Executive Function (S-REF) model (Wells, 1995, 2006), which views metacognition as central to psychological dysfunction. Both the ISM and the S-REF model, contrary to cognitive and behavioral theories of psychological disorders, posit that dysfunctional thought patterns and coping behaviors arise from metacognition influencing thinking processes. We will briefly discuss the S-REF model below.

In the late 1980s and early 1990s, the common belief was that attentional bias and worry operated as automatic processes. Additionally, mood and anxiety disorders were predominantly associated with the negative content of thoughts, not the manner of thinking. However, Wells and colleagues (e.g., Wells & Matthews, 1994, 1996) presented a contrasting view. They posited that attentional bias and worry are more closely related to an individual's deliberate strategies for evaluating and responding to threats. They argued that *how* thoughts are managed and controlled is more critical in causing psychological disorders than the actual *content* of these thoughts. This perspective is encapsulated in their model, which emphasizes top-down or conscious processes and self-regulatory strategies in explaining psychological disorders. The model suggests that problems arise when an individual's style of managing thoughts, emotions, and stress becomes counterproductive, exacerbating and perpetuating emotional distress. The way an individual thinks about and regulates their response to threats and challenges can either prolong emotional suffering or result in more fleeting emotional responses (Wells & Matthews, 1994, 1996).

The S-REF model, distinct from other cognitive models, highlights the significance of cognitive architecture by distinguishing between reflexive low-level processing and top-down, higher-level motivated strategies. It identifies a cognitive attentional syndrome (CAS) characterized by biased, persistent negative processing as a central coping strategy in disorders.[10] This differentiation is crucial for psychotherapy development, as the level at which a bias operates dictates the treatment approach: repeated exposure for low-level processes versus strategy modification and metacognitive knowledge revision for higher-level processes. Wells & Matthews (1994, 1996) proposed that individual differences

10 See Kowalski & Dragan (2019).

in self-focused attention across psychological disorders signify CAS, seen as a *universal mechanism* that causes or maintains psychological disorders. They argued that it is the perseveration in response to negative thoughts, or CAS, rather than the content of cognition that leads to psychological disorders.

The progression of the S-REF model led to recognizing the importance of developing techniques to regulate the CAS effectively. In this model, CAS is seen as a product of metacognitive knowledge, such as beliefs about the usefulness of worrying or focusing on threats and higher-order procedural metacognitions that function as modifiable processing programs. The model links psychological disorders to *maladaptive metacognitive beliefs* and the excessive use of negative thinking strategies for coping rather than skill deficits (Wells, 2006). Consequently, treatments should aim at enhancing flexible mental control, not just addressing skill gaps or challenging the content of schemas.[11] Working from similar assumptions as the S-REF model, MBB aims to enhance *flexible mental control* and how an individual *thinks about* and *regulates their response* to threats and challenges.

Traditional cognitive and behavioral theories of psychological dysfunction (Ellis, 1962; Beck, 1976) emphasize the role of cognitive bias and distorted or irrational beliefs. For example, Beck (1976) describes cognitive distortions such as arbitrary inference, catastrophizing, and personalization as underlying emotional disturbance and behavioral dysfunction. In the S-REF model, bias occurs in the style that thinking takes, which is derived from metacognitive knowledge stored as a library of information and plans or programs that direct processing. Like the S-REF model, the ISM views bias in metacognitive styles of thinking as a factor that leads to psychological disorders. In cognitive and behavioral approaches, the focus is on "*what*" people think; in the S-REF model, the focus is on "*how*" people think. In addition to "*how*" people think (in the ISM the "how" is referred to as Depressor or Fixer activity), the ISM also focuses on the "*who*" that does the "how" of thinking – the self in an I-System Functioning mode or Natural Functioning mode.

11 Wells, in his subsequent works (2005, 2006), further developed the S-REF model, incorporating emerging experimental data and insights from clinical practice. He detailed the inner structure of higher-order cognitive functions and elucidated the relationship between the metacognitive components of the model and the regulation of CAS. This ongoing development underscores the model's emphasis on metacognitive aspects and their role in psychological disorders.

In summary, in the ISM, the content of ordinary cognition is not of primary importance in understanding psychological disturbance. Rather it is a particular *style of thinking* and *ways of coping* with negative ideas and threats that are a fundamental feature of all psychological disorders. The particular *style of thinking* that is problematic, called I-System Functioning, consists specifically of recurrent and inflexible self-referential thinking, recyclical ideation in the form of worry and rumination, and fixation on threat that leads to impaired self-regulating, coping strategies, and behavior. Simply put, MBB aims to develop awareness and metacognitive understanding of the adverse effects of I-System activity and develop practices that reduce its adverse effects. A strength of MMB is that it provides a simple metacognitive heuristic that has been shown to have significant clinical utility.

I-System Functioning and Natural Functioning as Dispositional States

According to the ISM, I-System Functioning and Natural Functioning can be seen as mutually exclusive *dispositional* states or modes of being. Depending on context, an individual has a disposition for either of these states. These states can more specifically be described as *self-states,* which we will discuss in more depth later. Figure 1.1 illustrates these two dispositional states.

According to the ISM, Natural Functioning is defined as an activity without the interference of I-System activity. It further posits that I-System activity results when certain expectations or requirements held by the individual are violated. The ISM distinguishes between ordinary expectations or requirements and *I-System Requirements* (or *Requirements* for short) that relate to an individual's self-conception. Requirements are mental rules of how we, others, and the world should be that are relevant to an individual self-conception or identity.[12] The violation of a Requirement is experienced as a

12 According to Edmund Husserl, experience of any sort (perception, memory, imagination, etc.) has a common temporal structure such that any moment of experience contains a retentional reference to past moments of experience, a current openness (primal impression) to what is present, and a protentional anticipation of the moments of experience that are just about to happen (see Gallagher, 2011). The retentional structure of experience, (i.e., the fact that when we experience something, each passing moment of consciousness does not simply disappear at the next moment but is kept in intentional currency) constitutes a coherency that stretches over an experienced temporal duration.

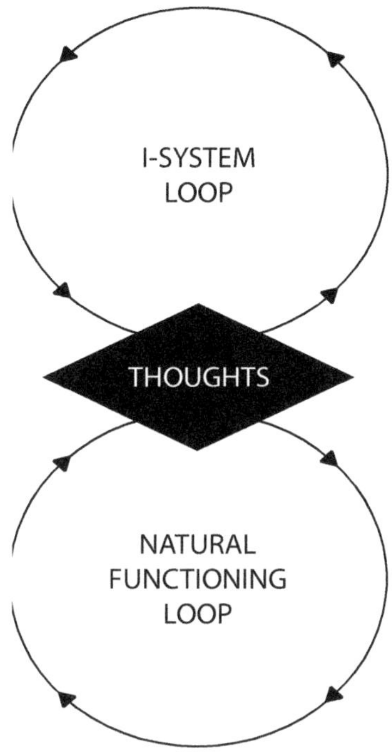

Figure 1.1 I-System loop and Natural Functioning loop.

self-threat, and I-System activity could be understood as a way of maintaining *self-integrity*. We will discuss this in more depth later.

I-System Functioning is viewed as the collective dynamics of Depressor and Fixer activity. The Depressor and Fixer are heuristics for metacognitive styles of thinking and ways of responding to self-threat.

In the ISM, Depressor activity results when a Requirement is violated (i.e., something does not conform to a "should" or "must"). Because a violated Requirement is interpreted as a *threat* to self-integrity, Depressor activity results in storylines about the flaw or inadequacy associated with the violated Requirement. These *Depressor Storylines* center on being inadequate or flawed (with associated feelings and sensations of embarrassment, humiliation, shame, and self-loathing) or on how others and/or the world is/are flawed. Depressor Storylines are compulsive and intrusive negative ruminations about oneself, others, or the world that suggest something needs to be "fixed," resolved, or compensated for. Consequently, Fixer activity is initiated to "fix," resolve (or even medicate) the unpleasant and often overwhelming affect states (feelings of humiliation, shame, and self-loathing) that result from Depressor activity. Fixer Storylines are simple or elaborate fantasies or "action plans" regarding how this "improvement" or "damage repair" will happen, or simply put, how to "fix it." Fixer schemas or plans can be understood as "solutions" for temporarily alleviating unpleasant and painful affect states caused by Depressor activity.

The interaction of Fixer and Depressor activity reciprocally reinforces each other in a nearly intractable habitual loop that can result in excessive rumination and prolonged emotion, which can lead to psychological dysfunction. The collective dynamic Depressor and Fixer activity is called the Depressor–Fixer dyad. In the ISM, the Depressor and Fixer are simplified heuristics for complicated psychological processes that provide clinical utility.

In conclusion, the therapeutic focus of MBB methodology consists of *awareness practices* that cultivate present-focused awareness of one's body, thoughts, and emotions, and *metacognitive strategies* (awareness of a particular style of metacognitive thinking related to responses to self-threats, i.e., Fixer and Depressor activity) that enhance awareness and understanding of one's thought processes that enhance executive functioning, resilience, and psychological flexibility in activities of daily living.

In the next section, we explore Depressor and Fixer activity as *modes of processing* through the lens of the Interacting Cognitive Subsystems (ICS) model.

Fixer and Depressor Activity as Modes of Processing

The Integrated Cognitive Subsystems (ICS) model explains the emergence of symptoms in psychological disorders as a result of multimodal information patterns (such as visual, propositional, and bodily states) activating or reactivating maladaptive schematic mental models (Teasdale, 1993, 1999; Cowdrey et al., 2017).

The ICS model posits that nine distinct mental codes are encoded by corresponding subsystems: acoustic, visual, body-state, object, morphonolexical (speech forms), propositional, implicational, articulatory, and limb. Each subsystem processes and transforms its specific mental code and maintains a unique memory store or "image record." These records are utilized during recollection, understanding situations, or predicting outcomes. Consequently, multiple records of a single event are stored across different subsystems (such as acoustic and visual), aligning with other theories' views on autobiographical memory storage (Brewin et al., 2010). Transformation within a subsystem and the inter-subsystem information exchange are crucial for effective information processing, resulting in the output code differing from the input code. Information processing involves a sequence of transformations heavily influenced by past experiences. For instance, seeing a frowning boss might trigger a visual code that activates a previous depressive episode's intrusive image (transformed within a subsystem into an "image record"), leading to somatic symptoms like slumped posture (Cowdrey et al., 2017).

In the ICS framework, how information is converted from one type of code to another is crucial. This transformation can happen in two modes: direct and buffered. The direct mode involves the immediate processing of limited incoming information, often called "on-line" processing. In contrast, the buffered mode allows for the accumulation of incoming information chunks before the transformation process begins, resulting in responses that are more reflective of the broader context due to the greater volume of information considered (Cowdrey et al., 2017). Furthermore, it distinguishes significantly between propositional and implicational meanings. Propositional code conveys specific, conceptual meanings that are subject to validation as true or false, such as the statement "My heart is beating faster" (Teasdale & Barnard, 1993). Implicational code, on the other hand, represents a broader, more holistic level of meaning that is less easily articulated linguistically and more akin to a felt sense. Examples include perceptions such as "self as anxious" or "self as weak and helpless." This more abstract level of meaning emerges from integrating specific propositional meanings with sensory elements. In the ICS framework, these recurrent patterns of implicational code are regarded as "schematic mental models" that shape our experience (Teasdale & Barnard, 1993).[13]

It is also critical to recognize the significant role of *attentional processes* in the ICS framework, particularly in influencing ruminative states. Attentional processes, such as selective attention and attentional avoidance, have been

13 Repetitive negative thinking is one of the features of I-System Functioning and is most often associated with Depressor activity. Substantial evidence suggests that repetitive negative thinking is prevalent among individuals with various emotional issues, marking it as a transdiagnostic process. See Ehring & Watkins (2008).

identified transdiagnostically as contributing to the maintenance of disorder (Mansell et al., 2008). *Mode of processing* refers to exactly how and where *attention is directed* within ICS. Different processing modes are characterized depending on whether buffered processing is occurring predominantly on the propositional, implicational, or one of the other subsystems (Teasdale, 1993, 1999). As the information processed by the buffered subsystem will dominate the whole processing configuration, it may give rise to different symptoms (Cowdrey et al., 2017).

Interlock is a good example of what happens if the propositional subsystem is buffered. In this scenario, awareness will become dominated by intellectualized and detached thoughts about perceived discrepancies and attempts to resolve these. This *mode of processing* is referred to as "*doing mode*" in the ICS model. Whilst "doing mode" can be adaptive – problem-solving being a prime example of this – persistent processing in this mode will result in high levels of repetitive negative thinking, which in turn will contribute to the regeneration of dysfunctional schematic mental models (Cowdrey et al., 2017). This *doing mode* of the ICS model may correlate with *Fixer activity* as articulated in the ISM.

Equally, when neither the propositional nor implicational subsystem is buffered, individuals will be unable to coolly reflect or demonstrate intuitive knowledge about their emotional experience; instead, individuals will become overwhelmed and immersed in it. Therefore, when both the propositional and implicational subsystems are in direct instead of buffered mode, the individual will enter a "*mindless emoting mode*" (Cowdrey et al., 2017). This "*mindless emoting mode*" of the ICS model may correlate with *Depressor activity* as articulated in the ISM. "Mindless emoting mode" is also experienced as highly aversive as individuals become "lost" in emotional experience (Teasdale, 1999). Therefore, "Modes of processing" in ICS, understood as Fixer and Depressor activity in the ISM, have the potential to explain how attentional processes contribute to the maintenance of disorders transdiagnostically.

The ICS also identifies another mode of processing called "*mindful experiencing mode*" or "*being mode*." In this mode of processing, attention is held at the implicational subsystem. Feelings, sensations, and thoughts are directly sensed as aspects of subjective experience rather than just thinking about them. The focus is on the present moment with reflexive awareness and a holistic, multisensory awareness of wider meaning. This "mindful experiencing mode" or "being mode" seems to correlate with the *Natural Functioning mode* as articulated by the ISM, as both are related to processing in the present moment with a focus on sensory and expanded awareness.

Like the ICS, the ISM views information from the body as playing an integral role in the production of emotion and as an important factor in the maintenance of psychological disorders. (For example, when doing Mapping practices, there is a significant focus on bodily sensation as a cue for I-System activity.) In the ICS framework's view of depression, bodily feedback, such as a slumped posture and diminished activity, is crucial in reinforcing the "interlock" between specific propositional and implicational meanings (Teasdale, 1993, 1999). A "doing mode" of processing, marked by an intense focus on intellectualized thoughts about internal and external stimuli, may perpetuate rumination and avoidance. Therefore, transitioning to an "experiential mode" of processing, where anxious thoughts and bodily sensations are viewed as transient events, could offer therapeutic benefits. The ISM holds a similar view, and the various skills suggested by MBB aim to shift an individual from a "doing mode" of processing, marked by an intense focus on intellectualized thoughts about internal and external stimuli, to an "experiential mode" of processing (Natural Functioning), where anxious thoughts and bodily sensations are viewed and experienced as transient events.

In summary, in the context of the above discussion, in the ISM, there are two primary modes of processing: (1) I-System Functioning mode composed of Depressor and Fixer activity, which may respectively correlate with the "mindless emoting mode" and "doing mode"; and (2) Natural Functioning mode which may correlate with the "mindful experiencing mode" or "being mode" as presented in the ICS model literature.

In the next section, we explore Requirements in more detail.

Propositional Attitudes and Requirements

A common assumption in phenomenology and philosophy of mind is that thoughts have *intentionality*. That is, they are about or refer to things and may be evaluated with respect to properties such as consistency, truth, appropriateness, and accuracy (Chalmers, 2002; Bayne & Montague, 2011). Intentionality is always directed at something called an *intentional object*, and intentional objects are represented in the mind as *mental representations* (Dennett, 1991, 2005).[14] An intentional state represents an object, real or unreal, and typically represents a whole state of affairs, which may or may not actually be obtained (Dennett, 1991, 1996, 2005).[15]

For physicalists, accepting that there are mental states that are both intentional and causal raises the question of how such states can exist in a physical world. Jerry Fodor's (1975, 1998) Representational Theory of Mind (RTM) is his attempt to answer such concerns. Broadly speaking, RTM claims that mental processes are computational processes and that intentional states are relations to mental representations that serve as the domain of such processes. In Fodor's (1975, 2008) version of RTM, these mental representations have syntactic structure and compositional semantics. Thinking thus takes place in an *internal language of thought*.[16] According to Fodor's (1975, 2008) language of thought hypothesis (LOTH), mental representation has a *linguistic structure*, or in other words, that thought takes place within a mental language. A representational system has a linguistic structure if it employs combinatorial syntax and compositional semantics (Fodor, 2008).[17] The hypothesis is sometimes expressed as the claim that thoughts are "sentences in the head."

14 The notion of a mental representation is, arguably, in the first instance a theoretical construct of cognitive science. In this broader construal, mental representation is a philosophical topic with roots in antiquity and a rich history and literature pre-dating the recent "cognitive revolution" (Chalmers, 2002; Clark, 2014).

15 The idea of representation has been central in discussions of intentionality for many years. But only more recently has it begun playing a wider role in the philosophy of mind, particularly in theories of consciousness. Indeed, there are now multiple representational theories of consciousness, corresponding to different uses of the term "conscious," each attempting to explain the corresponding phenomenon in terms of representation. More cautiously, each theory attempts to explain its target phenomenon in terms of intentionality and assumes that intentionality is representation.

16 The Representational Theory of Mind (RTM) (which goes back at least to Aristotle) takes as its starting point commonsense mental states, such as thoughts, beliefs, desires, perceptions, and imaginings. Such states are said to have "intentionality" – they are about or refer to things and may be evaluated for properties such as consistency, truth, appropriateness, and accuracy. RTM defines such intentional mental states as relations to mental representations and explains the intentionality of the former in terms of the semantic properties of the latter. RTM also understands mental processes such as thinking, reasoning, and imagining as sequences of intentional mental states (Dennett, 1991, 1996).

17 The LOTH is part of a broader cluster of theories including the causal-syntactic theory of mental processes (CSMP) and the RTM. The LOTH, along with CSMP and RTM, forms the basis of the computational theory of mind (CTM), which conceptualizes the brain as a computer and thinking as a computational process (Clark, 2014).

In essence, the language of thought hypothesis (LOTH) suggests that thinking takes place through a mental language, often referred to as *Mentalese*. This mental language shares several similarities with spoken language: it consists of words that can be combined to form sentences, these words and sentences carry meaning, and the meaning of each sentence is systematically determined by the meanings of its individual words and how those words are arranged.

Folk psychology commonly accounts for and anticipates behavior by referring to mental states such as beliefs, desires, intentions, fears, and hopes. These mental states, including belief and desire, are known as *propositional attitudes*. They can be specified using locutions of the form: *X* believes that *p*, *X* desires that *p*, *X* intends that *p*, *X* fears that *p*, etc. By replacing "*p*" with a sentence, we specify the content of *X*'s mental state. Propositional attitudes possess *intentionality* or *aboutness*, meaning they are directed toward a particular subject matter. Because of this, they are often referred to as *intentional states*. To believe, hope, or intend that *p* involves having an appropriate relationship with a mental representation whose meaning corresponds to *p*. The term "*propositional attitude*" was first introduced by Bertrand Russell (1918) and reflects his analysis that propositional attitudes relate to propositions. A proposition is an abstract entity that specifies a *truth-condition*. Propositional attitudes derive their semantic properties, including their truth-conditions, from the mental representations that are their objects.

In the ISM, certain propositional attitudes and their truth-condition (beliefs about self, others, and the world) are relevant to a certain *self-concept* at a particular moment, specifically to the *phenomenal* or *working self*. When the truth-condition, referred to in ISM parlance as a Requirement, is violated, it gives rise to a particular mental state and *thinking style* called I-System Functioning that is composed of Depressor and Fixer activity and *Storylines*. These Storylines can be seen as a particular form of *Mentalese*. In the ISM, a violated Requirement, a truth-condition of a certain propositional attitude that is related to the working self, is viewed as a *self-threat* or a threat to an individual's identity. I-System activity, in the form of Depressor and Fixer activity, is understood as a response to this self-threat in an attempt to maintain the coherence and integrity of the self.

We will discuss this in more detail in the following section.

Identity, Self-integrity, and Requirements

People's identities are complex and multifaceted, containing personal characteristics, roles, relationships, group memberships, autobiographical information, and other self-relevant representations. The notion of *self-concept* is defined as an "overall vision (as an integrated, coherent, and stable individuality) transcending the experiential and event content of self-awareness" (Lipiansky, 2008, p. 38). Given the size and complexity of their self-concepts, people can think about only limited aspects of their *identity* at any moment. The aspects of identity about which people are aware at a particular time have been called the phenomenal self (Rhodewalt & Agustsdottir, 1986), spontaneous self-concept (McGuire & McGuire, 1980), and *working self-concept* (Markus & Wurf, 1987). It is beyond the scope of this section to enter a debate regarding the nature of "personhood," self, or identity. We will mainly focus on the construct of the *working self-concept*.

According to the ISM, I-System activity results when a perceived threat exists to an individual's *working self-concept*. *Self-threat* refers to perceived or real doubt, diminishment, or devaluation of one's self-concept and self-esteem (Leary et al., 2009). The noxious incidents that induce self-threat can be implicit or explicit. According to self-affirmation theory (Steele, 1988), people are motivated to protect the perceived integrity and worth of the self. As Steele (1988, p. 262) observed, the purpose of the self-system is to "maintain a phenomenal experience of the self ... as adaptively and morally adequate, that is, competent, good, coherent, unitary, stable, capable of free choice, capable of controlling important outcomes."

As mentioned earlier, according to the ISM, I-System activity results when certain expectations or Requirements held by the individual are violated. The violation of a Requirement is experienced as a *self-threat*, and I-System activity can be understood as a way of maintaining *self-integrity*. I-System activity is phenomenologically experienced as a cascade of mind- and body-based reactions of Depressor and Fixer activity that can form looping Storylines by reciprocal reinforcement and lead to excessive rumination.

What is the function of self-integrity? And why do people go to such lengths to protect self-integrity, to the point of misrepresenting reality and misperceiving themselves? Although self-affirmation theory posits a self-system motivated to protect worth and integrity, it does not speak to the ultimate purpose of such a system. The benefits of positive self-illusions for psychological and even physical health suggest the adaptive value, and perhaps even evolutionary advantage, of maintaining self-integrity (cf. Colvin et al., 1995). It has been suggested that the "superordinate" function of self-integrity serves to stave off the existential terror that accompanies the knowledge of one's mortality, as highlighted by terror management theory (Solomon et al., 1991). According to this theory, people cope with the anxiety of impending mortality by identifying with a cultural worldview that provides meaning and the possibility of symbolic immortality through participation in culturally sanctioned projects.

We will now discuss Requirements from the perspective of self-affirmation theory (Steele, 1988), the psycho-social dynamic processing model of the self (Morf & Mischel, 2012), and the working self-perspective (Markus & Wurf, 1987).

In Morf & Mischel's (2012) psycho-social dynamic processing model of the self, the "self" or "personhood" is best conceptualized as an organized, coherent system. In such a system, the self and its directly relevant processes (e.g., self-evaluation, self-regulation, self-construction) may be conceptualized fruitfully as a coherent organization of mental-emotional representations interacting within a system of constraints that characterize a person distinctively. The self-system is responsive to contexts but is itself relatively stable in its organization and processing dynamics. In this sense, the self is both "stable and variable." The states within the system refer to the activation levels of the cognitions and affects at a given time (Shoda & Mischel, 1998). Morf & Mischel's (2012) conception of the self-system, from a systems perspective, is *constituted* by an array of *self-conceptions* and images. These elements represent various significant aspects or domains of an individual's life or the diverse bases upon which their self-worth is contingent, as Crocker & Wolfe (2001) outlined. The self-system can be understood as an intricate structure composed of various domains. These domains encompass roles (e.g., student, parent), values (e.g., religiosity, humor), social identities (e.g., group memberships, racial, cultural, and gender identities), and belief systems (e.g., political beliefs). Personal goals, like valuing health or academic success, are also integral components of the self (Markus & Wurf, 1987).

This self-system becomes particularly active when encountering a situation threatening *a significant self-conception* or image. Such threats challenge an individual's *preferred perception of themselves*. For instance, receiving negative feedback in an academic setting could undermine one's identity as a competent student; adverse health news might challenge one's self-view as a healthy person; shifts in public opinion could threaten one's patriotic identity; and awareness of social injustices might conflict with one's belief in a just world. These scenarios are perceived as *threats* because they impact the individual's overarching sense of *self-integrity* (Morf & Mischel, 2012).

These *threats to the self* (or self-threats) can lead to "fragmentation anxiety." According to Heinz Kohut (1971, 1977), fragmentation anxiety may emerge at crucial moments of psychic change when an existing maladaptive self-object organization is about to be given up. Even irrational systems of belief may be tenaciously retained because a threat to the coherence of their worldview is experienced as a direct attack on their sense of self and identity and conjures up powerful archaic fears of psychic fragmentation and annihilation. It must be noted that the fear of fragmentation is a universal human phenomenon, experienced unconsciously as a constant threat. This fear is rooted in the need for a coherent and integrated sense of self, which is developed through self-object functions provided by caregivers during early childhood.[18] As individuals develop, they form self-object systems with a wide range of human phenomena, including linguistic, cultural, imagistic, and behavioral routines and organizations. These systems serve to maintain a sense of coherence and continuity in the self, thereby reducing the threat of fragmentation. When these systems are threatened by confrontation with competing belief systems, the resulting disintegration anxiety can be intense (Kohut, 1971, 1977).[19]

18 In self psychology, developed by Heinz Kohut (1971), the term 'self-object' describes the experience of perceiving another person (referred to as an *object*) as an integral part of oneself, rather than as a distinct and independent individual. This typically occurs when the person's actions validate or enhance one's narcissistic sense of well-being.

19 From a logic-based therapy perspective (a philosophical counselling method developed by American philosopher Elliot Cohen), I-System Requirements could be seen as a conflict between demand and report premises. In LBT, this logico-linguistic conflict plays out on phenomenological and neurological levels. Elliot Cohen (2021, p. 37) notes:

> The upper forebrain system includes motivational feelings such as felt needs associated with images related to certainty, getting things fast, gaining the approval of others, being treated fairly, and being right about things. These are the phenomenological correlates of perfectionistic demands. Conflicts or inconsistencies arising between such felt needs and perception of reality, as expressed in perfectionistic demands and empirical reports in conflict with these demands, tend to generate negative, self-destructive emotions

According to Morf & Mischel (2012), the self-system, with its intricate organization and dynamic processing, employs metaphors from current connectionist theory and neural network models, as discussed in works by Mischel & Shoda (2008) and Morf & Horvath (2007). In connectionist networks, outputs are the result of a distributed activation pattern across numerous simple processing units. The characteristics of these outputs are contingent on and evolve with the connection weights between links and the fulfillment of mutual constraints among these links, as explained by Rumelhart & McClelland (1986). In a similar vein, the self-system does not store concepts as isolated entities. Instead, activation disseminates throughout the system via existing cognitive-affective links, each instance slightly altering and updating these connections. As Shoda & Mischel (1998) elucidate, self-constructs and units are essentially patterns of activation among much more fundamental units. Crucially, these constructs are always formed and reformed *in situ*, implying that they are *contextually generated* rather than retrieved in a pre-existing form. The *self-units or representations* within each individual are uniquely networked, shaped by a combination of genetic factors, biological history (such as temperament), and the individual's social learning and developmental experiences within their specific culture and subculture. This unique network organization is fundamental to determining which units are *activated* concurrently during interactions with the social environment. The structure of the self-system is thus defined by the stable links and connections among these units and the strength of their associations. Morf & Mischel (2012) explain that this *activation within the self-system* can arise from various sources.[20] Furthermore, the activation pattern within the self-system must satisfy, at least to some extent, the constraints represented by the network's connection

such as anxiety and depression (for example, as in the case of a felt need for approval in conflict with rejection by a former lover). Accordingly, identifying conflicts or inconsistencies between clients' perfectionistic demands and their perception of reality (in emotional reasoning) can often be helpful in getting at the roots of self-destructive behavioral and emotional disorders.

20 It may be triggered by social stimuli during interpersonal interactions, whether these encounters are spontaneous or initiated by the individual. Activation can also originate internally, through processes such as self-reflection and rumination. For instance, contemplating certain aspects of the self can spark associated affective responses (e.g., anxiety, shame, guilt, pride, eagerness, fear), which in turn may trigger a series of cognitive, emotional, and behavioral reactions (such as efficacy expectations, self-doubts, or defensive denials). These activations are not mere retrievals of pre-existing entities from memory; rather, they represent an active, context-dependent construction or reconstruction process (Morf & Mischel, 2012).

weights. This requirement leads to a relatively stable activation pattern among the units within each person's self-system.

In this sense, the self-system is "biased" because the connections are activated and updated in nonrandom, predictable ways distinctive for the individual. According to Morf & Mischel (2012), the variable expressions of the *states of the self* - the thoughts and feelings activated and the behaviors generated, plotted as a function of psychologically salient features of situations - emerge as stable, distinctive situation-behavior profiles. These profiles with characteristic elevations and shapes constitute the individual's characteristic *IF–THEN personality signature.* Morf & Mischel (2012) propose that the self-system comprises many IF–THEN contingencies, representing the different thoughts, feelings, and behavioral tendencies that are or could be activated in a given context. When these IF–THEN relations are *self-relevant,* they may be considered *signatures of the self* and the *self-system.*

In ISM parlance, these self-relevant *IF–THEN self-signatures* are related to what is heuristically referred to as *Requirements,* as they are relevant to our self-conceptions. For example, if someone has a Requirement that their wife should listen to them, the IF–THEN self-signature could be seen as "IF my wife listens to me THEN I feel and behave ..." and "IF my wife does not listen to me THEN I feel and behave ..." When the IF–THEN self-signature or Requirement is violated, it can be seen as a threat to the working self-concept within a specific context, which results in I-System activity. Simply put, when a Requirement is violated, it *threatens a self-conception.* Such *threats challenge* an individual's *preferred perception of themselves* - because they are perceived as *threats* they impact the individual's overarching sense of self-integrity. In basic terms, I-System activity can be seen as an attempt to maintain homeostasis within the self-system.[21]

21 What is also important to note is that I-System Requirements and Depressor and Fixer Storylines can be seen as performative "*speech acts.*" Elliot Cohen (2021) notes that in the 1950s, the philosopher J. L. Austin (1975) pointed out a different way to perceive the use of natural language. Instead of seeing the primary use of language as making true or false statements, Austin also focused on how it could be used to *do* things - to *perform various speech acts.* This emphasis on the *per-formative* use of language was key to the development of Albert Ellis' first cognitive-behavior therapy, which he later called Rational-Emotive Behavior Therapy (REBT). Ellis (1962, p. 21) notes, "The very facility with language which enabled them to be essentially human - to talk to others and to talk to themselves - also enabled them to abuse this facility by talking utter nonsense to themselves: to *define* things as terrible when, at worst, these things were inconvenient and

Morf & Mischel (2012, p. 35) state that "whereas the cognitions and affects that are activated at a given time in the self-system may change as the situation does, how they change, and the relations among them are assumed to reflect the relatively stable structure and organization of the self-system." For example, whenever a person encounters an individual with a configuration of features relevant to him or herself, the thoughts and feelings that are activated follow a particular predictable pattern, as illustrated in work on transference (Andersen & Chen, 2002) and narcissism (Morf et al., 2011). When the current situations change, so do the *self-states* that become activated, reflecting the person's interpersonal history and the distinctive organization of the self-system.

The notions of different *self-states* that are activated depending on the situation will be the focus of the next section. According to the ISM, and as a heuristic for clinical utility, there are two primary *self-states*: I-System Functioning and Natural Functioning.

annoying." Cohen (2021) highlights that Ellis italicized the word "define" to suggest that people do something linguistically to upset themselves. Yet the idea that these speech acts can cause emotional disturbance is an idea that goes back to Ancient Greece and was a central premise in Stoic philosophy. This has been highlighted by scholars such as the French philosopher Pierre Hadot (1992, 1995, 2002), who has contributed to a resurgence of interest in ancient philosophies and coined the term "philosophy as a way of life" (PWL). Hadot (1995) noted that many ancient philosophical schools, such as the Epicureans, Skeptics, and Stoics, viewed philosophy as "the art of living." In addition to ancient philosophy being an art of living, it also had a therapeutic agenda. Hadot (1995, p. 107) points out that ancient philosophy "presented itself as therapeutic, intended to cure mankind's anguish." The therapeutic agenda of these ancient schools aligns with the broader goals of modern psychotherapy *ante litteram*, and this was noted by Ellis (1962, p. 54), in his book, *Reason and Emotion in Psychotherapy*; when referring to the central premise of his emerging cognitive approach to psychotherapy he stated "[t]his principle, which I have inducted from many psychotherapeutic sessions with scores of patients during the last several years, was originally discovered and stated by the ancient Stoic philosophers, especially Zeno of Citium (the founder of the school), Chrysippus, Panaetius of Rhodes (who introduced Stoicism into Rome), Cicero [sic], Seneca, Epictetus, and Marcus Aurelius." Mainly through Ellis's writings, Stoic principles continued to influence Aaron T. Beck, the founder of cognitive therapy. Beck (1976, p. 3) opened his first book on cognitive therapy, *Cognitive Therapy and the Emotional Disorders*, by describing how his new style of therapy was founded upon the emerging consensus among researchers that cognitions play a central role in determining our emotions, but noted: "[n]evertheless, the philosophical underpinnings go back thousands of years, certainly to the time of the Stoics, who considered man's conceptions (or misconceptions) of events rather than the events themselves as the key to his emotional turmoil."

Self-states with Degrees of Complexity

In the following section we will explore I-System Functioning and Natural Functioning from the perspective of self-states informed by self-affirmation theory (Steele, 1988), working-self perspectives (Markus & Wurf, 1987), self-complexity theory (Linville, 1987), and the expandable selves perspective of Walton et al. (2012). These perspectives propose that the working-self can vary in its breadth, complexity, and structure and that it is "expandable" and "contractable."

We propose that I-System Functioning represents a "contracted" self-state, where the individual has fewer resources with which to function effectively in challenging situations, and that in Natural Functioning, an individual inhabits a more "expanded" self-state, with greater self-complexity and executive functioning.

As already mentioned, given the size and complexity of their self-concepts, people can think about only limited aspects of their identity at any moment, referred to as the *working self-concept* (Markus & Wurf, 1987). Theory and research on the *working self* emphasize how the contents of the active or working self change in different situations. Because the self contains too much information for all of it to be simultaneously active, only a subset of this information is activated, typically those contents of the self that appear *relevant* to the situation at hand. Thus, different contexts, roles, and identities can evoke *different working selves* (McGuire et al., 1979) that, in turn, guide people's attitudes, judgments, and behaviors.[22]

The type of self-state that an individual embodies significantly influences their behavior and how they deal with the situation at hand. According to self-complexity theory, these self-states can also differ in *complexity* (Linville, 1985). Self-complexity theory emphasizes how the structure of a more global and stable self can differ for different people. The complexity of this structure, in turn, can affect people's ability to cope with threats or failures and ultimately

22 For instance, McConnell's (2011) multiple self-aspects framework (MSF) portrays the self as "a collection of multiple, context-dependent selves" (p. 3). There is also, in MSF, attention to how the different aspects of the self that are activated in a given context may combine to produce psychological and behavioral outcomes. At the heart of this theory is the contextual nature of the contents of the self, the idea that the self is not unitary or constant but changes in reliable ways as situations evoke different context-dependent selves.

affect their overall well-being (Linville, 1985). In classic research, Linville (1987) found that people with greater self-complexity experience less stress and depression and show better physical health following stressful events, such as social and academic difficulties, financial problems, and work-related pressure (Showers & Zeigler-Hill, 2012). Research highlights that individuals who are high in *self-complexity* can more successfully suppress negative or distracting self-relevant thoughts by diverting their attention to positive aspects of self (Renaud & McConnell, 2002). By contrast, lower self-complexity is thought to lead to greater reactivity to life events because those events affect a larger proportion of the person's overall self-concept (and, in the face of negative events, there are fewer remaining positive aspects to which one may turn).

Combining insights from the working-self perspective and self-complexity theory, Walton et al. (2012) argue for an "*expandable selves theory*" and propose that the working self, depending on the situation, can vary in its breadth, complexity, and structure (vary in degrees of self-complexity) – that it is "*expandable*" and "*contractable*." Different situations may bring a wide range of aspects to the fore or only isolated aspects of the self. As a result, the working self in a situation may be *relatively broad* or *relatively narrow*. Consistent with self-complexity theory, they suggest that, in general, when the working self is narrow, it may be more vulnerable and have fewer resources with which to function effectively in challenging situations (Walton et al., 2012).

Based on the above discussion, we propose that I-System activity may result in a "contracted" working *self-state* of psychological narrowing with limited self-complexity that is characterized by a specific style of thinking involving recurrent and inflexible self-referential thinking, recyclical ideation in the form of worry and rumination, and fixation on a threat that leads to impaired self-regulating and coping strategies and non optimal behavior. In this limiting self-state, the individual has fewer resources with which to function effectively in challenging situations. In contrast, in the absence of I-System activity, an individual inhabits a more "expanded" working self-state of psychological broadening, with greater self-complexity and executive functioning, resulting in more optimal coping strategies and behavior.

In summary, the type of *self-state* that an individual embodies significantly influences their behavior and how they deal with the situation at hand. We propose that when there is a threat to the working self-concept due to a violated

Requirement, I-System activity is initiated that results in a contracted working self-state of psychological narrowing with limited self-complexity called *I-System Functioning*. In contrast, when there is little or no I-System activity, an individual inhabits a more expanded working self-state of psychological broadening, called *Natural Functioning*, characterized by greater self-complexity, executive functioning, adaptability, self-regulating, and coping strategies.

In the next section, we will briefly discuss how the theory presented thus far relates to addiction relapse prevention and the Recovery Resilience Program outlined in this manual.

Addiction Relapse Prevention and the Recovery Resilience Program

The Recovery Resilience Program is informed by the view that addiction may be conceptualized as a *disposition* to use psychoactive substances that is characterized by impaired control and harm. Robert West and colleagues define "disposition" in the context of cravings as "a latent characteristic that becomes expressed under certain conditions" (West et al., 2019a, p. 168).[23] This dispositional perspective highlights that individuals can vary in degrees of effective self-control depending on the immediate context or situation.[24] Accordingly, the Recovery Resilience Program incorporates a resiliency-focused and strength-based approach and highlights that individuals in recovery can have the capacity to *influence* this *disposition* either (1) by having trained awareness of factors that can make this disposition

23 In the *Routledge Handbook of Philosophy and Science of Addiction* (Pickard & Ahmed, 2019) Robert West and colleagues (West et al., 2019a, 160) highlight a pervasive challenge in the study of addiction: the "need to achieve clarity of constructs and develop consensus while at the same time recognizing that divergent views have utility," and that "[t]he science of addiction is being hampered by confusion in concepts and terms, and a multiplicity of models and theoretical approaches that make little reference to each other." They further state "that a general theory of addiction has yet to be developed, but a key requirement for such a theory is that it should recognize and accommodate multiple viewpoints on addiction, and not be limited to a single viewpoint such as the 'medical model' (construing addiction in term of a mental disorder, disease or disease process)" (West et al., 2019a, 163). West et al. (2019a) propose that one approach to developing a general theory of addiction, as well as addressing the conceptual challenges, is to focus on the ontology of addiction and to establish an Addiction Ontology (see Hastings et al., 2020). The notion of disposition will be central in any ontology of addiction (see West et al., 2019a, 2019b, 2024; Du Plessis, 2023).

24 See West et al. (2024), that highlights the notion of disposition as part of a comprehensive understanding of addiction.

(toward addictive behaviors) more likely or (2) by having access to resources, support, and practices that can make this disposition less likely to be acted upon. In summary, the Recovery Resilience Program can be understood as a person-centered, strength-based, and resiliency-focused relapse prevention and recovery-oriented intervention, as it emphasizes an individual's inherent strengths, and encourages those in recovery to view themselves as capable of resilience in the face of adversity.[25]

A central theme of the Recovery Resilience Program is that addictive behavior can be understood as part of a *mode of being*, meaning that it is a particular and habitual way of existing, relating, and living. An *addicted mode of being* (or *addicted mode* for short) refers to all the beliefs, thoughts, attitudes, and fantasies that support an individual's addictive behavior over time. An addicted mode can also be understood as the result of a particular *self-state* that accompanies addictive behavior over time. Once a person enters an addicted mode, their awareness, attitudes, and behavior *"contract" to the habitual patterns* of their addicted lifestyle. Anyone who has experienced addiction to substances will relate to the notion that the act of using a substance is merely one aspect of their addictive lifestyle. A premise of the Recovery Resilience Program is that an addicted mode is one of many dysfunctional modes of being resulting from I-System activity (Du Plessis et al., 2024). An addicted mode is not a permanent state, per se, but rather a *transitory mode* that is one of many possible modes of being (healthy or dysfunctional). An addicted mode can be understood as a disposition. It is not always active or present but rather a state an individual enters under certain conditions (it is context-dependent). Addiction can be seen as a *way of life* that has been taken *hostage* by a *particular mode of being.*

An example of a disposition is a vase standing on a table. It has a disposition to break under certain conditions, such as if it gets bumped off the table and lands on a hard floor. Therefore, it has a disposition for two possible states: being whole or being broken (under certain conditions). In the same way, one can have a disposition for inhabiting an addicted mode, and as we will highlight in this manual, there are some conditions or contexts that make this disposition more probable. A *Recovery Resilience Practice* is about learning how to shift from an addicted mode to a Natural Functioning mode, thereby lessening the power of the beliefs, expectations, thoughts, fantasies, and attitudes that comprise their addicted mode.

25 With its foundation in social work, the strengths-based approach focuses on an individual's self-determination and strength. See Hill (2008).

Simply put, an individual is more prone to addictive behavior in an addicted mode (I-System Functioning), which can be seen, based on the previous discussion, as the result of a contracted self-state of lower self-complexity. In this self-state, an individual has limited access to inner and outer data (and past experiences) and may make decisions that contradict motivations or plans that are reasonable (or have been decided) in more expanded self-states of increased self-complexity (e.g., giving into a craving to use alcohol or drugs even though one has made a conscious decision to stop). In an addicted mode, which results from a contracted self-state, giving into a craving may seem logical within the context of that self-state, even though it is incompatible or illogical with other more expanded self-states (contradictory with other self-states).

This perspective may help to account for the phenomenon of self-deception (and *akrasia*), a common attribute of behavioral disorders such as substance use disorder, in that an individual may have a belief of *p* in a certain self-state and a belief of ~*p* (*not p*) in another self-state, where each can lead to different decisions or behaviors.[26] This perspective could also possibly explain the common observation and enigma of why individuals suffering from substance use disorder can display various degrees of control over their use of substances depending on the context. A dispositional perspective highlights that certain context-dependent situations (for example, high-risk situations) can elicit a more contracted and limited self-state of lower self-complexity. In these self-states, using substances may seem like a rational response, even though it contradicts the intentions of the individual when in more expanded self-states.[27]

26 See Heather (2017).

27 The notion of disposition and self-state can provide additional explanatory value that seems to be lacking in "brain disease" models of addiction (cf., Volkow et al., 2002). The issue with physiological models of addiction is that they often conflate all aspects of addiction to neuro-adaptation. When understanding addiction as existing at various "levels" of ontological complexity (for example physical, psychological, and volitional), it highlights why certain models of addiction give rise to such reductionist explanations, with limited utility (see Du Plessis, 2014, 2018, 2023). They are good at explaining certain features of addiction, let's say in the realm of neuroadaptation, but methodologically and epistemologically they are incapable of explaining the features of addiction at higher orders of complexity, for example *akrasia* (see Heather, 1998). Addiction is observed across all levels of ontological complexity. As clinical psychologist and addiction researcher Nick Heather (1998, p. 3) points out:

> [A]ddiction ... is best defined by repeated failures to refrain from drug use despite prior resolutions to do so. This definition is consistent with views of addiction that see decision-making, ambivalence and conflict as central features of the addict's behavior and

In summary, the primary aim of a *Recovery Resilience Practice* is to facilitate the *shift* from an *addicted mode* (and I-System Functioning), which can be seen as a limiting and "contracted" self-state and mode of being-in-the-world, where the working self has limited self-complexity and has fewer resources with which to function effectively in challenging situations, and which can result in non-optimal functioning, to a *Natural Functioning mode*, an "expanded" self-state of psychological broadening with greater self-complexity, reflexive awareness, executive functioning, and multisensory awareness of wider meaning. Simply put, a Recovery Resilience Practice aims to facilitate a shift from a state where relapse is more likely (addicted mode) to one where relapse is less likely (Natural Functioning mode).

How a Recovery Resilience Practice Can Enhance Relapse Prevention Strategies

Earlier in the Introduction, we discussed that Relapse Prevention's (RP) main goal is to identify and address high-risk situations for relapses, involving client education on lapses and trigger identification, which could be emotional, social, or physical. RP emphasizes understanding cravings and urges, recognizing triggers, and developing coping strategies to manage high-risk situations and emotions, aiming to reduce the risk of relapse and recognizing substance use as a temporary coping mechanism. A major objective of RP is to develop effective strategies for managing high-risk situations, cravings, and difficult emotions. We previously highlighted six such *common strategies.*

The following section will briefly indicate how a Recovery Resilience Practice can *enhance* these common strategies. This is in line with the focus of the Recovery Resilience Program, which serves as an *adjunct* to existing

experience. On this basis, a three-level framework of required explanation is (needed) consisting of (1) the level of neuroadaptation, (2) the level of desire for drugs, and (3) the level of 'akrasia' or failures of resolve ... explanatory concepts used at the 'lower' levels in this framework can never be held to be sufficient as explanations at higher levels, i.e. the postulation of additional determinants is always required at Levels 2 and 3. In particular, it is a failure to address problems at the highest level in the framework that marks the inadequacy of most existing theories of addiction.

recovery practices and *enhances recovery resilience* or, simply put, enhances the capacity to draw on recovery capital effectively.

We will not present these strategies comprehensively again, so please refer to the initial discussion in the Introduction. In the discussion below, we will focus briefly on how a Recovery Resilience Practice can enhance these *common relapse prevention strategies.*

Comprehend Relapse as a Process and Identify Early Warning Signs

Typically, relapse prevention programs educate clients on viewing addiction as a chronic and cyclical condition, with relapse and recovery phases. This approach helps clients understand relapse as a process with early warning signs rather than a singular event. A Recovery Resilience Practice enhances this strategy by introducing the concept of an addicted mode. When in an addicted mode, one is more prone to relapse because using substances is often the default behavior of this mode. For each person, there are specific ways of thinking, attitudes, and behaviors that comprise their addicted mode. These can be seen as one's unique addicted mode warning signs. A Recovery Resilience Practice is comprised of exercises that bring awareness to a client's addicted mode – warning signs that often precede a lapse or relapse.

Identify High-Risk Situations and Develop Cognitive and Behavioral Coping Responses

To mitigate the progression from a lapse to a full relapse, it is crucial for clients to identify and adeptly manage high-risk situations, which include both interpersonal and intrapersonal factors. The key to relapse prevention lies more in developing and applying effective coping strategies than in the presence of high-risk situations themselves. Similarly, the Recovery Resilience Program emphasizes that the "*who*" (addicted mode or Natural Functioning mode) that is dealing with the high-risk situation is as important as the "what" or the situation itself. When in an addicted mode, it makes it even more difficult to manage high-risk situations. When in an addicted mode, it hinders a client's ability to draw on their recovery capital and skills and thereby limits their choices to a few habitual behaviors.

Enhance Communication Skills, Interpersonal Relationships, and Social Networks

Addressing substance abuse effectively requires also enhancing clients' relational skills, as neglecting this aspect can leave them unsupported. Clients are encouraged to engage with self-help groups and strategically build their recovery network. The Recovery Resilience Program places an emphasis on the notion that the quality of a client's relationships is imperative for sustained recovery. It proposes that one of the biggest hindrances to forming healthy relationships is Requirements for others, which often lead to disappointment and *resentment* and may eventually erode even their most valued relationships. It suggests that to maintain healthy relationships, which are crucial for sustained and successful recovery, there needs to be awareness of the Requirements we have for others. Otherwise, our relationships, which are meant to be supportive, can become a significant trigger or high-risk situation for relapse. This is the focus of the Recovery Resilience Practice called *Recognize and Defuse Requirements.*

Manage Negative Emotional States

Managing negative emotional states is crucial in addiction recovery, particularly since a depressed mood is often a significant relapse trigger for individuals recovering from alcohol addiction. Other emotional states, such as anxiety, tension, anger, and boredom, are also known to precipitate relapse. Educating clients about the adverse effects of negative emotions on recovery and aiding them in managing emotions is an essential component of relapse prevention. The Recovery Resilience Program emphasizes negative thinking and rumination as a central feature of the addictive mode and identifies *Depressor activity,* principally *Storylines,* that result in excessive rumination. This issue is addressed through the practice of *Defuse Depressor Storylines.*

Identify and Manage Cravings and Precursory Cues

Understanding cravings is crucial, with reward (positive) cravings linked to the desire for psychoactive substances' hedonic effects and relief (negative) cravings associated with avoiding withdrawal symptoms. Environmental cues can trigger cravings, leading to cognitive and physiological changes. Monitoring and recording cues and their associated cravings can increase client awareness and preparedness. The Recovery Resilience Program is based on the premise that in a Natural Functioning mode, a client is better able to manage their cravings than in an addicted mode. The suggested practice of *Sensory Awareness* can lead to greater acceptance of internal experiences such as cravings or other painful feeling states. It must be noted that Sensory Awareness differs from other mindfulness-based interventions (Bowen et al., 2011) that also practice tuning into the senses in that the aim is not to have detached awareness or merely observe thoughts but is also about "thinking about our thinking" to gain awareness of the adverse effects of I-System activity, and thus develop more adaptive metacognitive strategies for reducing I-System activity.[28]

Identify and Challenge Cognitive Distortions

Teaching clients to recognize and address their cognitive distortions, such as catastrophizing, jumping to conclusions, and overgeneralizing, is beneficial for recovery and relapse prevention. In addition to addressing cognitive distortions, the Recovery Resilience Program emphasizes the role of metacognition in addiction dynamics. In short, the content of ordinary cognition is important to understanding psychological disturbance and the capacity for flexible mental control. Traditional cognitive and behavioral theories of psychological dysfunction (Ellis, 1962; Beck, 1976) emphasize the role of cognitive bias and distorted or irrational beliefs. In cognitive and behavioral approaches, the focus is on "*what*" people think; in the metacognitive approaches, the focus is on "*how*" people think. In addition to "*how*" people think (in the ISM the "how" is referred to as Depressor or Fixer activity), the Recovery Resilience Program also focuses on the "*who*" that does the "how" of thinking – the individual in an addicted mode or Natural Functioning mode.

Simply put, the goal of a Recovery Resilience Program is for clients to develop awareness and metacognitive understanding of the adverse effects of I-System activity in their recovery process and gain practices that reduce its adverse effects as part of their recovery program.

28 The practice of Sensory Awareness shares similarities with the attention training technique (ATT) of metacognitive therapy. See Normann & Morina (2018).

Session 1

High-Risk Situations

SESSION OBJECTIVE

1. Provide overview and objective of the Recovery Resilience Program.
2. Discuss the concept of recovery capital.
3. Introduce the I-System.
4. Introduce the concept of a Recovery Resilience Practice.
5. Introduce Natural Functioning.
6. Introduce I-System Requirements.
7. Introduce the Mind–body Bridging Shift.
8. Discuss High-Risk Situations.
9. Introduce Sensory Awareness.
10. Assign homework.

SESSION DESCRIPTION

Session 1 introduces the Recovery Resilience Program and its fundamental concepts. In this session, the concepts of I-System and Natural Functioning are introduced and explained. The central premise of the program is highlighted: (1) that I-System activity can adversely affect a client's capacity to effectively apply their recovery tools and access their recovery capital, referred to as recovery resilience, and (2) that a Recovery Resilience Practice enhances recovery resilience (where they effectively apply their recovery tools and access their recovery capital).

How to Facilitate a Session

This manual is designed for those working with addicted populations (from lay counsellors to psychiatrists) who are delivering the Recovery Resilience Program (RRP). The RRP is a person-centered, strength and resiliency-based relapse prevention and recovery-oriented intervention that works in synergy with other models, especially 12-step programs. The RRP presents practices that enhance "recovery resilience" – an individual's capacity to effectively apply coping and self-regulation skills in dealing with cravings, triggers, stress, and high-risk situations without reverting to substance use. The program helps individuals to enhance and use their recovery capital at any stage of recovery, and ultimately reach recovery and life goals. It effortlessly integrates with other evidence-based relapse prevention programs, from the original cognitive–behavioral approaches to the newer mindfulness-based and metacognitive approaches. Written by clinicians who have worked with addicts and their families for many decades, the program is easy to implement and very little preparation is necessary, with handouts and PowerPoints included in each session.

Each Session offers exercises that can be presented as PowerPoint presentations or written on a whiteboard. We have included references for facilitators who want to further explore the source material or want to include references in their presentations.

Material that needs to be presented to clients is indented throughout the manual. Our instructions and suggestions to facilitators are not indented. It is important to note the "**sample dialogue**" and instructions provided are suggestive only. Facilitators are not required to present material verbatim or follow instructions exactly. Similarly, the information provided in the "**Discuss** the following information" sections does not need to be presented verbatim either. Rather, it provides philosophical, theoretical, and research-based context for discussion that supports the RRP exercises. We encourage facilitators to present material and exercises based on the needs of the client or group, and to present the material at a level that is conducive to the client's or group's understanding and stage of recovery. This manual is scalable and can be adapted to a client's or group's specific needs.

For each exercise, there is a client handout available in the Appendix that they can use to complete the exercise during the session or as part of their assigned homework. The sessions are designed to be experiential, so in most cases, it is best if clients complete the exercises during each session. We provide examples of completed exercises throughout the manual.

The exercises in this manual mirror those in the client workbook titled Building Recovery Resilience. Addiction Recovery and Relapse Prevention Workbook – An I-System Model Application. du Plessis et al.

Introduction to the Recovery Resilience Program

The following section aims to provide a brief introduction and overview of the purpose of the Recovery Resilience Program (RRP).

Discuss the following information to introduce clients to the theory that informs the Recovery Resilience Program:

> There are several understandable reasons why individuals continue to use mind-altering substances, even when the costs are so obviously high across their lives.[1]
>
> Research points out that one reason that many individuals fail to achieve and/or maintain sobriety is that they have inadequate coping skills for dealing with stressful situations and painful feelings.[2] Hence,

1 See Gire (2002), West (2005), Maté (2011), Ahmed & Pickards (2019), and West et al. (2019).

2 See Marlatt & Gordon (1980) and Miller et al. (1996).

they turn to psychoactive substances as an alternative coping mechanism since alcohol or other drugs provide immediate and quite effective short-term stress relief and comfort. Some researchers believe that the primary reason psychoactive substances are so addictive is because of their short-term capacity to reduce stress and regulate emotion. For individuals suffering from addiction, substance use often becomes their predominant response to coping with life's challenges.[3]

For those in an addiction recovery process, relapse, despite the best of intentions and efforts to stop, is a daunting challenge in any sustained and successful effort to escape addiction. Individuals working on behavior change, such as recovery from addiction, are confronted again and again with powerful cravings and compulsive thoughts regarding the maladaptive behaviors they are attempting to change. Research has revealed a direct correlation between relapse to substance use after rehabilitation and deficits in skills for coping effectively with high-risk and stressful situations.[4] Therefore, the key to preventing relapse is to gain and practice new skills for coping with both anticipated and potentially unforeseen challenges. Simply put, having reliably accessible and effective coping skills is a crucial predictor for successful and sustained recovery from substance use disorders. For this very important reason, relapse prevention books or programs typically focus on teaching such skills.

Simply acquiring these coping skills does not guarantee sustained recovery. One also needs to *effectively* practice these skills and work a sustainable recovery program. This is evidenced by the fact that addiction treatment and relapse prevention programs have high rates of relapse, despite individuals having a plethora of skills available to them and often being highly motivated for recovery (Xie et al., 2005).[5] What will be highlighted in the upcoming sessions is that there is a mind–body system that **hinders** individuals in recovery from **effectively applying** these skills and recovery practices, saps their motivation, and may cause them to veer off their chosen recovery pathways.[6]

3 See Litt et al. (2003) and Maté (2011).
4 See Connors et al. (1996), Brewer et al. (1998), and Irvin et al. (1999).
5 See Xie et al. (2005.)
6 See Block et al. (2016), Ho & Nakamura (2017), and Du Plessis et al. (2021).

Use the following **sample dialogue** to introduce clients to the central aim of the RRP:

> The Recovery Resilience Program outlined in these six sessions will teach you how to recognize and "befriend" this hindrance - so that instead of it being an impediment, it can serve as a compass that guides you to stay true to your chosen recovery pathways as you go about your activities of daily living.

The following material provides a brief overview of some of the premises that inform the RRP. The aim is to provide clients with some understanding of the purpose of the RRP and how it dovetails with other recovery approaches, especially 12-step programs such as Narcotics Anonymous (NA) and Alcoholics Anonymous (AA). Clients need to understand that the RRP is not meant to replace their existing recovery practices, but is designed to augment it.

Discuss the following information to highlight the theory that informs the RRP:

> The Recovery Resilience Program is informed by the **I-System Model,** which was developed by psychoanalyst, psychiatrist, and physicist Stanley H. Block, and his wife and collaborator, Carolyn Block. Mind-Body Bridging, a psychological intervention derived from the I-System Model, informs the exercises in this manual, and has successfully been used in the treatment of several mood and behavioral disorders and has been recognized as evidence-based for the treatment of substance use disorders.[7]
>
> Three central premises underlie the Recovery Resilience Program. The first premise, is that we possess an innate capacity for resilience and flourishing. Patricia Gianotti in her book, *Uncovering the Resilient Core,* put it this way: "From the very beginning of life, the mind (like the body) is in a continuing process of working to actualize itself. The process is inherent" (Danielian & Gianotti, 2017, p. 3). Yet, as the program will highlight there is a mind-body system that at times can obstruct and hinder this innate resilience and our natural capacity for flourishing.[8]

7 See Nakamura et al. (2015), Block et al. (2016), and Block & Du Plessis (2018).

8 We use the term "flourishing" as an umbrella term for "happiness," "well-being," and "quality of life," as we believe this is one of the best constructs to define one of the central aims of the Recovery Resilience Program, and why we have included the Flourishing Scale at the end of each session.

The practices outlined in these sessions have a primary focus on teaching how to identify and manage this hindrance as it manifests in their activities of daily living. Clinical experience highlights that by identifying and managing this hindrance, referred to as "befriending" it, we can access our natural resilience. This allows one to efficiently apply coping skills and effectively work a recovery program. Our activities of daily living become the *dojo* (the Japanese term for practice hall) for applying these practices, which help unleash our innate resilience and capacity for flourishing, and thus sustain us in reaching our recovery and life goals.

The second premise that informs the Recovery Resilience Program is how it views addiction, and how this relates to recovery.[9] Most addiction specialists and researchers agree on some key elements,[10] and the definition of addiction used for the Recovery Resilience Program is congruent with conventional wisdom, research, and experience, but stresses one important feature that has particular relevance to the practices outlined in this manual. The Recovery Resilience Program views addiction broadly and simply as a **disposition** to use psychoactive substances that is characterized by impaired control and harm. Simply put, it views it from a dispositional perspective (proneness or tendency) that is context dependent. Robert West and colleagues (West et al., 2019a, p. 168) define "disposition" in the context of cravings as "a latent characteristic that becomes expressed under certain conditions." This dispositional perspective highlights that individuals can vary in degrees of control over their addiction depending on the context of the situation. Accordingly, the Recovery Resilience Program incorporates a resiliency and strength-based approach and highlights that individuals in recovery can have the capacity to *influence* this disposition both by (1) having

9 We use the terms "addiction" and "substance use disorder" interchangeably. Although the techniques in this book can be applied to both substance use and behavioral addictions, the focus of the book is on the treatment of substance use disorders. In fact, we have found the use of the term "addiction" as sometimes preferable in work with our clients in recovery, insofar as the term derives from the Latin root, *addictus*, which means "bond-servant," or "slave." Hence, addiction might be understood as "servitude" as in the biblical concept, or "enslavement," the alternative to which is "liberation" or "freedom" – first-hand experiences with which virtually any individual addicted to substances might readily identify.

10 See West (2005), American Psychiatric Association (2013), West et al. (2019a, 2019b), and Du Plessis (2023).

awareness of external and internal factors that make this disposition *more likely* and by (2) having *access* to resources and practices that can make this disposition less likely.

The third premise, simply put, is that you cannot fix what is not broken. That is, we do not view people who experience addiction as broken. Best-selling author and recovery expert John Bradshaw presents the argument in his book, *Healing the Shame that Binds You,* that toxic shame is often the motivator behind addictive behaviors (as well as many other dysfunctional behaviors). He states that "toxic shame gives you a sense of worthlessness, a sense of failing and falling short as a human being. Toxic shame is a rupture of the self with the self" (Bradshaw, 2005, p. 29). Toxic shame is a deep-seated belief that one is fundamentally flawed and simply not good enough as a human being. Shame often fuels substance use in a futile effort to medicate the often-overwhelming feelings associated with shame. Because individuals in recovery often feel flawed, not good enough, or damaged, they may feel that they need to be "fixed." However, when individuals in recovery attempt to fix what is *not broken* it only reinforces that which hinders their recovery process.

Use the following **sample dialogue** to emphasize to clients that they are not broken or damaged and don't need fixing. Rather, there is a mind-body system (which they will soon learn about) that causes them to see themselves as broken and often drives them to try to fix what is not broken.

Some of you working this program might have thought this (that you are somehow fundamentally broken or damaged) for so long that you think that it is true, that this shame is "just who you are," which may drive you to continually try and fix yourself. But these efforts are futile because we cannot fix an illusion or fiction.

The Greek myth of Sisyphus might be a useful analogy here. Sisyphus is depicted as one whose tricks and cunning as well as his hubris condemned him to eternally push a boulder uphill. However, as soon as he reached the top of the hill, the boulder would roll down and Sisyphus had to push it back up again, eternally. In trying to fix ourselves, we, like

> Sisyphus, keep pushing the boulder up the hill, only for it to roll down again. No matter how we try, we are caught in a perpetual cycle of trying to fix the illusionary damage induced by a shame-based belief system. All types of addiction could be seen as one of being caught, like Sisyphus, in a futile and perceptual cycle. The practices introduced in these sessions will help you to stop trying to fix "what ain't broke," and break that shame-based cycle, as these practices do not aim to fix you, because, as you will see, there indeed is nothing to fix. Instead, you will learn to recognize when a mind–body system we'll be discussing is overactive. You can then use this awareness to shift to a more natural mind–body state wherein you experience your true, resilient, undamaged self.

Use the following **sample dialogue** to help clients understand that a Recovery Resilience Practice will enhance their capacity to effectively work a recovery and relapse prevention program. It does not replace their recovery practices but is designed to help them use their practices more optimally.

> These sessions will assist you in developing a **Recovery Resilience Practice** that will facilitate your addiction recovery process by enhancing your capacity to effectively work a recovery and relapse prevention program. The practices presented enhance "**recovery resilience**" – a term we use to refer to an individual's capacity to effectively apply coping and self-regulation skills in dealing with cravings, triggers, stress, and high-risk situations without reverting to substance use. Each session includes exercises that help you develop these practices.

Discuss the following information to highlight how the concept of recovery resilience has commonality with the notion of **recovery capital**, which is central within **recovery-oriented** approaches to treating substance use disorders, and situated within the larger framework of **recovery-oriented systems of care** (ROSC). All these approaches value community-based services and supports that are person-centered and build on the strengths and resiliencies of individuals, families, and communities to help addicted individuals achieve abstinence and improved health, wellness, and quality of life. In short, the RRP program is intentionally designed to methodologically and theoretically dovetail within the frameworks of recovery-oriented interventions and ROSC by supporting these interventions and support systems.

The concept of recovery resilience has commonality with the notion of **recovery capital**, a phrase used in recovery communities to refer to the sum of all internal and external resources that a person has available to initiate and maintain their ongoing recovery process (Cloud & Granfield, 2004). William White defines recovery capital as "conceptually linked to natural recovery, solution-focused therapy, strengths-based case management, recovery management, resilience and protective factors, and the ideas of hardiness, wellness, and global health" (White & Cloud, 2008, p. 23). The notion of recovery capital reflects a move away from a focus on pathology or brokenness to one of a resilience-based recovery approach – a notion that is congruent with the recovery resilience focus of this workbook. White defines three types of recovery capital: personal recovery capital – which includes an individual's physical and human capital; family/social recovery capital – these resources relate to intimate relationships with friends and family, relationships with people in recovery, and supportive partners; and cultural capital – these resources resonate with individuals' cultural and faith-based beliefs.[11]

Use the following **sample dialogue** to further emphasize that the RRP will help clients access and optimally employ their existing recovery capital and resources. It does this by teaching them how to identify when they are "getting in their own way" and take action to get back on their recovery pathway.

A Recovery Resilience Practice aims to strengthen your internal resources, by removing what hinders your capacity to draw upon or use all three aspects of your recovery capital (e.g., skills, tools, knowledge, etc.), which will help prevent relapse, promote flourishing, and enable you to live the good life.

A Recovery Resilience Practice has one simple aim – to help you stay true to your recovery pathway and help you reach your recovery and life goals, thus enabling you to flourish. Although there is a hindrance that can steer you off course, this program will teach you how to "befriend" it, which will allow you to course-correct moment-to-moment as you go about your **activities of daily living**. In this way, the hindrance becomes a compass that helps you stay on your recovery pathway.

11 See White & Cloud (2008) and Foote et al. (2014).

As mentioned in the Introduction the RRP is designed to be an adjunct to relapse prevention programs and the recovery practices of individuals in addiction recovery. The Recovery Resilience Practice clients will develop by completing this program is not meant to replace any of their existing recovery practices, but instead is designed to positively augment their unique recovery pathway and help them access and optimally use their recovery capital. It is important that this is clearly stated to clients. Moreover, a Recovery Resilience Practice is compatible with most recovery pathways, especially 12-step programs, and is designed to support and enhance these recovery-oriented interventions. It is important to highlight that the RRP will not be effective without clients having a solid foundational recovery program, especially a community-based support group like the 12-step program or a similar peer-support group.

Use the following **sample dialogue** to emphasize to clients that developing the foundation of a Recovery Resilience Practice requires consistent effort over several weeks or months.

> The six sessions of the Recovery Resilience Program outline a structured approach to learning practices that can be completed within a concentrated timeframe. Together, these practices, when practiced regularly, constitute your personal **Recovery Resilience Practice**. Each session serves as a building block for the next, introducing a sequence of exercises that teach, through direct experience, aspects of a Recovery Resilience Practice as well as providing the underlying rationale for each of these practices. There are two scales at the end of each session to help you monitor your Recovery Resilience Practice development and improvement in your subjective well-being or flourishing.
>
> It is recommended that you directly experience and live the practices introduced in each session for at least one to two weeks before moving on to the next chapter. As jazz saxophonist Charlie Parker observed: "If you don't live it, it won't come out of your horn." Which is to say: your Recovery Resilience Practice and your recovery will be sustainable only if you "live it."

The I-System

The next couple of exercises are designed for clients to become familiar with the activity of their I-Systems, which we also refer to as the "hindrance," that is, the hindrance to them working an effective recovery program. It is important that they learn to recognize their personal I-System signals. That is, how they experience their minds and bodies when their I-System is overactive and hindering their recovery.

The primary focus of Session 1 is on high-risk situations but before we discuss that we will provide clients with exercises that outline some of the basic concepts of the program.

Use the following **sample dialogue** to guide clients through completing a **Mapping** exercise that will help them recognize when the mind-body state they've been learning about is overactive.

> We begin with an exercise that will help you recognize when you are experiencing this mind-body system that acts as a hindrance, and how it interferes with your ability to effectively navigate high-risk situations. Recognizing when this mind-body system is overactive is the first step in increasing your recovery resilience.
>
> In Exercise 1.1 you will identify a situation that is currently causing you a great deal of trouble or distress (e.g., your current relationship or stress at work). You will use a template called a Map. In this exercise you will perform I-System Mapping, or Mapping for short, a core Recovery Resilience Practice that helps you, through free association, recognize the mind-body system that acts as a hindrance to your innate resilience and interferes in your daily life.
>
> Once you have identified a troubling situation, write it inside the oval on Map 1. Then take a couple of minutes to scatter your thoughts and feelings about that situation around the outside of the oval. Don't edit or second-guess; just write down whatever thoughts come to mind.

> After a couple of minutes, stop writing and at the bottom of the Map describe your body tension. Where do you experience it in your body? How do you experience it?

Use the **sample dialogue** below to guide clients through Exercise 1.2, which will have them complete another Map about the same situation after engaging in **sensory awareness**.

> Next, write the same troubling situation used in the Map 1 exercise you just completed in the oval of Map 2 using the template provided for Exercise 1.2. Before you write anything else on the Map, you will take a few moments to tune into your senses.
>
> Begin by first getting comfortable in your chair and focusing on what you are currently doing. Next, just sit and listen to the background sounds. As you listen feel your feet on the floor, the weight of your body on your seat. Feel the fabric of your clothing, or the tabletop, or just rub the tips of your fingers together while you continue to listen to the background sounds. If a thought distracts you, return to listening to the background sounds.
>
> Once you feel settled write the thoughts and feelings that come to your mind now about the situation around the oval. As you write, feel the pen in your hand and watch the ink flow onto the paper while continually focusing on the background sounds. As with the previous Map, don't edit. There are no right or wrong thoughts. Just let your thoughts stream while you are tuned into your senses.
>
> After a couple of minutes, stop writing and at the bottom of Map 2 provide a description of your body tension. Where do you experience it in your body? How do you experience it?

Use the **sample dialogue** below to facilitate a discussion about how clients' second Map differed from their first Map. Allow clients sufficient time to process how the second Map differed from the first. Most of them will have experienced a "shift" in their mind-body state. Have them share how they experienced the shift. Note that occasionally a client might not experience a difference between the Maps.

Completed example of Exercise 1.1

Map 1

What if I cannot live up to others' expectations of me?

I have to give up my life for this job

I don't feel like going into work today

Scared about losing my job

Stress on the job

I will be never be good enough

I don't know how to manage my supervisees at work

Anxious about being so far behind

What do I tell co-workers when they disappoint or frustrate me?

Description of body tension I feel so much tension in my neck & shoulders

Now, compare Map 1 and Map 2. In the template provided for Exercise 1.3 write down a very brief description of your experience of doing Map 1 and then do the same for Map 2. The troubling situation in the oval is the same on both Maps, but what is different about your experience with the two Maps? What, if anything, has shifted for you? Write down your thoughts.

Did you experience more tension in Map 1 than in Map 2? Did you experience less stress and more lightness when completing Map 2? Was there more mind-clutter in Map 1 than in Map 2? The answer to these questions is most likely "yes."

What caused the decrease in body tension and mind clutter? The reality of the situation did not change, but your orientation toward it did. When you did Map 1 you likely attributed all your distress to the troubling situation itself. But your body tension and mind clutter decreased when you did Map 2, even though the troubling situation is the same. So, if the troubling situation is not the sole cause of your distress, what is? This exercise demonstrates that there is something else besides the troubling situation that is causing your distress.

What you will discover as you complete this workbook is that excessive mental clutter (i.e., excessive worrying, rumination, obsessive thinking, and over-analyzing) and body tension are often signs that a certain mind–body state is prevailing and that this mind–body state is caused by a mind–body system. This mind–body system is operationalized as the short for Identity System – a construct for a self-referential mind–body system that when overactive interferes with optimal functioning and innate resilience. Your I-System was likely more active when you did Map 1 than it was when you did Map 2. Why? When you did Map 2, you literally "came to your senses" by focusing on the background sounds and your body sensations. Opening your awareness to what you are sensing quiets or "rests" your I-System.

When your I-System is overactive, it contracts your awareness and restricts your optimal functioning. These are the characteristics of the mind–body state called I-System Functioning. What does this have to do with your recovery? The I-System distorts how one perceives, thinks, feels, and acts. If not effectively managed, your I-System hinders your ability to draw on your recovery capital (skills and tools). What's more, it not only negatively affects your capacity to apply skills or tools, but it hinders all aspects of working a recovery program and living the good life.

As we previously outlined, the Recovery Resilience Program is based on the premise that we have an innate resilience toward growth and healing. You naturally experience and express this innate resilience when your I-System is rested and thus not hindering this access. Excessive mental clutter and body tension are "red flags" that you are experiencing I-System Functioning. Learning to recognize when you are experiencing this mind–body state allows you to use the other Recovery Resilience Practices taught in this workbook to transform your I-System into a powerful ally.

Recognize I-System Activity

Use the **sample dialogue** below to help clients understand that the I-System can be an ally when they learn to recognize its activity and signals.

Now you will learn how to transform your I-System from a hindrance to a helper and use it to help you stay on your recovery pathway instead of allowing it to veer you off course. When you recognize that your I-System is overactive by noticing that you are experiencing mental clutter and body tension, you are using a Recovery Resilience Practice called **Recognize I-System Activity**. When you recognize your I-System is overactive, it allows you to befriend it.

You befriend your I-System by using it as a compass that alerts you when you are off course from living your best life and from tapping into your innate resources. The mind clutter and body tension you experience are signals alerting you that your I-System is overactive. From now on, these signals can alert you that you are experiencing I-System

Functioning and thus not optimally prepared to deal with the situation at hand, so you can then act to correct course.

When you "came to your senses" while completing Map 2, you experienced this course correction - the shift in a mind-body state that occurred (i.e., from mind clutter and body tension to a lightness or calmness) when your I-System released its grip.

The Mind–Body Bridging Shift

Use the **sample dialogue** below to introduce and then process the next exercise (Exercise 1.4) which is designed to help clients experience what it's like to be off balance and regain equilibrium. This is analogous to shifting from an overactive I-System to a rested I-System (there is no handout for this exercise).

The following exercise will help to further illustrate the Recovery Resilience Practice of Recognizing I-System Activity. As you sit in your chair, lean to the left or right for about 10 seconds then bring yourself back to an upright centered position. When you leaned to the left or right, did you feel tension in your body? Did you feel a sense of imbalance? After you returned to an upright, centered position, did the body tension release? Did you feel more balanced?

Recognizing your I-System activity is like recognizing you are tilting off balance. The I-System alerts you to this imbalanced state. When you rest your I-System, you come back in balance. Simply put, the I-System creates this imbalanced state and sends signals alerting you that you are off course, and your Recovery Resilience Practice brings you back into balance. This shift is referred to as the **Mind–Body Bridging Shift** (the **Shift** for short).

I-System Functioning inhibits optimal functioning by causing you to "get in your own way" as your thoughts turn inward and away from the task or moment at hand. When you are in this mind-body state it distracts you from meeting the imperative of the moment and drawing on your recovery capital and effectively applying your recovery skills. It is important to note that the I-System is not bad, as it plays an important function. Our aim is not to eliminate the I-System, which is not possible, but instead to make it an ally. Without awareness of its overactivity, it is counterproductive. With awareness, it acts as a compass that guides us in our activities of daily living.

Let's consider the example of a plane that has an automatic pilot system to illustrate how this works. As the plane flies towards its destination the automatic pilot self-corrects, moment-to-moment, to keep the plane on course regardless of the conditions. In the same way, each time you befriend your I-System and experience the Shift you correct course and stay true to your recovery pathway and life goals.

Natural Functioning

Use the **sample dialogue** below to introduce clients to the concept of Natural Functioning, which according to the I-System Model is their innate and optimal mind–body state. Emphasize that clients will automatically shift to Natural Functioning when their I-Systems are not overactive. They do not need to be or do anything special to experience their Natural Functioning apart from resting their I-Systems. Also, emphasize that it is in their Natural Functioning that they have more access to their recovery capital.

Look at Map 2 again. Even though the situation was the same as the one used with Map 1, you likely had a different experience while doing this Map. When focused on the background sounds and your body sensations your I-System quieted down or was rested, your mind clutter and body tension reduced, and you most likely had a different perspective of the situation. The reality of the troubling situation did not change, but your orientation toward it did because you shifted toward a more expansive mind–body state.

In doing the second Map you likely shifted to a mind–body state termed **Natural Functioning**. Natural Functioning refers to our state or mode of being when focused on the present moment or activity without the hindrance of the I-System. Because it is your natural mind–body state, Natural Functioning spontaneously arises when you rest your I-System.

When you shifted to Natural Functioning, you were brought back into balance. Although there is often little you can do about external events, there is often a great deal you can do about your internal orientation to the event or situation. When you recognize that your I-System is overactive when dealing with any situation and take action to rest it, you are less at the mercy of the external event or situation and naturally more confident in your ability to cope with it.

One of the central premises of the Recovery Resilience Program is that in a Natural Functioning state, we are more resourceful and resilient, and we can tap into our innate capacity for flourishing. This point of view is shared by several scholars who assert that we have an innate resilience and drive toward self-actualization (sometimes referred to as the "true" or "real" self). The psychoanalyst Karen Horney (1950) proposed that the "real" self contains potential for growth, happiness, and willpower, and for achieving self-actualization. These scholars postulate that growth and flourishing spontaneously occur if one removes what hinders them from manifesting (Horney, 1950; Danielian & Gianotti, 2012, 2017). For example, plants have an innate capacity to grow when one places them in the right environment. They cannot be forced to grow. One can only create the right conditions for growth to occur. In this regard humans are not that dissimilar - when we access our natural resourcefulness we flourish.

The aim of developing a Recovery Resilience Practice is to simply remove the I-System's interference with your innate resourcefulness, resilience, and capacity for flourishing. You can therefore see that it is not just the "**what**" and "**how**" that comprise an effective and sustainable recovery lifestyle but also the "**who**" that is doing it. The "who" that is engaged in your recovery is the essence of the Recovery Resilience Practice. The "who" may often be much more important than "what." There are many books on "what" to do for a sustainable recovery, but this book focuses primarily on "who" is doing it - your Natural Functioning self or your I-System Functioning self.

The Recovery Resilience Program is based on the premise that your Natural Functioning mind-body state is central to achieving what the Greek philosopher Aristotle called *eudaimonia*, often translated as flourishing.[12] In a Natural Functioning mind–body state you meet the imperative of each moment without the hindrance of your overactive I-System. You automatically tap into your innate resources. This does not mean you act or behave perfectly but do your best, at that moment, unfettered by your I-System's interference. In Natural Functioning you are capable of *phronesis*, an ancient Greek word for a type of wisdom or intelligence relevant to practical action. In your Natural Functioning mind–body state, you have access to your innate resilience, your various recovery skills and tools (recovery capital), and your practical wisdom (*phronesis*) to meet the demands of the moment.

I-System Requirements

Use the **sample dialogue** below to introduce the concept of Requirements by having the client complete two Maps: *How I Would Like Certain People to Act* and *How I Would Like to Be*. These are teaching Maps, in the sense that they are designed to help clients understand the concept of a Requirement. The aim is for clients to recognize that it is a violated Requirement that causes their I-Systems to become overactive.

Now you may ask, what triggers the I-System to become overactive, creating this imbalanced state that causes you to get in your own way, impeding your capacity to work a recovery program, and veering you off your recovery pathway? This is an important question, and we are going to explore it by doing two Mapping exercises. First, you will complete a How I Would Like Certain People to Act Map followed by a How I Would Like to Be Map.

Using the template provided for Exercise 1.5: How I Would Like Certain People to Act, write down inside the circle how you would like certain important people in your life to act or behave. Then draw a line to the outside of the circle and write down the person's behavior when they contradict how you would like them to act. Then, for each of the items outside the circle write down the degree of your body tension and

12 See Kenny (1978).

degree of negative emotional response. Note it on a scale from 1 (low) to 3 (high). Refer to the example provided.

Use the **sample dialogue** below to help clients understand the difference between a Natural Functioning expectation and a Requirement, which is that the latter causes their I-Systems to become overactive whereas the former does not. Emphasize that their Requirements are tied to their sense of identity or their perceived self-concept. When Requirements are violated, they will feel like their identity or sense of self is threatened and their I-Systems will become overactive in an effort to defend them from the perceived threat and to maintain a stable sense of self or identity.

Note that on this "How I Would Like Certain People to Act Map" the items inside the circle may be natural expectations you have for that person. However, if you normally have a lot of mind clutter and body tension in response to the person's behavior outside the circle, it is your sign that your I-System becomes overactive when they behave like that.

We all have expectations. When some of these are violated, it does not bother us much if at all. But when some expectations are not met, we experience significant mind clutter and body tension, as you may have noticed when completing the exercise. When you experience significant mind clutter and body tension when an expectation is not met it is a sign that the unmet expectation has triggered your I-System. These expectations are **I-System Requirements** or **Requirements** for short. They are what cause your I-System to become overactive and interfere with your Natural Functioning.

Requirements are simply the "shoulds" or "musts" you have about a particular situation. Your I-System generates requirements each moment of how you, others, or the world absolutely should or must be. When you have a violated Requirement (i.e., reality does not conform to your Requirement), your I-System becomes overactive.

Why do Requirements over-activate the I-System? We will use an analogy to explain. All living systems strive to maintain homeostasis. When your body does not feel right, it instinctively works to restore its optimal functioning. For example, when your body temperature is too high, you sweat, and if it goes too low, you shiver. Your temperature-regulating system automatically tries to restore your body's optimal temperature.

Analogously, your I-System, instead of working to maintain an ideal temperature, works to maintain a certain "I-centered" fictional ideal of yourself, others, and the world. In other words, the reason that these "ideal pictures" or "mental rules" (I-System Requirements) of how you, others, and the world should or absolutely must be cause you distress when they are not realized is simply because your I-System believes that they have something important to do with who you are, your perceived sense of self or identity; hence, our shorthand term, I-System. When a Requirement is violated, it is not merely experienced as a minor disappointment, but rather as a major threat to your I-System's idealized picture of yourself or your I-centered reality. Karen Horney (1950) referred to this type of demand we have for an idealized view of ourselves as a "tyranny of shoulds."

There are many thoughts, memories, and stories that make up "who you think you are." When you experience excessive body tension and mental clutter (signs of I-System Functioning) you can bet that something is not conforming to the Requirements you have for yourself, others, or the world. When you recognize that a Requirement has triggered your I-System you are practicing a Recovery Resilience Practice called **Recognize Requirements**.

Now let's do another exercise to further illustrate the concept of Requirements. For the next exercise, you will do a *How I Would Like to Be Map*. Using the template provided for Exercise 1.6, write down the qualities you wish to have or possess. Write five of these qualities inside the circle. Then draw a line to the outside of the circle and write down the opposite of that quality. Now for each of the qualities outside the circle consider the degree of body tension and negative emotional response you experience when you display these qualities.

Use the **sample dialogue** below to process the *How I Would Like to Be Map* with clients. Emphasize that the way to differentiate between a Natural Functioning expectation and a Requirement is that the latter will have significant body tension and mental clutter associated with it whereas the former will not. Also emphasize that when they get caught up in their Requirements they will focus on the "what" or be situationally focused rather on the "who" or the self that is dealing with the situation, which is what they can control.

EXAMPLE 1.5

Completed example of Exercise 1.5

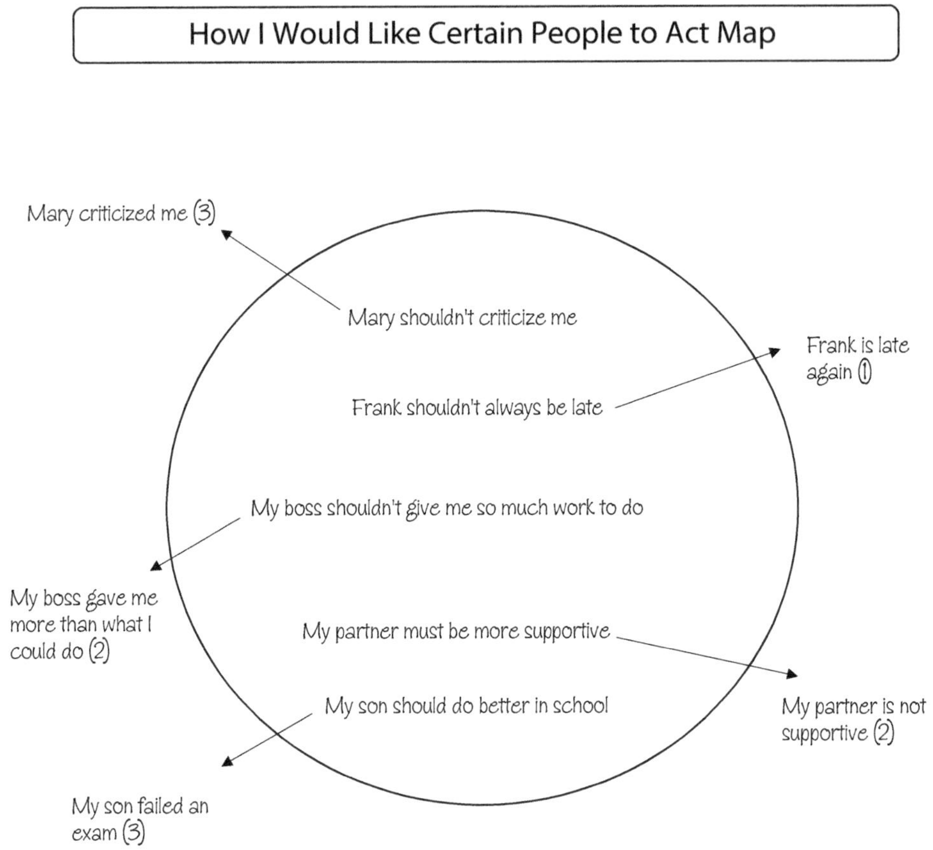

Like the previous Map, all the qualities inside the circle may be Natural Functioning expectations you have for yourself. But, if you have excessive mind clutter and body tension associated with the qualities outside the circle, it is a sign that they trigger your I-System. As mentioned, what over-activates your I-System are the Requirements inside the circle. For example, wanting to be successful is a natural expectation. However, when you fail (or feel as if you're failing) and you have mind clutter and body tension it signifies that it is an I-System Requirement, "I should be successful." That means that your ability to deal with the present moment is impaired because your I-System is over-active and interfering with your Natural Functioning. Simply recognizing that a Requirement has over-activated your I-System helps you experience the Shift.

Share and discuss the following information to highlight that a Recovery Resilience Practice does not focus on changing any given situation (the "what") but instead focuses on changing the "who" that is dealing with the situation. This does not mean that the situation (the "what") is distressing in itself, but often one does not have control over it, yet we can control how we (the "who") respond to it, either by creating more distress or dealing with the distressing situation more effectively.

As was previously mentioned, Recovery Resilience Practice does not focus on changing any given situation (the "what") (crucial insofar as many distressful situations or triggers may be unavoidable) but instead focuses on changing the "who" that is dealing with the situation. In *It Works How and Why: The Twelve Steps and Twelve Traditions of Narcotics Anonymous* it states: "It is a spiritual axiom that whenever we are disturbed, no matter the cause, there is something wrong with us" (Narcotics Anonymous World Services, 1983, p. 92). This is exactly what the I-System leads us to believe, that it is the "what" that's the problem. What we are attempting to point out is that it is not the "what" (situation) that distresses us – which, by the way, may not be amenable to change – but rather the "who" that is dealing with the "what." That is, when we deal with any situation or moment in I-System Functioning, we will experience body tension and mental clutter and have limited access to our recovery capital. When we deal with these "whats" in Natural Functioning, we have more access to our recovery capital and skills. Recognizing when a Requirement has activated your I-System is critical to making sure the right "who" that is best equipped to stay on the recovery path is in charge. The Stoic philosopher Epictetus highlights this point of view by stating, "It's not what happens to you, but how you react to it that matters" (in Taylor, 2021, p. 220). We would modify the second part of this statement slightly to "but the 'who' that reacts to it that matters."

Use the **sample dialogue** to emphasize that a Recovery Resilience Practice provides participants with a choice between I-System Functioning or Natural

Functioning. Point out that the ability to regulate their I-Systems is especially critical when they encounter high-risk situations, which is the focus of the next section.

Choosing to use Recognize Requirements and other Recovery Resilience Practices to rest your overactive I-System allows you to experience your innate resilience moment-by-moment and to live your best life. Making the same basic point, this time from an existential perspective,

EXAMPLE 1.6

Completed example of Exercise 1.6

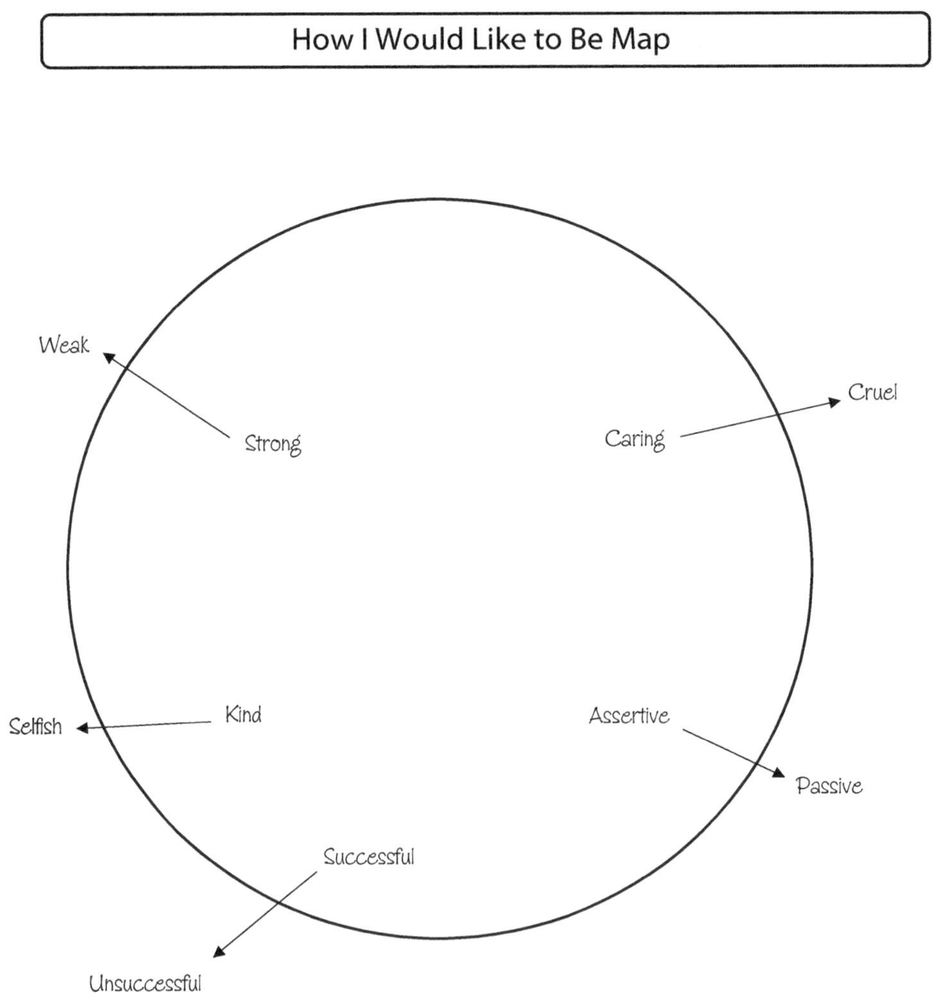

psychiatrist and Holocaust survivor, Dr. Viktor Frankl, asserted: "Everything can be taken from a man but one thing: the last of the human freedoms – to choose one's attitude in any given set of circumstances, to choose one's own way" (Frankl, 1969, p. 86). You can simply choose to befriend your I-System and use it as a guide as you travel on your recovery pathway, or you can choose to let it steer you off course – it is up to you.

Now let's see how what you've learned and experienced so far in the session relates to high-risk situations. Managing high-risk situations is an essential component of any recovery or relapse prevention process.

High-Risk Situations

Use the **sample dialogue** below to transition clients' focus to how their Recovery Resilience Practice relates to navigating high-risk situations. They will begin by identifying a few different kinds of high-risk situations they often encounter. Remind clients that the focus of this program is not just to provide an exhaustive set of relapse prevention skills and tools but, as importantly, to help them to consistently and effectively apply them.

As was pointed out, research has shown that having reliably accessible coping and self-regulation skills is a crucial predictor for successful, sustained recovery from addiction (Marlatt, 1985b; West 2005). With more effective skills, a person in addiction recovery develops increased confidence (Marlatt et al., 1995) in their ability to handle challenging situations without the use of substances, increasing their **recovery resilience**. As mentioned, your recovery resilience represents your ability to draw on your recovery capital to effectively cope with and manage stressful situations without reverting to substance use, as well as being able to self-regulate your inner world without the use of substances.[13] Recovery resilience is about having the right skills and the capacity to apply those skills. This is particularly important for situations that pose a high risk for relapse.

13 See Wills & Shiffman (1985).

High-risk situations can be understood as events and situations that, if not effectively managed, pose a potential risk for relapse (Brewer et al., 1998). What is important to note is that it is chiefly the individual's subjective perception of "risk" that plays a significant role in whether a situation is high risk or not. A high-risk situation poses a threat to one's perceived ability (what psychology calls "self-efficacy") to handle the challenging situation at hand (Greenfield et al., 2000). Therefore, by developing more effective coping skills, thereby increasing perceived self-efficacy, one can learn to manage a high-risk situation without defaulting to substance use (Earley, 1994).

Most relapse prevention programs provide various skills and tools for dealing with high-risk situations which are essential for sustained recovery. It is assumed that you already have these assets or are in the process of gaining them. Therefore, the focus of this program is not to provide an exhaustive set of relapse prevention skills and tools but to help you unlock your innate resilience so that you can effectively apply them. In this session and throughout the program we focus on helping you to develop a **Recovery Resilience Practice**, which will enable you to use these assets to maximum effect. More specifically, you will learn about a mind–body system that when overactive hinders your capacity to effectively use your skills and tools to deal with high-risk situations or any troubling situation, thereby causing you to veer off your recovery pathway. In other words, this mind–body system can, if not managed, restrict your recovery resilience thereby limiting your capacity to effectively deal with high-risk situations.

Share and discuss the following information to highlight that each person has a unique set of high-risk situations related to their experience of addiction. It is impossible to avoid all high-risk situations, but it is imperative for clients to learn to effectively manage these situations by managing the "who" that is dealing with them.

Each person has a unique set of high-risk situations related to his or her life and experience of addiction. Even so, there are nevertheless three generally agreed-upon categories most high-risk situations fit within: (1) negative or challenging internal, emotional states, (2) external social pressure, and (3) interpersonal conflict.[14] As an individual in recovery, it is impossible to avoid all high-risk situations and their associated internal or external triggers. It is imperative, however, for the sake of ongoing sobriety, to learn to effectively manage these situations by managing the "who" that is dealing with them.

Use the **sample dialogue** below to introduce Exercise 1.7:

Using the template provided for Exercise 1.7, you will make a list of potential high-risk situations using the three categories:

- intrapersonal (which occur internally, within yourself, for example, your attitudes, thinking, and emotional states);
- interpersonal (refers to things occurring between people, for example, your relationship with your partner); and
- environmental (for example, external stressors such as finances, work, and social events).

It is not important at this stage to be comprehensive in your list; rather, you must start with those items that are "on the front burner" or uppermost in your mind. See the examples provided to help you know what to do.

Use the **sample dialogue** below to explain how to "Map out" a high-risk situation.

For Exercise 1.8, you will once again use a **Map** template. As previously introduced, **I-System Mapping,** or **Mapping** for short, is a core Recovery Resilience Practice that helps you recognize your I-System activity. The central aim of Mapping is to help you "see" how your I-System works and interferes in your daily life, including your ability to handle high-risk situations when you encounter them.

For this exercise, you will choose one of the high-risk situations from the list you created in the previous exercise and write it inside the oval of Map 1 using the template provided for Exercise 1.8. Then take a couple of minutes to scatter your thoughts and feelings about that situation around the outside of the oval. Don't edit or second-guess; just write down whatever thoughts come to mind.

14 See Marlatt & Gordon (1980).

After a couple of minutes, stop writing and at the bottom of Map 1 describe your body tension. Where do you experience it in your body? How do you experience it?

Use the **sample dialogue** below to guide clients in "Mapping out" a high-risk situation after engaging in Sensory Awareness.

Now, using the template provided for Exercise 1.9, write the same high-risk situation used in Map 1 of the previous exercise in the oval.

Begin by first getting comfortable in your chair and focusing on what you are currently doing. Next, just sit and listen to the background sounds. As you listen feel your feet on the floor, the weight of your body on your seat. Feel the fabric of your clothing, or the tabletop, or just rub the tips of your fingers together while you continue to listen to the background sounds. If a thought distracts you, return to listening to the background sounds.

Once you feel settled write the thoughts and feelings that come to your mind now about the situation around the oval. As you write, feel the pen in your hand and watch the ink flow onto the paper while continually focusing on the background sounds. As with the previous Map, don't edit. There are no right or wrong thoughts. Just let your thoughts stream while you are tuned into your senses.

After a couple of minutes, stop writing and at the bottom of Map 2 provide a description of your body tension. Where do you experience it in your body? How do you experience it?

Use the **sample dialogue** below to facilitate a discussion about how clients' second high-risk situation Map differed from their first high-risk situation Map. Help them focus on what shifted for them.

Now, using the template provided for Exercise 1.10, compare Map 1 and Map 2. Write down a very brief description of your experience of doing Map 1 and then do the same for Map 2. The situation in the oval is the same on both Maps, but what is different about your experience of the two Maps? What, if anything, has shifted for you? Write down your thoughts.

Use the **sample dialogue** below to process the shift clients likely experienced between Map 1 and Map 2 even though the high-risk situation was the same. Emphasize that this means that the "who" that is dealing with the high-risk situation is as important, if not more so, than the "what" of the situation itself.

> As with the previous troubling situation Map exercise, did you experience more tension in Map 1 than in Map 2? Did you experience less stress and more lightness when completing Map 2? Was there more mental clutter in Map 1 than in Map 2?
>
> The high-risk situation did not change, but your orientation toward it probably did. When you did Map 1 you likely attributed all your distress to the high-risk situation itself. But your body tension and mind clutter decreased when you did Map 2, even though the troubling situation is the same. This exercise again demonstrates that there is something else (your I-System) besides the high-risk situation that is causing your distress.
>
> Map 1 helps you see that when there is I-System overactivity it makes it even more difficult to manage a high-risk situation. This is because when you attempt to deal with a high-risk situation or any troubling, stressful, or painful situation in I-System Functioning, it limits your awareness and ability to act optimally. When your I-System is active, it hinders your ability to draw on your recovery capital and skills and thereby limits your choices to a few habitual behaviors. And for those struggling with addiction, relapse is often the default response when confronted with stressful, painful, high-risk, and troubling situations.
>
> In Map 2 you likely experienced some release from I-System Functioning (i.e., the Shift). When you remove this hindrance your capacity to effectively deal with high-risk situations dramatically increases because you have full access to your recovery capital and skills.
>
> Earlier in the session you learned that I-System Functioning inhibits optimal functioning by causing you to "get in your own way" as your thoughts turn inward and away from the task or moment at hand, and that when you are in this mind–body state it keeps you from meeting the imperative of the moment optimally. Remember that the I-System

EXAMPLE 1.7

Completed example of Exercise 1.7

High-Risk Situations		
Intrapersonal (self)	**Interpersonal (others)**	**Environmental (the world)**
Self-pity	Arguing with partner	Social event
Anger	Isolating	Friend's house
Ungrateful	Problems with colleagues at work	Bills not paid

is not bad, as it plays an important function. You only need to learn to befriend it, which requires that you are aware of when it is active. Doing this transforms the I-System *from a hindrance to a compass* that tells you when you are getting off track and guides you back to Natural Functioning.

Use the **sample dialogue** below to guide clients in completing the next exercise that will help them "see" the Requirements they have regarding the high-risk situation they just "Mapped out."

In the next exercise, we are going to look for the Requirements associated with a high-risk situation that activate your I-System when they are violated.

Go back to Map 1 from Exercise 1.8 and circle the thoughts on the Map that cause a great deal of mind clutter and body tension. Then ask yourself how you would like these items to be. Sometimes the Requirement is as simple as being the opposite of the thought on the Map; other times you can identify a Requirement by asking the question "What is my Requirement for this situation?"

Completed example of Exercise 1.8

High-Risk Situation Map 1

What if somebody offers me alcohol?

It will be boring sober

I don't feel like going.

Scared

Holiday Party at Work

I will be socially awkward

I don't know how to socialize sober

Anxious

What do I tell people when they offer me a drink?

Description of body tension? Butterflies in stomach

> Write the thoughts you circled as "should" or "must" statements. Connect each circled thought to its should/must statement with a line. You may have written some of the thoughts on your map as should/must statements. If you did, just circle them. Refer to the example provided.

Use the **sample dialogue** below to help clients see that it is not only the high-risk situation itself that over-activates their I-Systems but the Requirements they have about the situation. Further emphasize that this means that they can deal with any high-risk situation optimally by recognizing the Requirements associated with it, which will prevent their I-Systems from becoming overactive and interfering with their recovery resilience.

> When you realize that a Requirement has been violated and has triggered your I-System you are using a Recovery Resilience Practice called **Recognize Requirements**. The aim of this practice is to become aware when a Requirement has been violated as you go through your daily activities. When you become aware of a Requirement it causes it to lose power to keep your I-System overactive. For example, let's say you have a Requirement that "Life should be fair." When you experience unfairness in some way or another, you will notice body tension and mind clutter, signs of I-System overactivity. When you notice these mind and body signals, you simply say to yourself, I have a Requirement that life should be fair. Doing this in the heat of the moment, when the Requirement is violated, initiates the Shift and quiets your I-System.
>
> As you have learned, it is not the situation (the what) that causes your I-System to become overactive, but rather the Requirements you (often automatically and out of awareness) have regarding that situation. It is frequently a violated Requirement associated with a high-risk situation that makes it more difficult to manage. Why? Because when the violated Requirement triggers your I-System your awareness and optimal functioning are restricted. Recognizing your Requirements related to high-risk situations will make it easier to manage the situation because you will do it in Natural Functioning where you can draw on your recovery capital and skills to deal with the situation more effectively.

Sensory Awareness

Use the **sample dialogue** below to introduce the Recovery Resilience Practice of **Sensory Awareness**:

When you completed Map 2, in Exercises 1.2. and 1.9, you likely experienced a shift from I-System Functioning to Natural Functioning, even though the troubling situation or high-risk situation was the same as the one on Map 1 (Exercises 1.1 and 1.8). What caused this shift? Simply put, when you completed Map 2 you literally "came to your senses" by focusing on the background sounds and your body sensations. When tuned into your senses the I-System automatically quiets and your mind clutter and body tension decrease. You shift from a limited and contracted state of being to a more expanded, flexible, and resilient state of being (refer to Figure 1.1). You don't have to stretch to move into Natural Functioning because it happens automatically when you rest your I-System.

When you did Map 2 you were performing a Recovery Resilience Practice called **Sensory Awareness**. It is as easy as listening attentively to the sound of an air conditioner, traffic outside, water going down the drain when you wash your hands, or the sound of a clock ticking. Any time in the day when you recognize that your I-System has become overactive, practice Sensory Awareness to initiate the Shift. This is particularly useful in high-risk situations, as it will help you deal with the situation in Natural Functioning.

It is important to note that sometimes when you experience excessive or overwhelming I-System activity (this happens to all of us) applying Sensory Awareness will not necessarily completely quiet your I-System. But with consistent practice, in the long run, you will find it to be a helpful component of your Recovery Resilience Practice.

Here is a list of various types of Sensory Awareness that you can practice throughout the day to quiet your I-System:

Awareness of Background Sounds

Your environment is full of sounds. During the day, pause and listen to background sounds, like the white noise of the heating or air-conditioning system, the wind blowing, traffic sounds, or the hum of the refrigerator.

Awareness of What You Are Touching

Be aware of what your fingers sense as you touch things such as glasses, phones, pens, keys, computers, and other objects. Are these surfaces smooth or rough, cold or warm, pleasant or unpleasant? Sense what it's like to feel the sun's warmth on your face or the breeze on your skin.

Awareness of Colors and Shapes

Pay attention today to what you see when you look at scenery and objects. Notice their colors, shapes, and forms.

Awareness of Your Body

Because of the unpleasant body sensations often associated with your overactive I-System, you may have developed a habit of trying to block out or get away from the feelings in your body. Pay attention to various bodily sensations or any tension or emotions experienced in the body. When you walk feel the sensation of your feet touching the ground. When you sit feel the pressure of the chair against your body.

Just for Today

To conclude Session 1, it would be helpful for clients who are active in 12-step fellowships to highlight how the practice of Sensory Awareness can augment the principle of living "just for today," a central feature of these fellowships. Explain that in 12-step fellowships members are advised to live "Just for Today."

Complete example of Exercise 1.9

High-Risk Situation Map 2

Description of body tension? Butterflies in stomach

Discuss the following information related to Sensory Awareness:

The practice of Sensory Awareness increases our capacity to live "Just for Today." Contrarily, active addiction brings with it a kind of "mindlessness," in which attention is distractible, a sense of purpose inaccessible, where being in the present moment is encumbered by cravings and/or withdrawal – and shame and self-judgment are the order of the day (Creswell et al., 2007; Teyber et al., 2011). On top of this, active addicts often apply ineffective and maladaptive coping strategies in stressful and troubling life situations. Sensory Awareness and being present in the moment, on the other hand, provide an alternative (Natural Functioning) for coping with stress, negative affect, and anxiety.[15] In the context of addiction, Sensory Awareness means "becoming aware of triggers for craving ... and choosing to do something else which might ameliorate or prevent craving, so weakening this habitual response" (Groves & Farmer, 1994, p. 189).

The practice of Sensory Awareness temporarily rests the I-System thereby facilitating recovery resilience. It increases and expands awareness, a necessary aptitude in recovery because activity without awareness is a feature of impulsive, mood-dependent, and addictive behavior (Lazarus & Folkman, 1984). Sensory Awareness is a way of cultivating and strengthening this awareness (Nakamura et al., 2015). Addiction, over time, distorts one's view of reality. More specifically, the defense mechanism of denial, which is one of the primary obstacles to initiating and sustaining successful recovery, is itself a profound narrowing of awareness. This in turn leads to a fragmented understanding of the widespread damage that goes hand-in-hand with addiction, which then only perpetuates the negative, addictive cycle. As Gestalt psychology pioneer Fritz Perls (1969, p. 66) put it: "Without awareness, there is no cognition of choice." Conversely, with increased awareness there is increased choice, and consequently increased ability to break the cycle of addiction.

Use the **sample dialogue** below to highlight the benefits of Sensory Awareness for their recovery and as a relapse prevention practice. Although Sensory Awareness is like mindfulness-based practices, there are some

15 See Baer (2003).

differences as the aim is not merely detached, non-judgmental awareness of thoughts, but also improved coping responses to both internal and external stressors.

When your I-System is overactive, your awareness contracts, leading to a more distorted and limited view of reality. When you practice **Sensory Awareness** and experience the **Shift**, a more balanced awareness expands spontaneously, which leads to a more comprehensive point of view that allows you to see things as they really are, and thus gain better insight into the true nature of your addiction and the consequences of using substances.

The practice of Sensory Awareness can also lead to greater acceptance of your internal experiences. In the context of the above discussion, it leads to greater acceptance of cravings or other painful feeling states rather than counterproductive shaming and self-judgment. Enhanced coping may also be experienced as the capacity for intentional inaction, which can be described as "letting go" and not acting on a craving or impulse to try to "fix" the negative feeling. (The Asian wisdom traditions speak similarly of "actionless action," or *wu wei.*) From this perspective the focus is on identifying and accepting the craving, thought, or feeling, rather than acting on it or attempting to fight it or fix it. This is sometimes referred to as "urge surfing" in relapse prevention programs. Instead of trying to eliminate the urge, one surfs it as they would a wave until it naturally fades away. Cravings typically only last for a limited time and will eventually run out of steam if they are not attended to.

It must be noted that Sensory Awareness skills differ from other mindfulness-based interventions (Bowen et al., 2011) that also practice

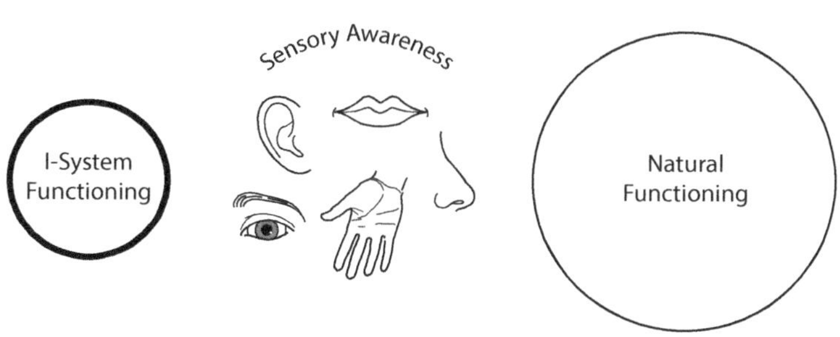

Figure 1.1 Sensory awareness skills.

tuning into the senses, in that the aim is not to merely have a detached awareness of our thoughts but to understand the workings of our mind (in psychology this is called metacognition – simply meaning, thinking about thinking).[16] As you have learned and will see in later parts of this workbook, we want to Recognize Requirements and label specific I-System thoughts and I-System narratives or stories. So instead of merely observing thoughts with detached awareness, we also want to be thinking about our thinking, and therefore "befriend" the various components of our I-Systems. Sensory Awareness is an important practice as it initiates the MBB Shift, however, on its own it is not sufficient. What is additionally required is an awareness of the components of your I-System, which is the focus of the other Recovery Resilience Practices introduced later in the Workbook.

Something stressed throughout this program is that it is not the written exercises by themselves that are your Recovery Resilience Practice, rather it is how regularly and habitually you learn to apply the practices in each moment of daily living – "just for today." At the beginning of your practice, it may feel awkward and mechanical, but with more practice, it will become second nature. Like in 12-step programs where participants are urged to apply the spiritual principles of the program in all their affairs, we suggest that a Recovery Resilience Practice is aimed at relating to all your activities in a state of Natural Functioning. When befriending the I-System it will act as a guide and compass alerting you when any of its Requirements have been violated, thus giving you an opportunity "shift" to relating to the situation in Natural Functioning, with expanded awareness and more practical wisdom and practical reasoning. Your practice hall or *dojo* is each moment.

I-System Functioning results in limited options for dealing with life because it restricts our capacity to use our recovery capital. It fundamentally results in a lack of creativity. The famous psychoanalytic thinker Otto Rank[17] argued that most of life's problems are due to a lack of creative responses. From the I-System Model perspective, we can see that Requirements limit our choices to those that are only congruent with our Requirements. When encumbered by Requirements we have

16 The practice of Sensory Awareness shares similarities with metacognitive therapy. See Normann & Morina (2018).

17 See Kramer (1995).

limited creativity to deal optimally with each moment in daily living and remain weighted down and boxed in them. In Natural Functioning, we do not have to force ourselves to be creative because in this state we automatically respond more creatively and resourcefully in the sense that the options we now have are expanded well beyond those imposed on us by our I-System's "tyranny of shoulds."

Conclude Session 1

Conclude the session by providing clients with exercise templates for any homework that is required before the next session and with the *Homework for Session 1* handout, which provides a summary of the Recovery Resilience Practices introduced in Session 1, as well as instructions for the *Flourishing Scale* and *Recovery Resilience Practice Scale*. The *Flourishing Scale* is designed to measure a client's subjective happiness, well-being, and quality of life. The *Recovery Resilience Scale* is designed to measure the frequency of a client's Recovery Resilience Practice. Indicate the frequency of each item occurring, whether "never," "hardly ever," "occasionally," or "regularly."

Please note that the way the sessions are outlined in this manual is suggestive only and facilitators can adapt this material to best match a given client's needs or what may be needed to adapt this curriculum within the structure of the facility within which they may be working.

Session 2

Cravings and Triggers

SESSION OBJECTIVE

1. Help clients deal effectively with cravings and triggers.
2. Introduce the concept of an addicted mode of being.
3. Introduce the concept of disposition and how it relates to addiction.
4. Introduce the notion that Natural Functioning enhances the capacity to manage cravings and triggers.
5. Discuss addicted mode warning signs.
6. Discuss the idea that recovery is a way of life.
7. Assign homework.

SESSION DESCRIPTION

The focus of this session is on helping clients to manage cravings and triggers. The notion of an addicted mode is introduced, and practices are highlighted that can assist clients in moving from an addicted mode to a Natural Functioning mode. The session aims to help clients understand that when they are in a Natural Functioning mode, they are more capable of dealing and coping with cravings and triggers. The notion of addicted mode warning signs is introduced and how to recognize these signs before it leads to a lapse or relapse.

Introduction to Session 2

Discuss the following information about the addicted mode with clients:

> Addictive behavior can be understood as being part of a mode of being, meaning that it is a particular and habitual way of existing, relating, and living. An **addicted mode of being** (or **addicted mode** for short) refers to all of an individual's beliefs, thoughts, attitudes, and fantasies that support their addictive behavior over time. An addicted mode can be understood as a particular mind–body state that accompanies all addictive behavior. Once someone enters an addicted mode, their awareness, attitudes, and behavior contract to the habitual patterns of their addicted lifestyle. Anyone who has experienced addiction to substances will relate to the notion that the act of using is merely one aspect of their addictive lifestyle. The premise of this program is that an individual's addicted mode is one of many possible dysfunctional and habitual mind–body states or modes-of-being they can experience when their I-System is overactive and that their addicted mode can only come into being when their I-System is overactive.

Use the **sample dialogue** below to introduce clients to the concept that an addicted mode is a disposition rather than a fixed state of being. With the claim that an addicted mode is a disposition we are not saying that addiction is not a permanent condition that spans long periods, but rather that individuals display various degrees of control over their addictive behavior depending on the situation or context – and that addictive behavior is one aspect of an addicted mode. Therefore, someone can be seen to suffer from addiction, but not necessarily be in an addicted mode. When one is in an addicted mode, addictive behavior is more likely, and therefore when an individual is in recovery and not in active addiction, they will still be prone to entering an addicted mode. However, if managed properly it will not lead to addictive behavior. In short, addictive behavior is a probable, but not necessary, outcome of being in an addicted mode.

> Some of you working this program might have thought you are broken or damaged. Your addicted mode is not a permanent or chronic condition, but rather a transitory mode that is one of many possible modes of being (healthy or dysfunctional). Your addicted mode can be

understood as a disposition, in the sense that it is not always active or present, but rather a state you enter under certain conditions (it is context-dependent) – that is, when your I-System is overactive. Natural Functioning can also be viewed from this perspective. It is a state you automatically experience when your I-System is resting. Addiction can be seen as a way of life that has been taken hostage by a particular mode of being.

An example of a disposition is a vase standing on a table. It has a disposition to break under certain conditions, such as if it gets bumped off the table and lands on a hard floor. Therefore, it has a disposition for two possible states, that is, being whole or being broken (under certain conditions). In the same way, one can have a disposition for inhabiting an addicted mode and subsequent addictive behavior, and as will be highlighted, there are some conditions or contexts that can activate this disposition. By learning how to rest your I-System, you can influence this disposition.

Your addicted mode and Natural Functioning mode are two distinct modes of being, each with its unique characteristics. You can only inhabit one of these modes at a time. When you rest your overactive I-System and consequently move into a Natural Functioning mode, it lessens the power of the beliefs, expectations, thoughts, fantasies, and attitudes that comprise your addicted mode. In your Natural Functioning mode, the possibility of relapse decreases significantly.

Cravings

Discuss the following information about cravings with clients. Highlight that their ability to manage cravings is a pivotal coping skill needed for sustained recovery from addiction.

It is often stated that cravings are a formidable adversary to those on a recovery pathway and that cravings are one of the major factors related to relapse (Marlatt, 1985a; Brewer, 2017). From an addiction treatment perspective, the management of cravings is a primary goal both in psychotherapy and pharmacotherapy. Individuals who lack effective coping responses and/or the confidence (self-efficacy) to deal with cravings and the situations that trigger them are at high risk for relapse (Miller, 1996). Consequently, your ability to manage cravings is a pivotal coping skill needed for your sustained recovery from addiction (Ahmed & Pickards, 2019).

Craving is often part of the habitual thoughts, emotions, attitudes, beliefs, and fantasies of an addicted mode. But cravings are also something we naturally experience. Some cravings are imperative for our survival. For example, if you do not crave water when your body needs water you could die. Cravings can also be a sign that our needs are not being met. Hence the acronym *HAALT-BB* (hungry, angry, anxious, lonely, tired, bored, and blue), which is inspired by a shorter version often used in 12-step communities that signifies certain emotional states and needs that when not met can lead to cravings. In any case, they are a natural and unavoidable aspect of any recovery process.

Cravings are best understood as existing on a continuum. On the one side are cravings that naturally arise and fade. On the other side are cravings that are amplified in various degrees of intensity when they are experienced in the addicted mode due to an overactive I-System. When one experiences cravings in an addicted mode, which limits access to one's recovery capital, the cravings can seem overwhelming.

Use the **sample dialogue** below to emphasize to your clients that in a Natural Functioning mode, they will better handle their cravings than they will in an addicted mode. You can use Figure 2.1 to explain this visually:

This program is based on the idea that in a Natural Functioning mind–body state or mode, you will better handle your cravings than you will in an addicted mode (overactive I-System mind–body state). To explain this metaphorically we will use two vessels - a one-ounce vessel and a 20-ounce vessel (see Figure 2.1)–to represent your internal experience of cravings and your mode of being. Imagine the one-ounce vessel is filled to the top with cravings - this represents being in an addicted mode with an overactive I-System. This vessel is so full there is no room for your recovery capital. Your existence is limited to relating to yourself, others, and the world only through the perspective of this addicted mode. In this overactive I-System mind–body state, overwhelmed by your cravings, you experience yourself as limited, and trapped within this addicted mode. You are cut off from your recovery capital and consequently, your ability to handle cravings (the empty space in Figure 2.1) is greatly limited.

When you rest your overactive I-System, you expand your internal capacity and mode of being. Metaphorically speaking, it's like pouring your "one ounce of cravings" into a 20-ounce vessel. Even though the same "amount" of cravings are present, they don't seem overwhelming. This is because in this Natural Functioning mind–body state – who you are without I-System interference – your innate resilience spontaneously emerges; you have full access to your recovery capital. The situation and cravings haven't changed, but your capacity to deal with them has increased. There is more space in the container, which represents a greater capacity to deal with the situation.

In Natural Functioning, the state of being which is symbolized in Figure 2.1 by the bigger vessel, you have expanded your sense of self and mode of being beyond your self-centered addicted mode. In the "Big Book" of Alcoholics Anonymous, it is stated that at the root of alcoholism is

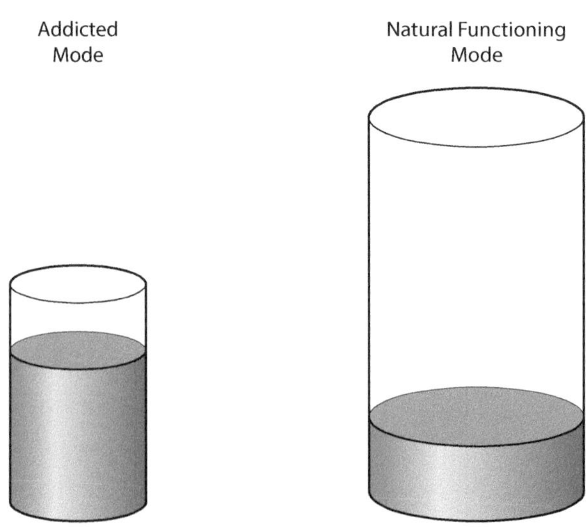

Figure 2.1 Addicted mode and Natural Functioning mode.

> self-centered fear (Wilson, 1976). This contracted and limited addicted mode of self-centered fear (you in the small vessel) is caused by your overactive I-System. In this self-centered state, you come to falsely believe that your addicted mode and its cravings and habitual behavior are who you are.

Discuss the following information with clients that further highlights the shift from an addicted mode to a Natural Functioning mode:

> In a letter addressed to Bill Wilson, the cofounder of Alcoholics Anonymous, the famous Swiss psychiatrist Carl Jung wrote: "You see, alcohol in Latin is *spiritus* and you use the same word for the highest religious experience as well as for the most depraving poison. The helpful formula therefore is: *spiritus contra spiritum*" (in Kurtz & Ketcham, 2002, p. 118). *Spiritus contra spiritum*, in the original Latin, translates as "spirit against [contra] spirit." Jung's suggestion can be interpreted to mean that we need "spirit" in the sense of an enlarged, or greater sense of self, to successfully counter the lesser spiritual facsimile (the literal "spirits" of alcohol). Jung was directly pointing out to Wilson that at the heart of a treatment for alcoholism there often is an existential/spiritual transformation. Jung believed that the thirst for alcohol "was the equivalent, on a lower level, of the spiritual thirst of our being for wholeness" – which is a transformation one experiences when one shifts from the limited, isolated, and self-centered "I" of the addicted mode (overactive I-System mind–body state) to the wholeness and interconnectedness found in one's Natural Functioning mind–body state or mode. This shift may be illustrated in the following quote by the German philosopher Friedrich Nietzsche: "I want to learn more and more to see as beautiful what is necessary in things; then I shall be one of those who make things beautiful" (Nietzsche, 2003, p. 157).

Triggers

Use the **sample dialogue** below to introduce your clients to and help them complete Exercise 2.1, which will help them identify triggers that can cause their I-Systems to become overactive:

In the next section, we are going to explore triggers, which are social, environmental, or emotional cues that remind people in recovery of their past drug or alcohol use. These cues bring about cravings that may lead to a relapse. One can often choose to avoid certain high-risk situations, but it is impossible to avoid all triggers.

Triggers can be external or internal. External triggers are people, places, activities, and objects that elicit thoughts or cravings associated with substance use. Internal triggers involve feelings, thoughts, or emotions formerly associated with substance use. Both external and internal triggers are related to past experiences of substance use that can lead to cravings. For example, when an alcohol-dependent individual drives past a bar the experience of seeing the bar is an external trigger that leads to a craving for alcohol. Similarly, when a cocaine addict feels lonely and bored, these emotions associated with past cocaine use are an internal trigger that leads to a craving for cocaine. In both examples, the use of substances is governed by reinforcement principles and has a direct effect on the pleasure centers of the brain (Bell et al., 2014). The euphoria produced by the stimulation of the pleasure center by drug use tends to positively reinforce addictive behavior and its associated triggers. Therefore, any trigger related to past positive experiences of using substances and/or internal state of mind or emotion can lead to intense cravings and memories of positive substance use experiences. As a result, the resumption of addictive behavior or substance use may be prompted by situational cues and/or internal, emotional triggers. Therefore, acquiring and using coping skills for dealing with cravings that result from triggers is central to a sustained recovery.

Like the exercise of identifying high-risk situations in the previous chapter, you will now make a list of potential triggers. Make a list of intrapersonal (for example, your thoughts, attitudes, beliefs, and emotional states), interpersonal (for example, your relationship with your partner), and environmental (for example, family beliefs and attitudes, peer group, and community) triggers that pose the biggest threat to you. It is not important at this stage to be comprehensive in your list;

EXAMPLE 2.1

Completed example of Exercise 2.1

Intrapersonal (self)	Interpersonal (others)	Environmental (the world)
Feeling sad	Criticized by my boss	Smell of a barbeque
Resentful	Argument with girlfriend	Walking past a bar
Self-pity	Not respected at work	Finances not in order

just pick those items that may be the most challenging for your sobriety that first come to mind.

Trigger Maps

Use the **sample dialogue** below to help your clients complete Exercise 2.2 which will have them "Map out" one of their triggers:

> For this exercise choose one of your triggers identified in the previous exercise and write it inside the oval on the Map. Imagine yourself being in the situation and then take a couple of minutes to scatter your thoughts and feelings about that situation around the outside of the oval. Don't edit or second-guess, just write down whatever thoughts come to mind.
>
> When you've finished writing your thoughts, answer these questions at the bottom of the map: How much body tension am I experiencing? Where in my body do I notice any tension? How do I describe it?

Completed example of Exercise 2.2

Trigger Map 1

What if I am going to get fired?

I should have a thicker skin with feedback from others

My boss should be more interested in what's going on in my personal life

I will feel uncomfortable now whenever I am around my boss or co-workers

Criticized by my boss

I shouldn't feel self-doubt

Anxious and worried

I don't know how to stand up for myself

Description of body tension? Tension in my chest, dry throat

Trigger Map with Sensory Awareness

Use the **sample dialogue** below to guide your clients through Exercise 2.3. The focus here is for clients to see that it is not only the external factor, in this case the trigger, that is relevant but also how they relate to the trigger:

> Now for Exercise 2.3, on Map 2 write the same trigger you wrote in the oval of Map 1 in the oval of this map.
>
> Begin by first getting comfortable in your chair and focusing on what you are currently doing. Next, just sit and listen to the background sounds. As you listen feel your feet on the floor, the weight of your body on your seat. Feel the fabric of your clothing, the tabletop, or just rub the tips of your fingers together while you continue to listen to the background sounds. If a thought distracts you, return to listening to the background sounds.
>
> Once you begin to feel settled write around the oval the thoughts and feelings that come to your mind now about the situation. As you write, feel the pen in your hand and watch the ink flow onto the paper while continually focusing on the background sounds. As with the previous Map, don't edit. There are no right or wrong thoughts. Just let your thoughts stream while you are tuned into your senses.
>
> After a couple of minutes, stop writing and at the bottom of Map 2 provide a description of your body tension. Where do you experience it in your body? How do you experience it?

Use the **sample dialogue** below to guide your clients through Exercise 2.4 which will help them see how they can relate differently to a trigger in Natural Functioning.

> Now, compare Map 1 (Exercise 2.2) and Map 2 (Exercise 2.3). In the space in Exercise 2.4 write down a very brief (one or two sentences) description of your experience of doing Map 1 and then do the same for Map 2. The situation in the oval is the same on both Maps, but what is different about your experience of the two Maps? What, if anything, has shifted for you? Write down your thoughts.

Like the previous high-risk situation Map, did you experience more tension in Map 1 than in Map 2? Did you experience less stress and more lightness when completing Map 2? Was there more mind-clutter in Map 1 than in Map 2?

The trigger did not change, but your orientation toward it probably did. When you did Map 1 you likely attributed all your distress to the trigger itself. But your body tension and mind clutter decreased when you did Map 2, even though the trigger is the same. This exercise demonstrates that there is something else (which you now know is your I-System) besides the trigger that is causing your distress.

Map 1 helps you see that when your I-System is overactive it makes it more difficult to manage a triggering situation. This is because when you attempt to deal with a trigger or any troubling, stressful, or painful situation in I-System Functioning it limits your awareness and ability to act optimally. When your I-System is active, it hinders your ability to draw on your recovery capital and skills and thereby limits your choices to a few habitual behaviors. And for those struggling with addiction, relapse is often the default response when confronted with triggers or high-risk situations.

In Map 2 you likely experienced some release from I-System Functioning, experiencing the Shift. When you release this hindrance your capacity to effectively deal with a trigger dramatically increases because you have full access to your recovery capital and skills. You become the larger vessel we referred to earlier.

Use the **sample dialogue** below to help your clients complete Exercise 2.5. The focus of this exercise is to help clients to see that it is not the trigger situation that causes their I-System to become active, but rather the Requirements they have regarding that situation.

In the next exercise, we are going to look for the Requirements associated with the triggers that get your I-System going when they are violated.

Go back to Trigger Map 1 and circle the thoughts inside the Map that cause a great deal of mind clutter and body tension. Then ask yourself how you would like each one you circled to be? Sometimes the

Completed example of Exercise 2.5

Trigger Map 1

Description of body tension? Tension in my chest, dry throat

Requirement is as simple as being the opposite of the thought on the Map, and other times you can identify a Requirement by asking the question "What is my Requirement for this situation?"

Write the thoughts you circled as "should" or "must" statements. Connect each circled thought to its should/must statement with a line. You may have written some of the thoughts on your map as should/must statements. If you did, just circle them.

As previously mentioned, when you realize that a Requirement has been violated and has triggered your I-System you are using a Recovery Resilience Practice called Recognize Requirements. As you have learned, it is not the trigger situation (the what) that causes your I-System to become active, but rather the Requirements we (often automatically and out of awareness) have regarding that situation. It is often a violated Requirement associated with a trigger situation that makes it more difficult to manage.

Recognizing your Requirements allows you to break free from the box the I-System puts you in and leads to the benefits of Natural Functioning, which permits you to better handle the situation at hand and move forward with your day. When you Recognize your Requirements, you will likely experience the shift from I-System Functioning to Natural Functioning.

Addicted Mode Warning Signs

Use the following **sample dialogue** to introduce the notion of addicted mode warning signs, their role in lapse and relapse, and the value of having the ability to recognize these addicted mode warning signs.

You have learned that your thinking, attitudes, and behavior can either be driven by Natural Functioning or I-System Functioning. You've also learned that all aspects of your addicted mode are caused or amplified by I-System activity. When in an addicted mode, one is more prone to relapse, because using substances is the default behavior of this mode.

Relapse is typically a gradual process that starts with a momentary feeling, craving, or temptation that builds toward a decision to use substances. The act of relapsing can begin days, weeks, and sometimes even months before the physical act is initiated. For each person, there are specific ways of thinking, attitudes, and behaviors that comprise their addicted mode. These can be seen as one's unique **addicted mode warning signs**.

The deeply embedded, default, and habitual patterns of one's addicted mode are entirely unique to each individual. It is therefore important that you can identify the unique characteristics of how your addicted mode manifests in your daily life. The next exercise (2.6) will help you identify your addicted mode's warning signs. You will complete an Addicted Mode Warning Signs exercise, which will help you articulate certain ways of thinking, attitudes, and behaviors that contribute to your addicted mode in relationship to yourself, others, and your external environment. The way you relate to yourself, others, and your environment is mediated through Natural Functioning or I-System Functioning. When your thoughts, attitudes, and behavior are mediated through I-System Functioning and your addicted mode, relapse is more likely. Therefore, recognizing when your I-System is overactive and taking action to rest it are essential skills for sustained recovery.

A common feature of an addicted mode is the habitual, compulsive thinking patterns associated with it. These habitual thinking patterns, often referred to in recovery culture as "stinking thinking," are typically characterized by thoughts and narratives that reinforce and rationalize your substance use. Examples of addictive, "stinking thinking" patterns are denial, rationalization, blame, excessive self-pity, self-obsession, resentment, projection, over-personalization, and other types of defense mechanisms and/or cognitive distortions.

When cravings and "stinking thinking" arise, it is crucial that you recognize that they are part of your addicted mode, made possible by your overactive I-System. Developing this awareness and coupling it with Sensory Awareness will help you shift to a Natural Functioning mode where you will be able to access your recovery capital and employ your recovery skills to cope with the cravings. When you experience a shift from I-System Functioning to Natural Functioning you know you are back on the recovery pathway.

There are two potential trajectories when confronted with addicted mode warning signs. One can lead to relapse (refer to Figure 2.2). The other follows the recovery pathway. At the crossroads is the opportunity to use your Recovery Resilience Practice to shift to Natural Functioning or to not use your practice and potentially slip into addicted mode. The ability to use various recovery skills or otherwise draw on your recovery capital, your recovery resilience, is influenced by whether the I-System or Natural Functioning is in the driver's seat. If the I-System is in control, then thinking and actions may occur within the addicted mode. Conversely, if the I-System is resting, thinking and actions will occur within the Natural Functioning mode. The mode you are in will influence your capacity to effectively apply all your recovery skills and tools.

To provide a general overview of how your addicted mode warning signs can manifest, we look at it from three general areas or perspectives: self, others, and the world.

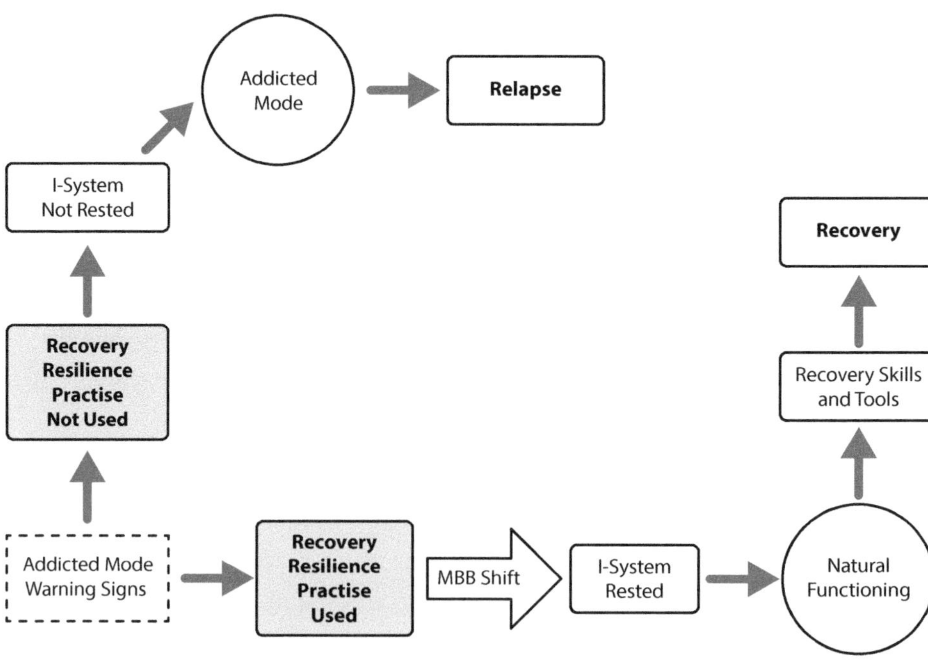

Figure 2.2 Relapse vs. Natural Functioning pathways.

(1) **Self**: refers to all aspects of you as an individual, which includes all aspects of your internal world and behavior and would include areas such as physical health and behaviors such as sleep and diet; your beliefs and thought processes; your emotional life and general psychological well-being; existential, that is, your goals and aspirations, and what you find meaningful, as well as your spiritual/religious beliefs.

(2) **Others**: refers to all your interpersonal, social relationships, and cultural influences.

(3) **World**: refers to your immediate environment, for example, the state of your house, and all your administrative, legal, and monetary dealings, as well as events and situations in the world.[1] We will keep referring to these three areas (self, others, and the world) throughout the program, as it provides a simple and fundamental framework for viewing our existence or what existential philosophers refer to as our "being-in-the-world." When our I-Systems are overactive, it distorts the way we think, perceive, and act within and across these dimensions of our lives, causing us to miss or dismiss warning signs when they arise. Conversely, when our I-Systems are rested, we see things, including warning signs, "as they really are."

Discuss the following information with clients that highlights how addicted mode warning signs can be understood as behaviors or signs that often proceed or can lead to a lapse or relapse.

Addiction expert Patrick Carnes (2008) would refer to the addicted mode warning signs in these areas as "middle circle behavior/signs" as these are behaviors or signs that often proceed or can lead to a lapse or relapse. Simply put, the more of these behaviors or signs that are present, the greater the chances are that an individual may relapse. This is a very common point of view in all addiction treatment and relapse prevention programs – what influences a sustainable recovery program is one's behaviors and attitudes toward oneself, others, and the world. When you are not coping with and managing all the essential features of your life then there is a chance that you will revert to your habitual coping style – using substances. One of the key insights of effective recovery approaches that incorporate notions like recovery capital is that recovery is not merely about your intentions, the

1 Adapted from the six recovery dimensions in Du Plessis (2018), which was informed by Ken Wilber's (2000) integral metatheory.

amount of therapy you do, or your psychological well-being, but also other factors such as a healthy diet, adequate sleep, exercise, managing finances, relationships, finding meaning, etc. Relapse prevention and addiction treatment programs that only focus on psychological change are limited – as addiction permeates all aspects of one's life. In line with the 12-step philosophy, a successful and sustainable recovery program requires a complete lifestyle change.

Use the **sample dialogue** below to guide clients through Exercise 2.6 which focuses on identifying addicted mode and relapse warning signs.

Using the template provided for Exercise 2.6, write down, in the space provided – for self, others, and the world, respectively – which of your

EXAMPLE 2.6

Completed example of Exercise 2.6

	Addicted Mode Warning Signs
Self	Eating too much sugar Resentful towards my parents Obsessing about the past Did not do any step work this week Feeling hopeless about my life
Others	Isolating Turning down invitations Arguing with partner Poor relationship with co-worker
The World	Spent too much money on clothes House not kept clean Late with taxes Procrastinating with my studies Not paying bills on time

thoughts, attitudes, and behaviors normally accompany or precede your substance use and have typically been a part of your addicted mode. In other words, you will identify relapse warning signs in each of these three areas. Try and be as comprehensive as possible. For example, for self: it may be poor sleep hygiene, eating junk food, euphoric recall (of prior intoxicated states), rationalization, thinking about positive aspects of using, dwelling on negative feelings such as anger or sadness, attitudes such as self-pity or resentment, lack of meaning, and/or hopelessness about the future. In assessing the category of “others” you might identify being socially isolated, not going to your support group, or not reaching out to your support system when going through a difficult time. In assessing the world, it might include being reckless with your spending, your house being untidy, consistently arriving late for work, procrastinating with studies, being upset about politics, etc.

Use the **sample dialogue** below to process Exercise 2.6 with your clients:

What you wrote down in each area can be understood as warning signs, or red flags, which indicate that your thinking, attitudes, or behavior (factors that are in your control) that are associated with and feed your addicted mode are making you more prone to relapse (increasing your disposition towards addictive behavior). The aim of developing a Recovery Resilience Practice is to develop a lifestyle where your daily activities and coping strategies are mediated through Natural Functioning instead of an addicted mode (I-System driven). It is therefore important to understand the “who” that is influencing your thinking, attitudes, and behavior – you in Natural Functioning or you in your addicted mode.

As you develop the ability to notice that you are entering into an addicted mode (noticing addicted mode warning signs) and that your I-System is overactive (by practicing Recognizing I-System Activity), it allows you to do something proactive about it. For example, if/when you have a day where you feel particularly ungrateful with excessive thoughts of self-pity and you recognize that these thoughts are associated with I-System activity and your addicted mode, you can then use your Recovery Resilience Practice (e.g., Mapping, Sensory Awareness) to shift to Natural Functioning. Doing this will allow you to see things more realistically instead of falling victim to your addicted mode and I-System's mirages.

Recovery as a Way of Life

Use the **sample dialogue** below to discuss the notion that both addiction and recovery could be seen as a way of life:

> When you incorporate a Recovery Resilience Practice into your daily activities and recovery program, they will not only help prevent relapse and build recovery resilience but also will help you over time to flourish in all aspects of your life. The approach outlined in this program is based on the premise (similar to the 12-step philosophy) that addiction is a dysfunctional way of being in the world and that stopping the use of substances is only one aspect of a sustainable recovery process. In short, one needs a complete lifestyle change – a change from a lifestyle dominated by the I-System and the addicted mode to one guided by moment-to-moment Natural Functioning. Without a lifestyle change, the I-System-driven addicted mode will likely prevail and thereby hinder your ability to use your recovery capital and skills to stay on the recovery pathway. Instead of accessing your coping and self-regulating skills, you may eventually gravitate back to your previous habitual and addictive mode of being-in-the-world.
>
> This lifestyle change is done, "just for today," moment-by-moment. The "Big Book" of Alcoholics Anonymous highlights this notion, which is that recovery is a "way of life" and emphasizes the necessity of engaging in activities of daily living that are guided by a desire for personal growth:
>
> AA is not a recovery plan that can be finished and done with. It is a **way of life**, and the challenge contained in its principles is great enough to keep any human being striving for as long as he lives. We do not, cannot, out-grow this plan ... we must have a program for living that allows for limitless expansion ... However, this isn't as rough as it sounds ... for

> we find that we are more than compensated for a consistent effort by the countless dividends we receive (Wilson, 1976, p. 311).

Discuss the following information with clients which points out that the notion of *recovery as a way of life* highlights that a sustainable recovery is a lifestyle where their basic human needs are met through healthy means in contrast to an addictive lifestyle where their needs are met through substance use.

> The notion of recovery as a way of life highlights that a sustainable recovery is a way of being-in-the-world where our basic human needs are met through healthy means in contrast to a lifestyle where our needs are met through substance use and other dysfunctional methods. Simply put, substance use and addiction can be seen as a dysfunctional way of attempting to satisfy basic human needs (Du Plessis, 2022).
>
> To highlight this, we will look at the relationship between substance abuse and altered states of consciousness and preferred styles of coping. Anybody that has used psychoactive substances would agree that it results in an alteration of consciousness or an altered state of consciousness. In fact, the aim of using psychoactive substances is to enter a certain altered state, and various types of substances create various types of altered states. Some researchers believe that humans have an innate drive to seek altered states of consciousness (McPeak et al., 1991; Winkelman, 2001; Du Plessis, 2018), and that individuals who abuse psychoactive substances follow a normal human motive to achieve altered states of consciousness, but use maladaptive methods because they are not provided with the opportunity to learn "constructive alternative methods for experiencing non-ordinary consciousness" (Winkelman, 2001, p. 340).
>
> From this viewpoint, substance use is then understood as a dysfunctional method to meet a basic human need. Alcoholics Anonymous echoes this view and suggests its participants find "a new state of consciousness and being" to replace the self-destructive pursuit of alcohol-induced altered states of consciousness with a healthier life-enhancing approach (Wilson, 1987, p. 106). Similarly, psychologists Richard Ulman and Harry Paul in their book *The Self Psychology of Addiction: Narcissus in Wonderland* (Ulman & Paul, 2006, p. 63) point

out the need for individuals in recovery to find healthy means to achieve altered states of consciousness. They state that "[s]uch an altered state of consciousness may eventually supersede and supplant [an individual's] dependence on an addictive state of mind."

Our innate need for altered states of consciousness is also related to how we cope with stress and psychic pain. Feeling good and avoiding unnecessary pain are universal needs. To feel good, we seek out activities that alter our brain chemistry. Addiction can be understood as this normal need gone awry. Addicts have found a dysfunctional way to meet this innate need through substance use or certain behaviors to which they have become addicted. One fascinating line of research has discovered a striking correlation between preferred coping styles and one's drugs of choice. The researchers found that individuals who preferred depressants, like heroin, used passive withdrawal, as well as reduced sensory stimulation, as their primary coping skills (Milkman & Sunderworth, 2010), whereas those who preferred stimulants, like amphetamines, were prone to confront a hostile environment with intellectual or physical activity. Those who used hallucinogens, like lysergic acid diethylamide (LSD), sought daydreaming and imagery to aid in reducing tension.

Addiction researchers Harvey Milkman and Stanley Sunderworth (2010, p. 19) state that "After studying life histories of drug abusers, we have seen that drugs of choice are harmonious with an individual's usual means of coping with stress." They go on to state that:

> the drug group of choice depressants [satiation], stimulants [arousal], or hallucinogens [fantasy] – is the one that best fits the individual's characteristic way of coping with stress or feelings of unworthiness. People do not become addicted to drugs or mood-altering activities as such, but rather to the satiation, arousal, or fantasy experiences that can be achieved through them (Milkman & Sunderworth, 2010, p. 19).

Based on the above discussion, it is imperative for individuals in recovery to find healthy activities related to their preferred coping style (satiation, arousal, or fantasy), in light of the research finding that this preferred coping style often correlates with their drug of choice. Natural Functioning is the state of consciousness and mode of being-in-the-world that sustains recovery whereas I-System Functioning derails it. Thus, the aim of this program is for you to develop a Recovery Resilience Practice that leads to moment-by-moment Natural Functioning where you are naturally more creative and thus have more capacity to access healthy ways of coping and find healthy ways to meet your basic human needs. Simply put, in Natural Functioning mode, you have more options and will find more creative ways to take care of yourself and stay on the recovery pathway.

Use the following **sample dialogue** which further highlights that clients can either respond in an addicted mode or Natural Functioning mode to situations and events.

In summary, we have seen that any activity is driven either by I-System Functioning or Natural Functioning. What is of primary importance is not only what you are doing, but who is doing it – your I-System (addicted mode) or you in Natural Functioning. That is, are your daily activities and how you meet your needs driven by your I-System, or are they guided by Natural Functioning? Asking yourself "*who*" is responding to triggers and cravings when they occur and "*who*" is doing the thinking and perceiving as you engage in your activities of daily living will help you develop a sustainable recovery lifestyle.

Recovery Resilience Journal

Use the **sample dialogue** below to introduce clients to and help them complete Exercise 2.7. In this exercise, the practice of a **recovery resilience journal** is introduced. There is a recovery resilience journal client handout at the end of each session.

Step Ten of the 12-step program suggests that individuals continue to take personal inventory. For many people in 12-step programs and those working other recovery programs a personal inventory or daily journal is often one of their core recovery practices. It is easy to see why because it allows one to do daily psychological "house-cleaning." In Step Ten, personal inventory, it is often suggested to look for emotional disturbances and attitudes that can trigger one to return to misusing drugs or alcohol. Watching for these disturbances and attitudes daily – and taking a daily inventory – is an important part of recovery.

Therefore, regularly incorporating awareness of addicted mode warning signs into your daily journaling can be of great benefit. With this awareness comes the power to act. You do not have to be a hostage to your I-System and addicted mode. For this reason, it is strongly recommended that you start, if you have not already started, the practice of keeping a daily journal or inventory. Consider incorporating the Recovery Resilience Journal template as part of your daily inventory. Or, if you have a book that you use as a journal you can do a similar exercise in your book.

EXAMPLE 2.7

Completed example of Exercise 2.7

	Addicted Mode Warning Signs	Recovery Resilience Practice
Self	Eating too much sugar Resentful towards my parents Obsessing about the past	Sensory Awareness Recognize Requirements Experienced the Shift when I recognized Requirements
Others	Isolating Arguing with partner Poor relationship with co-worker	Mapping Recognized my I-System and experienced the Shift Recognized Requirements
The World	Spent too much money on clothes Procrastinating with my studies Not paying bills on time	Used Sensory Awareness Mapping Asked myself "who" is making these choices? Recognized I-System Activity

In the next exercise (2.7) you will practice completing your daily journal. On the blank Recovery Resilience Journal template provided, write down how addicted mode warning signs have manifested in these life domains: self, others, and the world. Also, write down the Recovery Resilience Practices you used in these domains and note how you have experienced the Shift. See the example provided to help you see how to do this. While developing your Recovery Resilience Practice it will be useful to use the template. Eventually, you can incorporate it into your daily journal or Step Ten daily inventory in a less structured manner. Keep in mind that while the journal is completed at the end of the day your Recovery Resilience Practice is implemented in each moment of your activities of daily living.

Conclude Session 2

Conclude Session 2 by providing clients with exercise templates for any homework that is required before the next session. Provide them with the Homework for Session 2 handout that summarizes the Recovery Resilience Practices introduced in Session 2, as well as instructions for the Flourishing Scale, Recovery Resilience Practice Scale, and Addicted Mode Warning Signs template.

Session 3

Depressor and Fixer Activity

SESSION OBJECTIVE

1. Discuss the relationship between negative emotional states and substance use.
2. Introduce the Depressor and Depressor Storylines.
3. Discuss how Depressor Storylines fuel the addicted mode.
4. Discuss the Depressor and the abstinence violation effect.
5. Discuss the Depressor and toxic shame.
6. Teach clients how to Defuse Depressor Storylines.
7. Introduce the Fixer and Fixer Storylines.
8. Discuss how Fixer Storylines fuel the addicted mode.
9. Teach clients how to Defuse Fixer Storylines.
10. Discuss the Fixer and fundamental human needs.
11. Assign homework.

SESSION DESCRIPTION

The focus of this session is to help clients explore the relationship between their Depressor and Fixer activity. The session introduces the concept of the Depressor–Fixer Dyad and how it sustains addictive thinking and behavior and introduces practices that can aid in managing the adverse effects of Fixer and Depressor activity.

Introduction to Session 3

Discuss the following information with clients that highlights how the use of substances can be understood as a coping mechanism, and that an essential component of recovery is learning healthy coping strategies.

> There is a strong link between the capacity to cope with negative emotional states and substance abuse (Baumeister, 2001). As already discussed in the Introduction, it has been proposed that substance use may be a form of self-medication that individuals use to cope with their painful and unstable inner worlds (Khantzian, 1999). Philip Flores (1997, p. 233) believes that addiction can be
>
> > viewed as a misguided attempt at self-repair. Because of unmet developmental needs, certain individuals will be left with an injured, enfeebled, uncohesive, or fragmented self ... alcohol, drugs, and other external sources of gratification (i.e., food, sex, work, etc.) take on a regulating function while creating a false sense of autonomy, independence, and denial of need for others.
>
> When individuals use substances as a coping mechanism, this strategy may be effective in the short term but often proves maladaptive in the long run. The use of alcohol and drugs provides both negative reinforcement (namely, the reduction of painful feelings via self-medication) and positive reinforcement (that is, the pleasant experience of being high via positive outcome expectancies). The self-medication hypothesis applies when the individual is using a substance to cope with negative emotions, conflict, or stress (negative reinforcement). From a positive outcome expectancy perspective, the person is

focusing on the positive aspects and euphoria of using a substance (positive reinforcement), while ignoring the negative consequences (Brown et al., 1985).

Use the following **sample dialogue** to introduce the aim of the next exercise and the value of learning healthy coping skills.

> An essential component of recovery is learning healthy ways to self-regulate and cope with stress and painful emotions, and the negative thoughts and rumination associated with them. Without healthy coping skills, a key component of recovery capital, individuals in recovery will continue to seek dysfunctional ways of coping and self-regulation (Levin, 1995; Winhall, 2021). Distressing emotional states can be a by-product of I-System Functioning. In the previous chapters of this workbook, you learned that your Requirements, which are mental rules you have about how you, others, and the world should be, are what activate your I-System when they are violated. You also learned that mental clutter and body tension are signals alerting you that you have drifted off your Natural Functioning course. In the next section (Depressor Map), you will learn about a particularly destructive form of mental clutter with which we are all too familiar – intrusive negative thoughts and rumination (repetitive thinking or dwelling on negative feelings). Negative thinking and rumination are a central feature of the addictive mode.
>
> In the next exercise, you will learn about one of the subsystems of the I-System, called the **Depressor**, that often lies at the core of your negative thinking and rumination.

Depressor Map

Use the following **sample dialogue** to guide clients through Exercise 3.1. The focus here is for clients to experience Depressor activity.

Completed example of Exercise 3.1

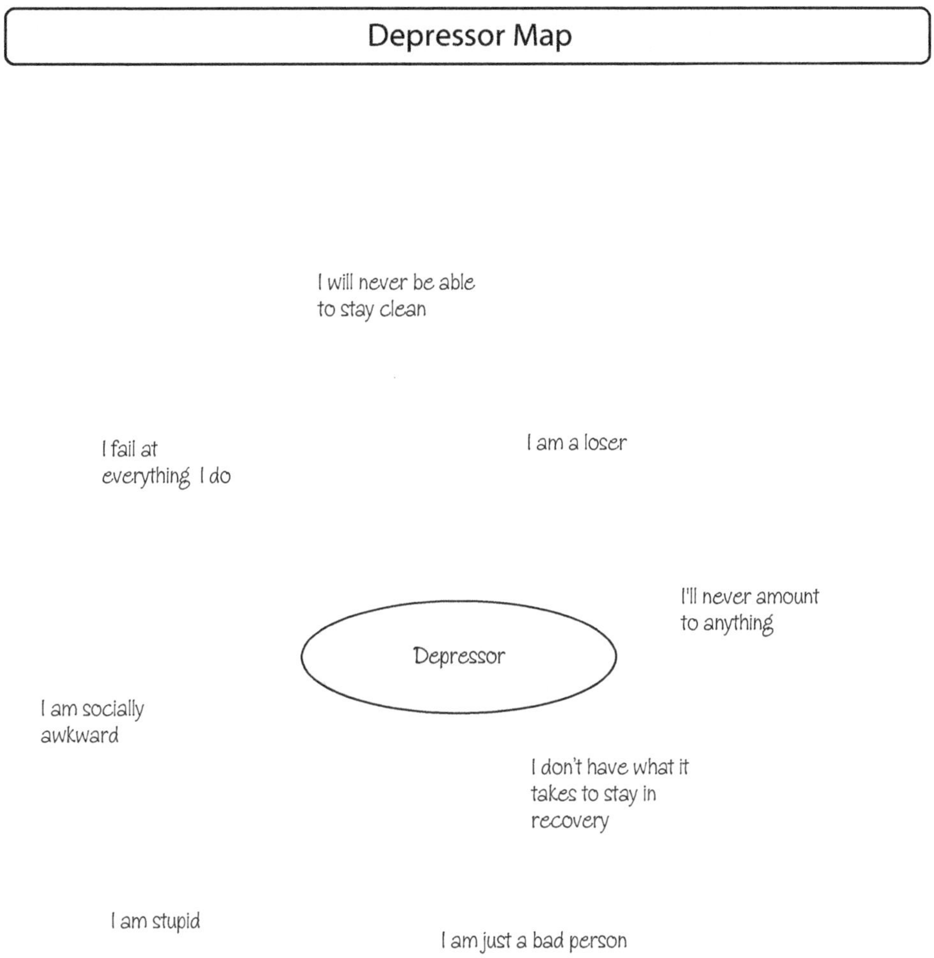

Write the words "My Depressor" inside the oval on the Map template provided. Around the oval, write down all the negative thoughts you've had about yourself, thoughts you've had when you were feeling down and being self-critical (e.g., I am lazy, I will never amount to anything, etc.). Don't edit or second-guess, just write down whatever thoughts come to mind.

Look at the thoughts on your Map. Each of them is just a Natural Functioning thought that happens to be negative. Some of these thoughts may create a little distress and some may create a huge amount of distress. However, the problem is not with your negative thoughts but with your **Depressor**, a component of your I-System that spins storylines about them, keeping you in a cycle of negative rumination.

Negative and self-critical thoughts come and go. What is problematic is when we are caught in a cycle of rumination about these thoughts.

We will investigate this more in the next section (Depressor Storylines).

Depressor Storylines

Use the following **sample dialogue** to help clients complete Exercise 3.2 which introduces the concept of Depressor Storylines.

Using the template provided for Exercise 3.2, take one of the negative thoughts from your Exercise 3.1 Depressor Map that has the most associated body tension and write down a story related to that thought that you tell yourself.

EXAMPLE 3.2

Completed example of Exercise 3.2

Thought: I am a loser.

Story: Every time I try to do anything I screw it up. People must think I'm useless. I'll never get things right. Why should I care or try?

Use the following **sample dialogue** to help clients process Exercise 3.2:

> What you have written down, whether it consisted of a couple of thoughts or a lengthier story, is called a **Depressor Storyline**. Depressor storylines are generally about not being "good enough" and being "damaged" (various feelings and sensations of embarrassment, humiliation, shame, and self-loathing such as "I will never amount to anything"). Depressor Storylines can also be about others and your environment or the world (e.g., storylines associated with "People cannot be trusted"). Depressor Storylines may play out in your mind many times throughout the day, cluttering your mind, and creating mental lapses, errors, misperceptions, misjudgments, and/or procrastination.

Use the following **sample dialogue,** which highlights the relationship between Depressor Storylines and lapse/relapse.

> I-System Functioning and your addicted mode are sustained by Depressor Storylines. For sustained and successful addiction recovery, it is helpful to be aware of Depressor Storylines. The negativity you experience when these types of storylines are playing in your mind and body has been consistently shown to be a significant contributing factor in relapse (Marlatt & Gordon, 1980). Below are some common thoughts that may have accompanied Depressor Storylines:
>
> - I am a failure at everything I do.
> - I don't think I can handle life without using.
> - Life won't be fun – I won't be fun – without using.
> - I'm worried I will turn into someone I don't like.
> - I am boring sober.
> - My cravings will be overwhelming; I won't be able to resist them.
> - If I stop, I'll only start up again; I have never finished anything.
> - I'm worried that I have been so damaged by my addiction that I won't be able to recover.
> - People cannot be trusted.
> - Life is unfair.

> What triggers your Depressor to generate these Storylines? It is a violated Requirement. For example, you may have a Requirement that "*I should be successful*," and when you fail at something, your Depressor starts to spin Storylines around the thought "*I am a failure at everything I do*." Whenever a Requirement is violated, it always activates the Depressor.

Use the following **sample dialogue** to wrap up Exercise 3.2:

> Go back to the "How I Would Like to Be" Map from Session 1 (Exercise 1.4) and focus on how you felt when your Requirement for yourself was violated. (For example, if the item inside the circle was "I should be successful," you confirmed it was a Requirement by the body tension and negative emotional response associated with the opposite item outside the circle, i.e., experiencing yourself as a failure.) The negative emotions and body tension you experienced were caused by your Depressor.
>
> Remember, the purpose of your Requirements is to support a certain self-image and identity. The Requirements you identified like "I should be strong" are intended to support this self-image. These Requirements are the fabric or glue that holds together a mental picture or self-schema of who you think you are. Self-schemas are stable and often rigid beliefs about oneself and one's relationship with others and the world. Basically, these schemas form the glasses through which we look at the world.
>
> The problem is that your I-System can construct an overly rigid and limited mental picture of who you think you are through the generation of Requirements. When these Requirements are violated, your Depressor starts to generate negative storylines associated with the violated Requirement. Simply put, your Requirements support a

certain self-image or mental picture of *who you think you are*, and when this is *threatened* by the violation of a Requirement, it results in the generation of Depressor Storylines. These Depressor Storylines are usually accompanied by very painful emotional states and, consequently, there is often the desire to medicate or counteract these painful feelings.

Depressor Storylines Can Fuel the Addicted Mode

Use the following **sample dialogue** to guide clients in completing Exercise 3.3 which will help them begin to see how Requirements are linked to Depressor Storylines.

Now we will look more in-depth at how Depressor Storylines can fuel your addicted mode.

Using the template provided for Exercise 3.3, write down three Requirements that underlie high-risk situations or triggers related to yourself, others, and the world, and which normally elicit a strong, negative emotional response. For example, "My partner should not argue with me." Then opposite it, write down a situation or event (internal or external) that would violate the particular Requirement (e.g., "My partner complained and argued with me").

Use the following **sample dialogue** to guide clients in completing Exercise 3.4 to help them begin to recognize their Depressor Storylines.

Now choose one of the situations or events from the Exercise 3.3 "What Violates the Requirement?" list and using the template provided for Exercise 3.4, write down a negative story you tell yourself when that situation happens. There is no right or wrong answer; it does not matter how irrational your thoughts or stories may be. Simply try to be as honest as you can and write down your thoughts in the form of a story without editing. It is not important to be comprehensive, just try to write down the essence of the story. Refer to the example provided to help you see how to do this.

Use the following **sample dialogue** to guide clients in processing Exercise 3.4 which highlights the relationship between Depressor Storylines and the feelings of shame that often accompany the addicted mode.

Depressor Storylines are a core aspect of your addiction mode and the toxic shame that accompanies it. Simply put, the Depressor makes an

EXAMPLE 3.3

Completed example of Exercise 3.3

Requirement	What Violates the Requirement?
My partner should not argue with me	My partner argues with me
I should not feel so sad	When I feel sad
Life should be fair	An earthquake that killed thousands of people

EXAMPLE 3.4

Completed example of Exercise 3.4

Situation: I feel sad and have a Requirement that I should not feel so sad.

Story: I seem to always feel sad. I don't think I'll ever not feel sad again. It seems like the only time I don't feel sad is when I'm using. I'll never figure this out. Why can't I just be happy? What's wrong with me?

unpleasant situation or disappointment far more unbearable by creating a narrative that makes you feel ashamed and not good enough as a human being, or excessively disappointed in others and the world. There are many things we are not good at, and sometimes we make mistakes, which lead to healthy feelings of disappointment, guilt, and a desire to improve. But the feelings of self-loathing and thoughts that we are just not good enough as human beings are Depressor-driven, self-shaming I-System fictions. When these narratives clutter your mind, your ability to draw on your recovery capital is severely compromised. And, perhaps most destructive of all is their impact on your self-image. If you tell yourself these stories long enough, they come to falsely define who you think you are.

In the next section (The Depressor and the Abstinence Violation Effect), we will look at the role the Depressor plays in relapse.

The Depressor and the Abstinence Violation Effect

Discuss the following information with clients that points out the relationship between Depressor activity and the abstinence violation effect that often follows a lapse and can consequently result in an extended relapse.

The thoughts and feelings of Depressor-driven toxic shame often precede and follow a lapse or relapse. A lapse can be understood as a one-time, typically brief episode of drinking or using substances, whereas a relapse represents a total immersion back into an addicted lifestyle. The Depressor is very active after either a lapse or relapse and therefore tills the soil for future relapse. It becomes a vicious cycle, where after each relapse there are more powerful Depressor Storylines, which in turn make you more prone to subsequent relapse. "I used to drink," writes John Bradshaw (2005, p. 36) "to solve the problems caused by drinking. The more I drank to relieve my shame-based loneliness and hurt, the more I felt ashamed."

In the context of the relapse process, the Depressor contributes to what is called the "abstinence violation effect," which is the self-blame, guilt, shame, and loss of perceived control that individuals often experience after the violation of self-imposed rules (Curry et al., 1987). An individual may have the Depressor Storyline that "*Now that I have failed and lost my clean time, I might as well just keep on using*" or "*I am such a loser that I will never be able to stay clean for long.*" A person may experience the abstinence violation effect when after some clean time he/she experiences a lapse, for example, there may be feelings of guilt, shame, and hopelessness. This is often triggered by the discrepancy between one's present lapse into addictive behavior and one's prior identity as an abstainer. The thoughts associated with the abstinence violation effect are more likely to progress to relapse if an individual views a lapse as an irreparable failure (Miller, 1996). However, if the same individual interprets the lapse as a transitional learning experience, then the progression to relapse or full-blown addiction is far less likely (Curry et al., 1987). Those individuals who perceive a lapse as a learning experience will be more likely to use alternative coping strategies in the future which may lead to more effective responses in high-risk situations (i.e., increased recovery capital).

Many practitioners can vouch for the palpable difference in outcomes experienced by individuals in an inpatient or outpatient treatment program for addiction between those who view relapse as a failure (often as the result of Depressor Storylines) versus those who see relapse as a learning opportunity. Not infrequently, for example, when a client returns to treatment after discharge, often directly in the wake of relapse, they are encouraged and supported to share their relapse experience – including events leading up to it – with the rest of the treatment center group. This way, all group members can benefit and contribute useful strategies for moving forward. Most importantly, the individual who experienced the relapse is not only not shamed by others but is actually seen as providing valuable learning "grist for the mill." Suffice it to say, the whole treatment milieu becomes one of supportive facilitation rather than shame or being otherwise ostracized.

> The I-System's Depressor will take the natural feelings of disappointment after a lapse or relapse and spin them into a Storyline of unbearable thoughts and feelings of disappointment and shame. This fuels one's addicted mode, making continued use more likely in the immediate future. This is important to remember as you may experience a lapse or relapse at various stages of your recovery journey.

Use the following **sample dialogue** to help clients complete Exercise 3.5 which will help them see how their Depressor activity relates to their lapses and relapses:

> For Exercise 3.5 recall the negative self-talk or Depressor Storylines that you experienced with past lapses or relapses. Think of those times when you did not want to use but did, and how you felt afterward. It is not important to be comprehensive, just write down the essence of the story using the template provided.

Use the following **sample dialogue** to wrap-up Exercise 3.5:

> Learning how to manage your Depressor and its Storylines is imperative to managing a lapse or relapse. Recognizing when your Depressor has spun up a story is a key Recovery Resilience Practice. Recognizing these storylines allows you to defuse them in real time, as they happen. You will learn how to do this. But first, we will explore how the Depressor causes toxic shame.

The Depressor and Toxic Shame

Discuss the following information with clients which further highlights the relationship between Depressor activity and toxic shame.

> As has been mentioned, Bradshaw argues that toxic shame is the motivator behind addictive behaviors (as well as many other dysfunctional behaviors). Bradshaw makes the distinction between healthy shame and toxic shame. Healthy shame lets us know that to be human is to be limited and provides us with a healthy sense of humility. Healthy shame

is an emotion that teaches us about our limits, and like all emotions, it moves us to get our basic human needs met. On the other hand, toxic shame is a deep-seated belief that we are fundamentally flawed and simply not good enough as human beings. As Friedrich Nietzsche said, "Everyone needs a sense of shame, but no one needs to feel ashamed" (in Bradshaw, 2005, p. 1).

A shame-based belief system is essentially composed of negative thoughts and storylines about being fundamentally flawed, and not good enough, and that you need to be fixed. When the Depressor is active it replays these stories and generates additional stories about not being good enough. People use substances in a futile effort to repair the illusion that they are not good enough and to numb the painful and often overwhelming feelings associated with toxic shame. As Bradshaw highlights, "This deep internalized shame gives rise to distorted thinking. The distorted thinking can be reduced to the belief that I'll be okay if I drink, eat, have sex, get more money, work harder, etc." (Bradshaw, 2005, p. 1).

Use the following **sample dialogue** which highlights that Depressor activity results in a distorted and fictitious view of oneself that limits one's choices and options to those that are congruent with this false sense of self.

It is impossible to rid yourself completely of negative thoughts and it wouldn't necessarily be advisable to do so even if you could. Some negative thoughts play an important regulatory role psychologically, for example, when you have negative thoughts associated with guilt. Toxic shame, on the other hand, is tied to the idea that it is you who is fundamentally "bad" or "broken" rather than the behaviors you sometimes engage in. It is the Depressor that drives these thoughts of toxic shame. The I-System tries to convince you that *you are* these shameful thoughts.

Shame is an example of when negative thoughts become problematic due to I-System overactivity; when they lead to "broken record" rumination, and/or chronic discomfort in your body. If you don't recognize them for what they are, you can come to believe that you are who your Depressor portrays you to be (i.e., "This is just who I am"). This distorted and fictitious view of yourself limits your choices to those that are congruent with this false sense of who you are. If you take just the example of a fiction that is common with addicted populations, the shame-based and Depressor-based belief that you are "damaged and not good enough," you can immediately see how this fiction could limit your choices and hinder your ability to draw on your recovery capital and to live each moment optimally.

You can learn to stop the Depressor from spinning all these stories about yourself, others, and the world. You cannot do much about negative thoughts that arise in the moment, but you can control what the Depressor does with these negative thoughts. This will be the focus of our next discussion.

Defuse Depressor Storylines

Use the following **sample dialogue** to teach clients how to Defuse their Depressor Storylines.

Recall that lacking adequate coping skills to deal with negative emotional states as well as distressful situations are two strong predictors of drug use and possible relapse when in recovery from addiction. Negative thoughts are just as natural as positive thoughts. Our minds can't have one without the other. For there to be a positive there must also be a negative. Therefore, understanding and knowing how to deal with the negative thoughts, feelings, and body sensations associated with the Depressor is imperative for sustained recovery. The good news is that you can develop these crucial skills, and with practice, protect your much-cherished sobriety.

Once your I-System is activated, due to a violated Requirement, your Depressor starts to spin Depressor Storylines about the situation, which clouds the moment with negativity. The Depressor activity impairs your ability to take care of yourself and your responsibilities. When you realize your Depressor has spun storylines about a negative thought after one of your Requirements was violated, you can use a Recovery Resilience Practice called **Defuse Depressor Storylines**. This can be

> done by recognizing when the Depressor has spun a storyline about a negative thought and then labeling the thoughts of the Storyline by saying to yourself "I'm having the thought that _______." Repeat this slowly several times and note what happens. You may even add "It's just a thought" or "So what else is new?" Try listening to background sounds as you label your thoughts. You will see how labeling a Depressor Storyline allows you to see the truth, which is that a thought is just a thought and that you are not who these thoughts portray you to be.
>
> By labeling your thoughts or storylines you don't ignore or neglect their content, you are just stopping the Depressor from generating more storylines that keep the I-System active and fuel your addicted mode, leaving you at a far greater risk of relapse.
>
> It is important to realize the power that Depressor Storylines have on your mind and body each moment. Without recognizing your Depressor's activities, it is very difficult, or even impossible, to see things as they really are. Shining your light of awareness on and interrupting these storylines helps you access your Natural Functioning. Recognizing and defusing these storylines will help you experience the Shift.
>
> As we have mentioned, the arena of your practice is your activities of daily living. The aim of your Recovery Resilience Practice is to improve how you live your life and help you stay on the recovery pathway. As we have highlighted, your I-System is like a compass and provides a signal when you are off course.

Use the following **sample dialogue** to help clients complete Exercise 3.6 which has them practice defusing their Depressor Storylines.

> To practice Refuse Depressor Storylines, using the template provided for Exercise 3.6, list the Depressor Storylines from the previous exercise and then thought-label each of them. This exercise may seem unnecessary but doing this will help you to use this practice in real time. The bottom line is how you address situations as they evolve.

Use the following **sample dialogue** to help clients differentiate Natural Functioning negative self-talk from Depressor negative self-talk.

What differentiates Natural Functioning negative self-talk (which is a normal and unavoidable aspect of human existence) from the Depressor negative self-talk you have written above is the disproportionate intensity of the unpleasant and painful thoughts, feelings, and body sensations that accompany it. Negative thoughts that are part of Natural Functioning come and go. We don't over-identify with them. They don't clutter our minds or fill our bodies with tension. Because we over-identify with them (i.e., we think *we are* these feelings), the shame-based feelings caused by the Depressor are often unbearable, and you cannot simply sit with them for extended periods. This results in an overbearing feeling or desire to do something about it – a compulsive need to fix the unpleasant and painful shame-based mind–body state caused by your Depressor's activities.

This compulsive need and desire to fix the unpleasant and shamed-based mind–body states caused by the Depressor will be our next topic of discussion.

The Fixer

Use the following **sample dialogue** to guide clients in completing Exercise 3.7 which introduces the notion of Fixer activity:

Using the template provided for Exercise 3.7, write around the oval your thoughts about how you are going to improve your life. Don't edit or second-guess, just write down whatever thoughts come to mind. Refer to the example provided.

Now, contemplate each item on the map, and for each of them rate (on a scale from 1 to 3) the amount of body tension you experience as you think about trying to reach your self-improvement goal.

What was the difference in energy you experienced when doing this Map compared with your previous Depressor Map? Do you feel more energized by this Map? What is the difference in body tension? All these

Completed example of Exercise 3.7

How I Am Going to Improve My Life Map

I am stopping drinking

Save money

Go to the gym

Try harder

How I Am Going to Improve My Life

Lose weight

Find a romantic partner

Get a degree

thoughts may be natural and normal plans you have about how you are going to improve your life. But as you will see, when they are captured by your I-System, these thoughts become problematic. We are going to explore this in the next exercise.

Use the following **sample dialogue** to guide clients in completing Exercise 3.8 which helps them begin to recognize Fixer activity:

For Exercise 3.8, you will go back to the Exercise 3.1 Depressor Map you did at the beginning of this session and write down what you feel you need to do about the negative thoughts on the Map. It is normal when experiencing the negativity and shame associated with Depressor thoughts and storylines to try and do something about them. It is difficult and even unbearable to sit with this negativity for very long.

Look at the thoughts on your Depressor Map and write down next to each of them what you feel driven to do about the thought.

Use the following **sample dialogue** to help clients process Exercise 3.8 which introduces the concept of the Fixer.

As highlighted previously, when your Depressor is active you are often overcome by an overwhelming desire to do something to rectify unpleasant feelings or mind–body state caused by your Depressor's activities.

Some of what you feel driven to do about your Depressor thoughts may be healthy Natural Functioning thoughts concerning how to take care of yourself and your responsibilities. These thoughts will not have much body tension associated with them. Any thoughts that have excessive body tension and mind clutter connected with them are associated with Depressor Storylines. Thus, these actions and intentions are driven not by wanting to take care of yourself, but by what you feel driven to do to fix the unpleasant mind–body state that's caused by your Depressor Storylines. These thoughts, intentions, and action plans are generated by a component of the I-System called the **Fixer**. These Fixer thoughts or plans can be seen as "solutions" that can counteract the shame generated by the Depressor. The Fixer attempts to fix the damaged self-image (self-esteem). Remember the I-System springs into action when

Completed example of Exercise 3.8

your Requirements are violated, when things don't align with your I-System's picture of how you, others, or the world should be, and your sense of self or identity is threatened.

Notice the energy level and feeling tone of the thoughts written down and then contrast them with the energy and feeling tone of the corresponding Depressor thoughts. You may notice that the Fixer's thoughts and plans may make you feel better, more positive, or even hopeful. Sometimes these Fixer thoughts may even be grandiose. They often tend to overcompensate for feelings of shame. As Bradshaw points out "Toxic shame also wears the face of grandiosity. Grandiosity is a disorder of the will. It can appear as narcissistic self-enlargement or wormlike helplessness. Each extreme refuses to be human. Each exaggerates: one is more than human; the other is less than human" (Bradshaw, 2005, p. 41).

Use the following **sample dialogue** to help clients understand the relationship between the Fixer and Depressor.

The Depressor and Fixer work as a dyad. The Storylines of the Depressor make you believe that you (or others or the world) are damaged and need fixing. The Fixer is the Depressor's partner that drives overactive, never-ending thoughts, plans, fantasies, and stories about how to fix yourself, others, and the world. In other words, the job of the Fixer is primarily to fix the unpleasant feelings of shame, self-loathing, and feelings of being fundamentally flawed, caused by the Depressor. The Depressor creates feelings of shame and unworthiness that are so unbearable that you absolutely must do something to get rid of them (e.g., use substances). The Fixer tries to fix the painful state that the Depressor creates with plans and often euphoria-producing fantasies. It is a normal aspect of our human nature to have a strong impulse to try to remedy painful and unpleasant feelings, but when this impulse is driven by your Fixer it either makes things worse or attempts to create temporary relief, the latter of which unfortunately often leads to negative consequences in the long run. Even though Fixer thoughts and fantasies may consist of various "good" feelings and sensations (e.g., euphoria, ecstasy, elation, and exhilaration), the Depressor is ever-present and ready to remind you that, despite these "good" feelings, you are still not good enough. We refer to this as the Depressor–Fixer Cycle.

All the energy you spend on the Depressor–Fixer Cycle is for naught. The Fixer's plan to repair the feelings of shame, of being broken and not being worthwhile is based on a Depressor fiction. You cannot fix what is not broken. Therefore, another problem associated with the Fixer is that it will perpetually try and fix something it cannot. And as stated in the Introduction this will keep you, like Sisyphus, trapped in an endless cycle of trying to fix what is not broken.

From the Recovery Resilience Practice perspective, substance use, or any addictive behavior, is often an attempt to "fix" the feelings of pain and shame associated with the Storylines the Depressor creates. Addictive behavior is Fixer-driven. You can easily see why it is no coincidence that using drugs is often referred to as getting a "fix."

To summarize, the Fixer is the Depressor's lifelong, faithful partner that drives you to repair the painful shame-based state the Depressor has caused or exacerbated. The Fixer is energized by the false belief (caused by the Depressor) that you are damaged or not good enough, then tries to fix you. A central feature of the addicted mode is that as your addiction progresses your choices become limited to certain predictable and habitual Fixer-driven behaviors, over which you feel more and more powerless.

The Fixer not only drives addictive behavior but also many of our daily actions and future goals. One way to recognize if a past behavior was Fixer-driven is to notice whether, when it was achieved, you experienced peace of mind and a sense of well-being and accomplishment. If the answer is a resounding "No," then it was very likely Fixer-driven. Why? Because regardless of your accomplishments the Depressor just spins another story about how you are still not good enough – and this creates an endless cycle.

Fixer Storylines

Use the following **sample dialogue** to help clients complete Exercise 3.9 which introduces them to Fixer Storylines:

Using the template provided for Exercise 3.9, choose one of your Depressor Storylines from the previous exercise and write down the thoughts or stories you tell yourself about how you are going to fix what your Depressor tells you is broken or damaged. These thoughts or stories can consist of a couple of ideas or can be an elaborate plan or fantasy. It is not important to be comprehensive; just try and write down the essence of the story.

Use the following **sample dialogue** to help clients process Exercise 3.9:

What you have written is called a **Fixer Storyline**. The Fixer creates never-ending thoughts, stories, and fantasies about how to fix the unpleasant and painful thoughts, feelings, and body sensations created by the Depressor. While on the surface some of these Fixer Storylines seem helpful, in reality they are counterproductive because they are driven by a misguided intention, i.e., to fix feelings of shame created by the Depressor. Fixer storylines are elaborate "schemas" and "action plans" regarding how this "fixing" or "damage repair" will happen (for example, "I am going to get straight As," "I am going to lose weight," etc.). Fixer-driven behavior is the implementation of these schemas or plans to try to live according to our I-System's demands (Requirements) so we can feel comfortable inside our skin once again. Put another way, these so-called solutions are just an attempt to make your Requirements come true. These "solutions" are often short-lived because they are trying to fix something that does not need fixing. For example, wanting and striving to get physically fit is perfectly fine, but if it is an attempt to

Completed example of Exercise 3.9

EXAMPLE 3.9

Depressor Storyline: I fail at everything I do.

Fixer Storyline: I will work harder and longer and make more money to prove to myself and others that I am not a failure.

"fix" feelings of shame, then it is misguided because no amount of physical fitness will resolve deep-seated feelings of shame. Substance use can be viewed in the same way. No drug can resolve the Depressor's shame-based beliefs.

Some fantasies and goals of achieving power, wealth, fame, and success may be entirely Fixer-driven. In these situations, these goals are simply shame-based manifestations of proving to ourselves and others that we are good enough. The problem with Fixer-driven goals is that no matter how successful we are the Depressor is always there to remind us that we are still not good enough after achieving the goals. When we are trapped by a Fixer-driven goal, the only two outcomes are: being successful and not feeling good enough; or being unsuccessful and not feeling good enough. The former represents, at best, a hollow victory, the latter, only defeat.

In contrast, when our plans and goals are situated in Natural Functioning, we will feel good enough whether we achieve our goals or not. Moreover, the Fixer is very goal-oriented; all that matters is success or failure. Whereas in Natural Functioning, while success and failure are important, one is also able to enjoy the process of striving toward the goal. Apply, for example, this to our previous discussion of relapse behavior. Recovery as a process implies that any temporary setback may serve as useful feedback for moving forward. Whereas when recovery goals are Fixer-driven there is no allowance for setbacks or "failures," including lapses or relapses. When goals and behaviors are Fixer-driven, it is usually an "all-or-nothing" proposition.

How the Fixer Can Fuel Addictive Behavior

Use the following **sample dialogue** to help clients complete Exercise 3.10. The exercise aims to help clients see how their Requirements and Depressor and Fixer Storylines are interconnected and manifest in high-risk situations.

Using the template provided for Exercise 3.10, list three high-risk situations or triggers that have caused or may cause cravings and that may

Completed example of Exercise 3.10

High-Risk/Trigger	Requirement	What Violates the Requirement?	Depressor Thought/Storyline	What Do I Feel Driven to Do About It? (Fixer)
My partner arguing with me	My partner should not argue with me	My partner argues with me	I am useless in relationships	Give up hope on our relationship ever working; in fact, maybe I should just break up now
Feeling sad	I should not feel so sad	When I feel sad	I am just a loser in whatever I try	Go the bar for a drink
Dwelling on unfairness in the world	Life should be fair	An earthquake that killed thousands of people	I am too sensitive to live in a world where bad things happen to good people	Smoke a joint and binge-watch TV programs

pose a risk for relapse. Then write down your Requirements related to the situation. Then next to each Requirement write down "What violates the Requirement." Next, write down a Depressor thought or storyline (a short, edited version) that is associated with the violated Requirement. Finally, write down what you feel driven to do (or not do) about the situation or event (Fixer). See the three examples provided to help you see how to do this.

Use the following **sample dialogue** to help clients process Exercise 3.10:

All of the actions or intentions in the "What Do I Feel Driven to Do About It?" section could be healthy thoughts about how to take care of yourself and your responsibilities. However, in this exercise, when they are the result of your Depressor, these actions and intentions are driven not by wanting to take care of yourself, but by what you feel driven to do to fix the unpleasant mind-body state that's caused by your Depressor. Now some of the "What Do I Feel Driven to Do About It" actions involved the use of substances, but others fuel your addicted mode and keep you in a cycle of addiction (e.g., isolating or watching too much TV).

This exercise illustrates that it is the cycle that the Depressor and Fixer keep you in that fuels your addicted mode and increases the risk for relapse. From the Recovery Resilience perspective, substance use (or any addictive behavior) is often an attempt to "fix" the feelings of pain and shame associated with the Storylines the Depressor creates. This sentiment is echoed in the following quote, "Addiction has been described as the belief that whenever there is 'something wrong with me,' it can be 'fixed' by something outside of me … It is no wonder, then, that 'locating divinity in drugs' becomes a kind of spiritual death" (Kurtz & Ketcham, 2002, p. 120).

Discuss the following information linked to how Fixer Storylines often drive outcome expectancies related to substance use:

From a substance use perspective, Fixer Storylines often drive outcome expectancies related to substance use, which are the anticipated effects the individual expects when consuming a mind-altering substance (Jones et al., 2001). However, the individual's drug use outcome expectancies may not necessarily correspond with the actual effects experienced after consumption. For example, an individual may expect to feel more relaxed, happier, and social after using a drug, but the person's actual experience may also include increased tension, sadness, and regret. Research conducted on treatment outcomes has shown that positive outcome expectancies (often Fixer Storylines) related to drug use are associated with poorer treatment outcomes (Connors et al., 1993), and negative outcome expectancies related to drug use are related to improved treatment outcomes (Jones & McMahon, 1996).

Simply put, overly positive and often unrealistic expectations driven by the Fixer may motivate individuals to use substances, while negative expectations (often much more realistic when viewed in Natural Functioning and framed within the context of the consequences substance use may have) may keep individuals from drinking or using. One reason for this is that when we are in an addicted mode our focus is on immediate reward and in this limited and contracted state of awareness (I-System Functioning) we don't always have ready access to past experiences and insight into possible consequences or our recovery capital. When this happens, we fail to see things as they really are, thus using can seem like a rational and good idea.

Defuse Fixer Storylines

Use the following **sample dialogue** to introduce Exercise 3.11 which shows clients how to defuse Fixer Storylines and recognize common Fixer activity and signs:

> As we have discussed, from a Recovery Resilience Program perspective, every activity we engage in is either driven by our Fixer or inspired by Natural Functioning. The Depressor works to make you believe that you are damaged or broken and need fixing. But the truth is you are not broken or damaged and you don't need fixing, because in Natural Functioning – who you really are – you are good enough. The activity of your Depressor leads to Fixer Storylines that focus on what you feel you absolutely must do to get rid of the unpleasant and painful thoughts, feelings, and body sensations associated with Depressor Storylines. Fixer Storylines then drive behavior that is not optimal for the imperative of the moment (e.g., substance use). When you realize your Depressor has generated storylines and your Fixer is generating storylines about how to fix the unpleasantness caused by your Depressor activity, you can use a Recovery Resilience Practice called **Defuse Fixer Storylines**. This is done by labeling the thoughts associated with the Fixer Storyline. Merely bringing awareness to your Fixer Storylines will help to break the cycle in which your Depressor and Fixer keep you locked. When labeling your Fixer Storylines, you don't ignore or neglect the content of the thoughts, you are just stopping the Fixer from generating additional stories that keep the I-System active, which fuels your addicted mode and increases your risk of relapse.

If an action is being driven by the Fixer, no matter how hard you try, nothing you do will ever be good enough because the Depressor is still there to disapprove or raise the bar. Fixer behavior/activity will never provide an adequate solution to Depressor Storylines no matter how hard you work at it. Therefore, learning to Defuse Fixer Storylines in action is critical to your recovery resilience and well-being.

Below is a list of common **Fixer signs**.

- Cravings to use (with limited or no awareness of past damages of substance use).
- Trying to meet Requirements at all costs (for example, at the cost of relationships, your physical and mental health, etc.). Note that it is often the ordinary Requirements we encounter every day that do the most damage.
- Excess mental pressure or urgency.
- Sense of being excessively driven.
- Over-preparation and perfectionism.
- Excessive controlling behavior.
- Mental obsession.
- No sense of satisfaction, well-being, or peace of mind with accomplishment.

Use the following **sample dialogue** to help clients complete Exercise 3.11 which has them practice defusing Fixer Storylines:

> To practice Defuse Fixer Storylines, use the template provided for Exercise 3.11 to list the Fixer thoughts and Storylines from the previous exercise and then to thought-label them. This may seem unnecessary but doing this will help you recognize your Fixer storylines when they happen in real time.

The Fixer and Fundamental Human Needs

Discuss the following information related to how Fixer activity can drive the satisfaction of fundamental human needs. It highlights how individuals in recovery must change from having their needs met through Fixer-driven behavior to meeting them through behaviors grounded in Natural Functioning.

Chilean economist Manfred Max-Neef, who developed the Theory of Human Needs, asserted that we have innate fundamental human needs that we all strive to fulfill and that an individual's quality of life is correlated with the actualization of these needs. According to Max-Neef, any "fundamental human need not adequately satisfied generates a pathology" (Max-Neef et al., 1991, p. 22). We all have various ways or methods of satisfying our basic human needs. These methods he calls "satisfiers" (satisfying the need), and various types of "satisfiers" are proposed: violators or destroyers, pseudo-satisfiers, inhibiting satisfiers, singular satisfiers, and synergic satisfiers.

Violators or destroyers are paradoxical because when they are applied to satisfy a need, "not only do they annihilate the possibility of its satisfaction over time, but they also impair the adequate satisfaction of other needs" (Max-Neef et al., 1991, p. 31). Pseudo-satisfiers "generate a false sense of satisfaction of a given need. Although not endowed with the aggressiveness of violators or destroyers, they may on occasion annul, in the not too long term, the possibility of satisfying the need they were originally aimed at fulfilling" (Max-Neef et al., 1991, p. 31). Inhibiting satisfiers tend to over-satisfy a given need, consequently limiting the possibility of other needs being satisfied. Singular satisfiers tend to satisfy one specific need. They are neutral concerning the satisfaction of other needs. Synergic satisfiers satisfy a given need, "simultaneously stimulating and contributing to the fulfillment of other needs" (Max-Neef et al., 1991, p. 34).

In the context of Max-Neef's model, Fixer behavior, like addictive behavior, can be understood as being like violators or destroyers, and pseudo-satisfiers. Addictive behavior is always directed at satisfying a need, but what differentiates addictive behavior (violators or destroyers) from other methods (or other satisfiers) of meeting needs is that it paradoxically destroys the individual's capacity to meet the need(s) as well as their capacity to meet other needs. As an addictive lifestyle progresses, an individual's capacity to have most of his or her needs met is diminished, until there is a near-total reliance on the substance or addictive behavior (Fixer) to meet the most fundamental human needs.

This discussion highlights that developing a recovery program and lifestyle is a process of replacing destroyers/violators with synergistic and singular satisfiers as our methods for getting our fundamental needs met. In other words, taking an I-System Model perspective, we need to change having our needs met through our Fixer-driven behavior to meeting them through behaviors grounded in Natural Functioning. When we "are in Naturally Functioning" it is more likely that we can have our needs fulfilled. Conversely, when we are in I-System Functioning, our Fixer-driven behavior (like substance use) will not meet our needs no matter how hard we try. Rather, we will always be left feeling unfulfilled and dissatisfied.

Recovery Resilience Journal

Use the following **sample dialogue** to guide clients in completing Exercise 3.12 which has clients integrate Depressor and Fixer activity into their Recovery Resilience Journal:

Now that we have introduced the Depressor and Fixer you can now include those I-System components into your daily journal. See the example provided. It is important to have an awareness of how your daily activities are influenced by the Depressor and Fixer.

Conclude Session 3

Conclude Session 3 by providing clients with exercise templates for any homework that is required before the next session. Provide the Homework for Session 3 handout which provides a summary of the Recovery Resilience Practices introduced in Session 3, as well as instructions for the Flourishing Scale, Recovery Resilience Practice Scale, and Addicted Mode Warning Signs template.

Completed example of Exercise 3.12

	Addicted Mode Relapse Signs	Requirements	Depressor/Fixer Activity in Daily Living	Recovery Resilience Practice
Self	Feeling bummed out	I should not feel sad	Depressor: I will always feel sad. What's the point of living sober Fixer: Daydreaming about times when I didn't feel sad while using	Defuse Depressor and Fixer Storylines Used sensory awareness to shift to Natural Functioning
Others	Angry at my boss for not promoting me	My boss should reward my hard work	Depressor: My boss could care less about me Fixer: Fantasizing about how I will tell him off	Defuse Depressor and Fixer Storylines Shifted to Natural Functioning and got on with my workday
The World	Ruminating about the political situation, politicians	Politicians should listen to and do what's best for their constituents	Depressor: Politicians are going to ruin the economy and cause me to lose my job Fixer: Spend time surfing and posting on social media	Defuse Depressor and Fixer Storylines Stopped wasting time on social media

Session 4

The Addiction Cycle

SESSION OBJECTIVE

1. Introduce the Depressor–Fixer Cycle and how it sustains an addicted mode.
2. Discuss how I-System Functioning and Natural Functioning can be a choice.
3. Introduce and discuss the Two-Loop Diagram.
4. Discuss how a worldview that is influenced by Natural Functioning rather than I-System Functioning is central to sustained recovery.
5. Assign homework.

SESSION DESCRIPTION

The focus of this session is to introduce clients to the Depressor–Fixer Cycle and to help them see how it fuels their addicted mode. It introduces the Two-Loop diagram which presents a visual representation of the various components of the I-System and its functioning. This session also highlights how a worldview that is influenced by Natural Functioning rather than by I-System Functioning is central to sustained recovery.

Introduction

Discuss the following to introduce to clients the aim of the session which is to learn how I-System activity sustains the cycle of addiction and how a Recovery Resilience Practice can help break this habitual cycle. Highlight to clients that the RRP is a strengths-based approach.

> The Recovery Resilience Program can be understood as a strengths-based approach because it highlights an individual's self-determination, focuses on their innate strengths, and promotes individuals in recovery seeing themselves as resourceful and resilient when they face adverse conditions. Informed by a strengths-based perspective this session highlights how an individual can draw on their strengths to break the addiction cycle.
>
> Session 3 highlighted that to sustain resilience in the face of cravings and temptations that accompany recovery it is imperative to understand Depressor and Fixer activity. This is not only crucial to preventing relapse and to building recovery resilience but also to improving quality of life. As individuals learn more healthy coping skills and develop a Recovery Resilience Practice they will rely less on unhealthy Fixer behaviors.
>
> A key aspect of a Recovery Resilience Practice is understanding the **Depressor–Fixer Cycle**. The Depressor–Fixer Cycle refers to the way the Depressor and Fixer interact with each other. Whenever there is Depressor activity there will be Fixer activity and vice versa. In this session, clients will experience how the Depressor–Fixer Cycle operates in and interferes with their day-to-day living as well as how it can lead to a lapse and/or relapse. Recognizing the Depressor–Fixer Cycle helps to lessen the power the I-System has over one and can assist in breaking the cycle of addiction.

The Depressor–Fixer Cycle

Use the following **sample dialogue** to illustrate how the Depressor–Fixer Cycle functions:

> The Depressor and Fixer "dance" with each other, keeping you in an addicted mode and/or creating additional, internal distress in your life.

The dynamics of the Depressor–Fixer Cycle may help explain why many of your attempts to reach certain goals have either failed or did not seem good enough even when you reached them. Your Depressor responds to a violated Requirement by spinning storylines about how you, others, or the world are broken, damaged, or not good enough. Your Fixer comes up with never-ending fantasy-driven storylines that focus on how to fix yourself, others, and the world. Your Fixer tends to bring a sense of urgency and pressure to your activities. Moreover, no matter what you accomplish, the Depressor is ever-present to remind you that it was not good enough. As long as your Depressor spins storylines about some type of inadequacy, your Fixer is going to overcompensate for that perceived inadequacy. Figure 4.1 illustrates the Depressor–Fixer Cycle.

Discuss the following information to illustrate how the Depressor–Fixer Cycle is associated with lapse and relapse, and how it manifests in an addicted mode. See Figure 4.2.

In Session 1 we discussed how individuals with ineffective coping responses will experience decreased self-efficacy. This self-perception, together with the expectation that the use of a substance will have a

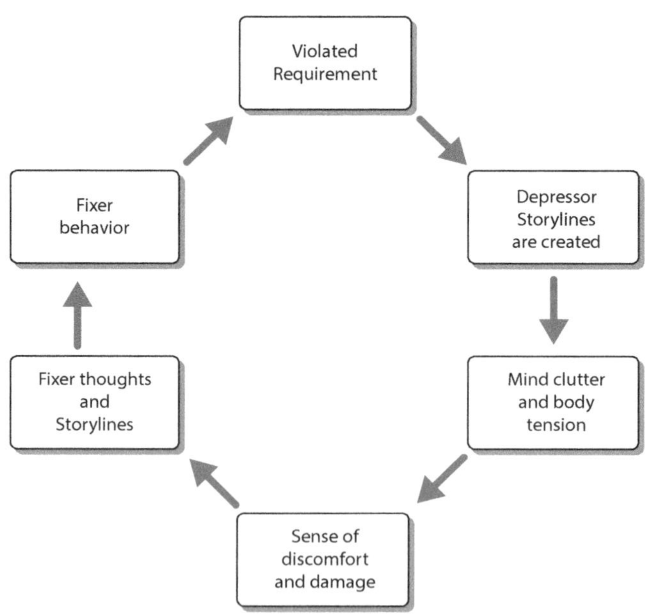

Figure 4.1 Depressor–Fixer Cycle.

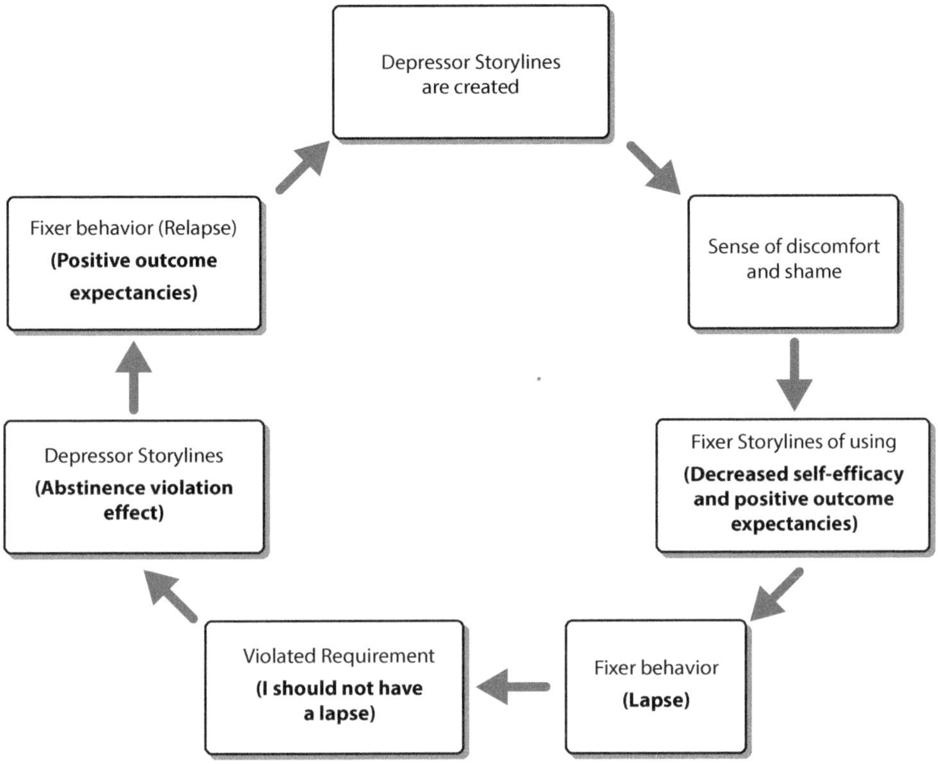

Figure 4.2 The addicted mode's Depressor–Fixer Cycle.

positive effect (i.e., positive outcome expectancies), may well lead directly to an initial lapse back into addictive behavior. This lapse, in turn, often results in feelings of shame and failure (i.e., abstinence violation effect). Figure 4.2 shows how the Depressor–Fixer Cycle manifests when in an addicted mode and how it could lead to a lapse and then full-blown relapse – and as anybody who has struggled with addictive behavior knows, once one is trapped in the addicted mode cycle it is very difficult to break, and it takes on a life of its own.

Use the following **sample dialogue** to guide clients through completing Exercise 4.1 which helps them see how the Depressor–Fixer Cycle has operated in their lives:

In Exercise 4.1 you will have the opportunity to explore in detail a situation that activated your Depressor–Fixer Cycle. Using the template provided for Exercise 4.1, write down a situation that really got your

I-System going (i.e., where you experienced significant mind clutter and body tension). The situation may represent a high-risk situation, trigger, or any troubling situation that comes to mind. Then identify the Requirement connected to this situation that was violated.

Next, in each of the boxes, describe the progression of your Depressor–Fixer Cycle activity related to this situation. Refer to the example provided to see how to do this.

Use the following **sample dialogue** to introduce Exercise 4.2 and Exercise 4.3 which help them see how the Depressor–Fixer Cycle has interfered with their lives and played a role in their addiction.

When you contemplate your life do you recognize how pervasive your Depressor–Fixer Cycle has been over the years? Do you see how that cycle has played a role in your addiction as well as your daily activities and distress? In the next two exercises, you will write down on the templates provided for Exercise 4.2 and Exercise 4.3 how your Depressor–Fixer Cycle has interfered with your life in general and how it has played a role in sustaining your addiction.

For Exercise 4.2 write down how your Depressor–Fixer Cycle has interfered with your life. Try to write down specific examples.

For Exercise 4.3 write down how the Depressor–Fixer Cycle has played a role in your addiction.

I-System or Natural Functioning

Use the following **sample dialogue** to introduce clients to the two-loop diagram, which is a simple visual representation of all the components and dynamics of I-System activity (Figure 4.3).

Through a Recovery Resilience Practice, you have the capacity and choice to break your Depressor–Fixer Cycle and live your life guided by Natural Functioning. In Figure 4.3 we show the two possible paths or loops that can mediate your experiences: I-System Functioning and Natural Functioning. This diagram highlights that when your I-System is not active you automatically inhabit a Natural Functioning state. In

Completed example of Exercise 4.1

Situation: I ran into someone I drank with in the past and started to crave alcohol.

Violated Requirement: I should not have cravings.

Depressor Thoughts and Storylines

I am ashamed and weak for craving alcohol.

Mind Clutter and Body Tension Experienced

My mind is occupied with thoughts and stories about craving and shame.
My chest is heavy and my neck is tight.

Fixer Thoughts and Storylines

Would it hurt to have one drink with an old friend?

Fixer Behavior

I swapped war stories from my drinking days with the former drinking buddy.

Depressor Response

I shouldn't think and talk this way. I'm just a hopeless addict. I will never get it right.

this state, you are naturally resourceful, creative, psychologically flexible, and resilient, and in this state, you can more readily access your recovery capital.

When a Requirement is violated, the I-System hijacks your Natural Functioning, filling your mind with storylines and your body full of tension, and distorting how you perceive, think, feel, and act. This is often the cause of your poor decisions and suffering, and many of your dysfunctional mind-body states, including your addicted mode.

As we have discussed, you can alter which mind-body state you are in – Natural Functioning or I-System Functioning. The primary focus of a Recovery Resilience Practice is on recognizing when you are in the

I-System mode and addicted mode and shifting to the Natural Functioning mode. Now obviously that is easier said than done. You will very often slip into the I-System loop without realizing it. The good news is that with practice you will become more aware of your I-System's signals (mental clutter and body tension) and increase your capacity to use your I-System as a compass that shifts you to get back on your

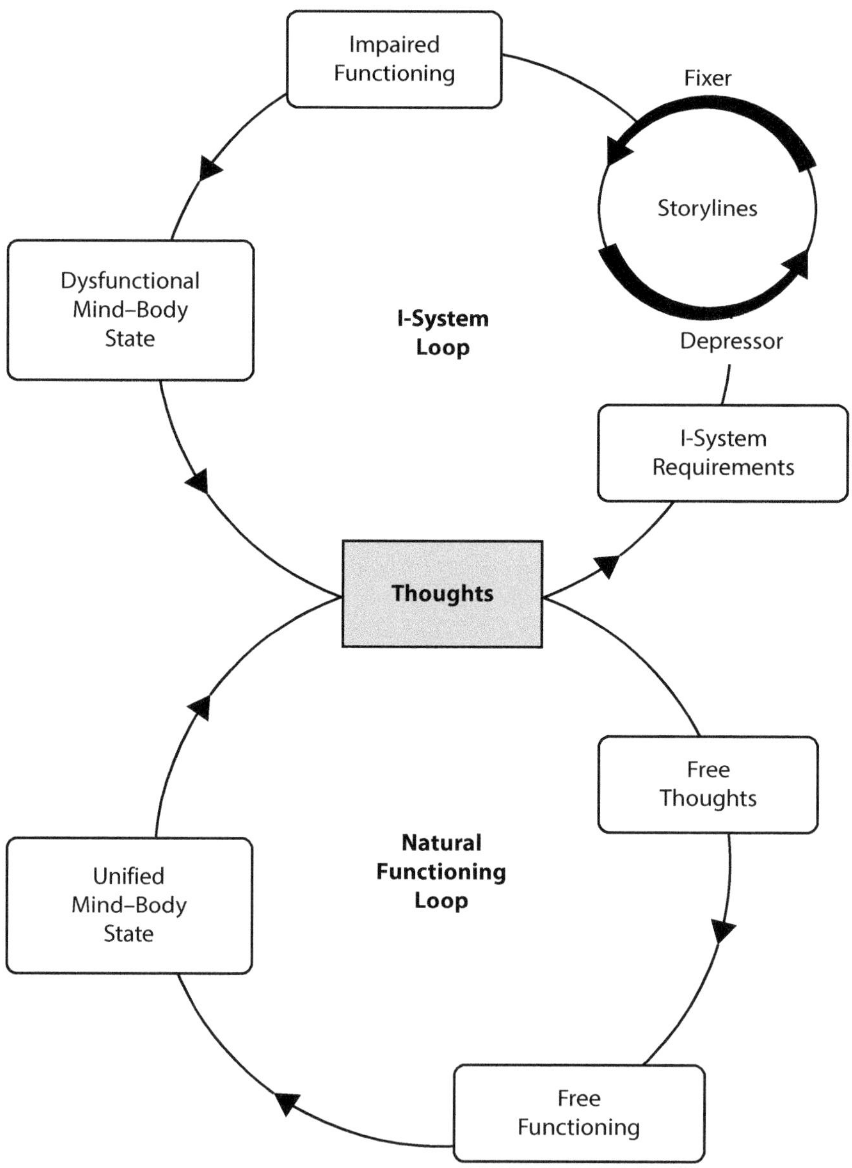

Figure 4.3 The I-System loop and the Natural Functioning loop.

Naturally Functioning course. In this Natural Functioning mode, you can more fully draw on your recovery capital to deal with high-risk situations as well as your day-to-day activities.

A Change of Worldview

Discuss the following information that highlights how an essential feature of transitioning from an addicted lifestyle to a recovery lifestyle, and the culture of recovery,[1] is a changing in worldview. The importance of this cannot be overstated.

Addiction is characterized by cognitive distortions fueled by defense mechanisms such as projection, denial, and/or repression (Brewer, 2017; West, 2017). Much of the therapeutic process of working a personal recovery program focuses on cognitive restructuring, which helps to work through defenses toward finding a more accurate perspective on the nature and consequences of addiction, as well as what life in recovery may look like. For those who have completed a primary care process, this cognitive restructuring was likely a primary focus of their therapy.

A pivotal feature of moving from an addicted lifestyle to a recovery lifestyle is a change in worldview. One's worldview is how we understand ourselves, others, and the world, and our place in society. As we have pointed out, the I-System, particularly its Depressor and Fixer Storylines, greatly influences or distorts one's worldview. An addicted lifestyle is sustained by a worldview that rationalizes substance use. Alongside other recovery practices individuals may have, a Recovery Resilience Practice will help change their worldview from one that sustained their addiction to one that sustains their recovery.

The exploration and transformation of one's worldview is a central feature within all 12-step programs. In *It Works How and Why*, it states, "[W]e need to change how we perceive the world and alter our role in it" (Narcotics Anonymous World Services, Inc., 1983, p. 37). Carl Thune believes one of the reasons Alcoholics Anonymous and other 12-step

1 See White (1996) for a comprehensive discussion about the cultural transition that underscores sustained recovery. This cultural transition encompassed a significant change in worldview.

programs are effective is because its members share their life histories in 12-step meetings and are "taught how to interpret their past in a way that gives meaning to the past and hope for the future" (in Flores, 1997, p. 281). Thune states, highlighting the value of an alteration of worldview for an individual in recovery:

In a sense, then, one of the first lessons AA must teach new members is that their lives were incoherent and senseless as they knew them. Simultaneously, it must reveal the "correct" understanding and interpretation of the drinking alcoholic's vision of the world before a new member can accept the full benefits of the program – a program which offers a different coherence and meaning to their active alcoholic lives. ... More abstractly, it is not just a revised and now coherent vision of the world which AA offers, but one which has altered the relation between its components (in Flores, 1997, p. 281).

Depressor and Fixer Storylines are supported by idealized and perfectionistic Requirements, which create a distorted view of ourselves, others, and the world. When individuals develop a worldview that is based in Natural Functioning, it strengthens their resilience and protects them from addicted mode thinking patterns – individuals start to perceive themselves, others, and the world more realistically. Their life and vision for the future become more meaningful – even the suffering of their past and addiction become more meaningful within the fuller context of their life and recovery. Viktor Frankl (1953) believed that when we can place our suffering within some meaningful context or worldview, we are not defeated by it but are helped to transcend it. Similarly, in AA members share "the kinship of suffering" and recovery depends on the mutual sharing of suffering. AA teaches the person dependent on alcohol that to be fully human is to need others and provides alcohol-dependents with a universally shared explanation for their suffering. Flores (1997, p. 280) states that "[w]ith Socrates, we argue to 'know thyself.' In this fashion, AA members are taught to believe that the authentic existence advocated by the AA program holds the key to self-examination, self-knowledge, emancipation, cure, and eventual salvation."

Again and again, the authors have observed clients in recovery humbly acknowledging an existential shift in worldview and some version of the following: "Were it not for my prior addiction, and now committed recovery,I would not be nearly the person I am today. And for that, I am immensely grateful." Simply put, their past suffering has now become meaningful within a newfound worldview.

Finding Meaning in Life

Discuss the following information which highlights an existential perspective of recovery, in the sense of how essential it is that a recovery way of life needs to provide new and healthy sources of meaning and purpose.

> When people have a personal meaning to their lives, they are far less likely to engage in addictive behaviors (Du Plessis, 2019b). Viktor Frankl (1953) proposed that people are driven to search for a sense of meaning in their lives and that people without a sense of meaning in their lives experience an "existential vacuum," a state largely characterized by boredom and purposelessness. Substance use represents an inadequate and often self-destructive coping mechanism to escape the feelings associated with meaningless, inner pain, and boredom resulting from Frankl's existential vacuum, and addiction can be understood as a misguided quest for meaning. As Medard Boss (1983, p. 283) noted, "Addiction, whatever its form, has always been a desperate search, on a false and hopeless path, for the fulfilment of human freedom." The Italian Jungian practitioner Luigi Zoja echoed a similar sentiment, highlighting the existential motives that may drive substance use, "It is almost impossible for many young people to feel in any way useful in today's society. Why should we be so amazed that so many take drugs, and why should we interpret addiction as a regressive renunciation of the ego when the person making this choice is actually seeking a few moments of heroic identity?" (Zoja, 1989, pp. 15–16).
>
> For recovery to be sustainable, one needs to develop a worldview that has a clear sense of meaning and purpose. With a Recovery Resilience Practice, your worldview will systemically shift to one that resonates with Natural Functioning. Right at the center of such a transformed worldview will be a personal foundation of meaning, values, and purpose that serves you well in a sustained, successful recovery. Viktor Frankl (1953, p. 84) in his book, *Man's Search for Meaning,* quoted

Friedrich Nietzsche: "He who has a why to live [personal meaning and value and purpose] can bear with almost any how," which highlights how having a meaningful worldview is essential for developing the resilience needed for sustained recovery.

One of the unfortunate features of the Fixer is that it can influence what we find meaningful (your "whys") and taint it with perfectionistic and idealized outcomes. In the same way, your Fixer can taint your recovery goals. It is important to be mindful of this happening instead of your life and recovery goals bringing you joy.

Use the following **sample dialogue** to help clients complete Exercise 4.4. This exercise aims to help clients see how the I-System can hijack their meaningful pursuits and goals.

In Exercise 4.4, you are going to write down meaningful pursuits and goals and explore whether any have been tainted or even hijacked by your I-System. In the space provided, write down your goals. Then ask yourself what Requirements do I have about these goals? Remember that Requirements are mental rules your I-System creates regarding how you think you, others, or the world should be. Write these Requirements next to your goal. Then write the Depressor and Fixer Storylines that are associated with the Requirements in the third and fourth columns. Note the body tension you experience in connection with the Depressor Storylines.

It must be noted that it is entirely normal for your goals to be influenced by your I-System, but the aim here is to become aware of when the pursuit of goals becomes predominantly Fixer-driven. You can know when a goal is Fixer-driven when you experience a disproportionate sense of urgency coupled with body tension and mental clutter associated with it. Conversely, when a goal is set and pursued in Natural Functioning,

EXAMPLE 4.4

Completed example of Exercise 4.4

Goal	Requirements	Depressor Storylines	Fixer Storylines
Get fit	I must do it quickly	You will fail at it like most things	I will work out five times a week

you are more likely to have realistic expectations and may also enjoy the process of striving toward the goal, and not simply be hyper-focused on its outcome.

Recovery Resilience Journal

Use the following **sample dialogue** to help clients complete Exercise 4.5 which has them integrate the Depressor–Fixer Cycle into their Recovery Resilience Journal.

Completed example of Exercise 4.5

	Addicted Mode Warning Signs	Requirements	Depressor/ Fixer Activity	Recovery Resilience Practice
Self	Thinking about skipping 12-step meeting	I should always want to go to meetings	D: I must not be committed to my recovery F: I'll find even more meetings to attend	Defuse Depressor and Fixer storylines Recognized Requirement Returned focus to what I needed to do in that moment
Others	Argument with partner	My partner should agree with me	D: My partner does not support me, never takes my side F: I just won't talk to her about this situation	Defuse Depressor and Fixer storylines Recognized Requirement Was able to have a productive discussion with partner
The World	Ruminating about how life is unfair, meaningless after watching a documentary	Life should be fair and meaningful	D: Life is pointless. Good people get the short end of the stick. Bad people get all the breaks. F: Have a "screw-it" attitude toward life. Be apathetic.	Defuse Depressor and Fixer Storylines Recognized Requirement Able to see life as it is – there is good and bad, beauty and ugliness, suffering and joy

EXAMPLE 4.5

Now that we have introduced the Depressor–Fixer Cycle you can now include these I-System components/dynamics in your daily journal.

Concluding Session 4

Conclude Session 4 by providing clients with exercise templates for any homework that is required before the next session. Provide the Homework for Session 4 handout which includes a summary of the Recovery Resilience Practices introduced in Session 4, as well as instructions for the Flourishing Scale, Recovery Resilience Practice Scale, and Addicted Mode Warning Signs template.

Session 5

Defuse Requirements

SESSION OBJECTIVE

1. Discuss the relationship between Requirements and resentment.
2. Discuss the relationship between Requirements and suffering.
3. Discuss the relationship between Requirements and motivation.
4. Help clients practice Defusing Requirements for themselves, others, and the world.
5. Review I-System Mapping.
6. Assign homework.

SESSION DESCRIPTION

The focus of this session is on how to defuse Requirements as they arise during activities of daily living. Various Maps are presented that assist clients to practice defusing Requirements for themselves, others, and the world. At the end of the session, clients are shown how to do an I-System Map that incorporates all aspects of a Recovery Resilience Practice.

Introduction

Discuss the following information with clients about resentment and its relationship to Requirements. The notion of dealing with resentment is a central component of 12-step programs and is understood as a significant risk factor for substance use and relapse. As this Session will highlight there is a strong relationship between Requirements and resentment, therefore learning how to adequately manage Requirements is a useful skill for those in recovery and supports the practices in 12-step programs.

The "Big Book" of Alcoholics Anonymous states that "resentment [is] the number one offender, and that it destroys more alcoholics than anything else" (Wilson, 1976, p. 64). When we look at the etymology of the word "resentment" it derives from "re-sentiment," with "re" indicating something repeating itself and "sentiment" related to feeling. Resentment can thus be understood quite literally as "feeling again," especially in terms of the habitual recycling of perceived injustices towards us and their accompanying feelings. This mental habit of resentment has a significant cost psychologically and even physically, yet ironically does next to nothing to aid the resolution or closure of the original event. Simply put, resentment binds us in a kind of emotional enslavement to the offending person or event. It should come as no big surprise then that the root word in Latin, *addictus*, means "bond servant" or "slave." Hence, addiction might best be understood as being bound or enslaved by any substance, behavior, or attitude that is ultimately self-defeating in the long term.

According to Alcoholics Anonymous what fuels resentment is having expectations. In 12-step programs, members are warned about the danger that holding expectations has for their recovery. This sentiment is expressed by the slogan: "Expectations are premeditated resentments" (Wilson, 1976, p. 45). As pointed out in Session 1 we made a distinction between natural expectations and I-System Requirements. A key insight of the recovery resilience approach is that when you are faced with a situation that violates one or more of your Requirements your I-System becomes active. Akin to the 12-step philosophy, we argue that these Requirements will fuel your addicted mode and that recognizing them will take away their power to do so. The *Big Book of Alcoholics Anonymous* observes: "My serenity is inversely proportional to my expectations. The higher my expectations of other people are, the lower is my serenity. I can watch my serenity level rise when I discard my expectations" (Wilson, 1976, p. 45).[1]

In addition to fueling resentments, Requirements also affect how we relate to potential high-risk situations, triggers, and stressful events in general. Chapter 1 of this Workbook highlighted that oftentimes it is not the situation or event itself that creates your emotional distress, but the Requirements one has (often automatically and out of awareness) for the situation or event that activated our I-Systems. Thus, a Recovery Resilience Practice does not focus on changing any given situation (crucial insofar as many distressful situations or triggers may be unavoidable) but focuses instead on changing the "who" we bring to that situation – our Natural Functioning self or our I-System Functioning self.

There are clear antecedents for this concept in the writings of the ancient Stoic philosophers, Marcus Aurelius, Seneca, and Epictetus. For example, in his *Meditations,* Marcus Aurelius writes, "If you are pained by any external thing, it is not this thing that disturbs you, but your own judgment about it. And it is in your power to wipe out this judgment now" (in Kaufman, 1997, p. 63). Similarly, in *It Works: How and Why* of Narcotics Anonymous – in a discussion of Step Four and taking responsibility for our resentments – it states, "[we] need to change how we perceive the world and alter our role in it" (Narcotics Anonymous World Services, Inc., 1983, p. 37). The good news is that through a Recovery Resilience

1 AA's view on resentment is significant when considering that socially deterministic approaches to addiction and harm reduction have increasingly gained traction. This view promotes a reductionistic and deterministic view of addiction based on the premise that social pathologies are addiction's root cause. The pitfall here is when social factors, which of course contribute to patterns of drug use, are considered determinate and prioritized over the multitude of other etiological factors. Nobody would deny that there are socio-economic factors that influence an individual's behavior, but when epistemologically prioritized a socially deterministic view of addiction can imply that individuals have little or no free will, are psychologically homogeneous, and are at the mercy of their environment – and this can lead to resentment. Consequently, in the context of addiction recovery, counsellors need to be careful when promoting a worldview that often seems to promote resentment, when according to AA "it destroys more alcoholics than anything else" (Wilson, 1976, p. 64).

Practice, one can "change how you perceive the world and alter your role in it" by simply living one's day-to-day life in Natural Functioning mode, which brings with it the ability to cope in optimal ways with triggers, high-risk, and other distressing situations. As one experiences this shift from an I-System Functioning mode to a Natural Functioning mode many times throughout the day, one will gradually change one's perception of oneself, others, and the world to one that is no longer dominated by self-defeating expectations.

Requirements and Suffering

Discuss the following information with clients about the relationship between Requirements and suffering.

The human experience includes various degrees of suffering, distress, and trauma (Maté, 2011; Badenoch, 2017; Winhall, 2021). These are unavoidable. However, a significant portion of this suffering – the part over which you have considerable control – is due to Requirements you have concerning how you, others, and the world should be.

The I-System can either cause suffering where none is warranted or add unnecessary suffering to an already distressing situation. When clients practice the recognition of Requirements, their distress related to any situation will often be reduced to a sizable degree or may, in some circumstances, even melt away entirely as their I-System releases its hold on them. When you shift to a state of Natural Functioning, you will be in a more optimal position to deal with the situation, either in the form of an action or perhaps, instead, a nonaction, that is, accepting the situation as it is (often referred to as "letting go" in the recovery community).

The 12-step Program, Buddhist, and Stoic philosophy all share the perspective that suffering is caused by our unwillingness to accept the world as it is and our insistence on trying to make it fit our expected ideas or fantasies. Addiction is, in essence, a refusal to accept things as they are and an attempt to avoid the reality of necessary suffering (unavoidable existential experiences of loss, disappointment, boredom, struggle to find and maintain meaning in one's life, etc.). This refusal to accept things as they are leads to a disproportionate need for control – a central feature of addictive dynamics. Ulman & Paul (2006) indicate how at the core of addiction dynamics, there is a fantasy of having an unrealistic sense of control of oneself, others, and things/events in the world:

> In the case of addiction, such a narcissistic fantasy centers on a narcissistic illusion of a megalomaniacal being that possesses magical control over psychoactive agents (things and activities). These latter entities allow for the artificial alteration of the subjective reality of one's sense of one's self and one's personal world. Under the influence of these intoxicating fantasies, an addict imagines being like a sorcerer or wizard who controls a magic wand capable of manipulating the forces of nature – and particularly the forces of human nature. Eventually, a person becomes a captive of these addictive fantasies and then becomes an addict, lost in a wonderland (Ulman & Paul 2006, p. 6).

In recovery, we learn that there are various aspects of our being-in-the-world in which we are not in control, and this is not something to be ashamed about – but rather something which makes us human. An important aspect of recovery is realizing the inevitability of suffering and letting go of our unrealistic demands. Flores (1997, pp. 195–196) highlights this shift for an individual in recovery:

> [m]any existential writers believe that in such a confrontation between the realistic acceptance of the world as it is and the self-centered demands for unlimited gratification [self-centered focus of I-System narratives], reason would prevail and the individual would choose more realistically between the [two distinct] alternatives: continued unhappy struggles with old patterns of expectations [Requirements] or authentic existence with expanded freedom of choice and responsible expression of drives and wishes [Natural Functioning].

Discuss the following information with clients regarding Friedrich Nietzsche's re-evaluation of suffering to provide a perspective of suffering that may be useful in the context of recovery. Additionally, Nietzsche's view resonates with the practice of "acceptance" and the notion of "life on life's terms" as suggested in 12-step programs.

Nietzsche's view of suffering is a crucial component of his concept of the "will to power." He views suffering as a component of happiness. Embracing the idea that happiness and suffering are inextricably linked leads to a need for re-evaluating suffering.[2] Nietzsche asserts, "How little you know of human happiness ... for happiness and unhappiness are sisters and even twins that either grow up together ..."[3] Nietzsche's notion of the will to power radically alters our conception and significance of suffering – that the will to power is best understood as man's "desire for the activity of overcoming resistance" (Reginster, 2006, 132). Nietzsche's analysis implies that the fundamental human impulse is not to avoid suffering but to find meaning in suffering, which is tantamount to affirming life itself.

When one considers that addiction can be understood as an escape to the fantasy of a "wonderland" where there is less or no suffering, Nietzsche's conceptualization of suffering and the will to power can be a powerful antidote to addiction. In Nietzsche's formulation of the will to power, he explicitly accentuates the idea of overcoming resistance, and the will to power is therefore the will to strive against something that resists. Considering that striving against is an effort to overcome, it can be claimed that the will to power is the will to overcome resistance. Addiction recovery requires great effort to overcome the resistance posed by addiction, and thus the successful overcoming of addiction can be seen as a manifestation of the will to power. The suffering implied in the overcoming of the resistance of addiction is then the bedrock for the recovering addict's will to power.

In conclusion, successful addiction recovery, in Nietzschean terms, can then be understood as relinquishing the fantasy of "wonderland" of active addiction, embracing suffering, and the overcoming of the resistance posed by addiction – and thus as a manifestation of the recovering addict's will to power (Du Plessis, 2024).

In *Ecce Homo*, Nietzsche (1992, 37–38) writes: "My formula for greatness in a human being is *amor fati*: that one wants nothing to be different, not forward, not backward, not in all eternity. Not merely bear what is necessary, still less conceal it ... but love it."

2 See Reginster (2006).
3 Nietzsche (1974, p. 270).

The notion of *amor fati* provides a powerful antidote to resentment, when considering that in the "Big Book" of Alcoholics Anonymous it states, "resentment [is] the number one offender. It destroys more alcoholics than anything else."

Requirements and Motivation

Use the following **sample dialogue** with clients, related to the connection between Requirements and motivation.

In the first two sessions, we saw how Requirements underlie high-risk or triggering situations. When these Requirements are unmet or violated, they activate your I-System, making you more prone to entering an addicted mode where cravings are amplified. Thus, you can begin to gain an appreciation for how helpful, even vital, it is to be able to Recognize your Requirements in your activities of daily living.

Maintaining positive motivation is a crucial factor in sustained recovery and relapse prevention. Sadly, your Requirements often directly reduce your motivation for continued abstinence or working a truly successful personal recovery program.

It may be helpful here if we further unpack this concept of motivation as it relates to recovery. Motivation informs relapse prevention through two antagonistic principles at war within the psyche of the addicted individual: (a) motivation for positive behavior change (choosing *not* to drink or use) versus (b) motivation to engage in the problematic behavior (choosing *to* drink or use).

The Requirements an individual has for their recovery process can lead to disappointment or even shame. For example, individuals who have committed to recovery may have the Requirement that once they have made this commitment, they should not experience cravings. Yet, when they experience triggers, high-risk situations, or stress, cravings may return. When this happens, the I-System will, if the Requirement is not recognized, become overactive – paving the way for their addicted mode to manifest. This means that Recognizing Your Requirements is essential for the "long haul" of lifelong recovery.

Defusing Requirements in the Moment

Use the following **sample dialogue** to introduce the next batch of exercises that will help clients Defuse Requirements as they arise in the heat of the moment.

> Recognizing Your Requirements while doing Mapping is very useful and makes you aware of Requirements that may arise in similar future situations. When Mapping you may experience an "a-ha" when you recognize a Requirement. However, this is not the end but rather the beginning of this part of your practice. The Requirement will likely arise again when you encounter the same situation. The fact that you have recognized a Requirement via Mapping will help you recognize and defuse that Requirement when it surfaces again, allowing you to face that situation in Natural Functioning. To effectively deal with Requirements is to recognize them as they arise "in the heat of the moment." We call this **Defuse Requirements**. When you defuse your Requirements when they come up you shift to Natural Functioning. Requirements are like the fuse in a stick of dynamite. If the fuse is lit (a Requirement is violated), but then is quickly cut before it can ignite the dynamite (Requirement is recognized and defused), the dynamite remains inert (the I-System continues to rest, and Natural Functioning prevails).
>
> Although all Requirements are essentially the same in terms of the role they play in activating the I-System, it can be useful to categorize them. A simple way to classify the various types of Requirements is under the categories of (1) Requirements for self, (2) Requirements for others, and (3) Requirements for the world. In the next exercises, you will practice Recognizing all three types of Requirements. As you complete these exercises keep in mind that you can only defuse a Requirement "in the heat of the moment." These exercises will help you "see" your Requirements but Defusing them happens in real time as you experience them "in the heat of the moment."

Requirements for Self

Use the following **sample dialogue** to help clients complete Exercise 5.1 which will help them identify high-risk situations related to their attitudes, thinking, emotional states, and behavior that have or could cause their I-Systems to become overactive:

> In Exercise 5.1 you are going to look at any high-risk situations or triggers related to your attitudes (for example, self-pity, being ungrateful, resentment, etc.), thinking (euphoric recall, etc.), emotional states (anger, sadness, excitement, etc.), and behavior (overworking, withdrawing, etc.) that have in the past or could in the future activate your I-System and possibly lead to an addicted mode. In the chart below list some of the most distressing high-risk situations or triggers that could activate your I-System. Then, using the template provided, write down how you normally act in the high-risk situation or when encountering the situation or trigger.

Use the following **sample dialogue** to help clients complete Exercise 5.2, which has them "Map out" a high-risk situation related to their attitudes, thinking, emotional states, and behavior:

EXAMPLE 5.1

Completed example of Exercise 5.1

High-Risk Situation/Trigger	How do I act
Anger	Say mean or hurtful things
Self-pity	Isolate
Resentment	Ruminate and distracted at work

> Choose one of the high-risk situations or triggers from Exercise 5.1 that is the most distressing (i.e., has the most body tension and mind clutter associated with it). Write it inside the oval on the Map on the template provided. Then take a couple of minutes to scatter your thoughts and feelings about that situation around the outside of the oval. Don't edit or second-guess, just write down whatever thoughts come to mind. At the bottom of the map describe your body tension.

Use the following **sample dialogue** to guide clients in completing Exercise 5.3 which has them recognize Requirements they have for themselves that are connected to a high-risk situation:

> In the next exercise see if you can recognize on the Map you just completed any Requirements ("shoulds" or "musts") you have for **yourself** in connection to the high-risk situation. List them in the box provided.

Use the following **sample dialogue** to conclude this group of exercises:

> Now that you have recognized some of the Requirements you have for yourself, you can defuse them in real time as they arise in your daily activities. Recognizing and Defusing Requirements "in the heat of the moment" will prevent them from causing your I-System to become overactive as you shift toward Natural Functioning.

Requirements for Others

Discuss the following information with clients regarding Requirements for others. The discussion also highlights that the quality of a client's relationships is imperative for sustained recovery, a perspective of those that view addiction as a type of "attachment disorder," which further highlights that healthy relationships are essential for sustained recovery.

> The presence of consistent social support makes a major difference between a sustained recovery process or risk of relapse. Positive social support is correlated with long-term abstinence rates across several addictive behaviors. On the other hand, negative social support, either

Completed example of Exercise 5.2

Situation Map (Example)

People are idiots

I feel out of control

My partner and kids don't listen unless I get upset

I can't sleep

Anger

My boss pushes my buttons

Judgmental people piss me off

Politics at work

My partner doesn't trust me

My "bad attitude" holds me back at work

Description of body tension? Chest gets tight. Clenched fists

EXAMPLE 5.3

Completed example of Exercise 5.3

Requirements for Self
I should not lose control
I should sleep better
I should have a better attitude

in the form of interpersonal conflict or social pressure to use substances, is correlated with an increased risk for relapse (Barber & Crisp, 1995).

Scholars who support the "self-medication hypothesis" maintain that addicts often struggle to regulate their feelings and self-esteem which dates back to suboptimal responsiveness in key relationships formed early in life (Levin, 1995). As a result, they may find themselves particularly prone to external sources of gratification (e.g., substance use) in later life (Kohut, 1977). Khantzian (1999, p. 231) asserts that "[p]ersons with substance use disorders suffer in the extreme with their feelings, either being overwhelmed with painful affects or seeming not to feel their emotions at all. Substances of abuse help such individuals to relieve painful affects or to experience or control emotions when they are absent or confusing."

It is for this reason that the capacity to form healthy relationships is of utmost importance for an effective and sustainable recovery process. If any addictive patterns are rooted in failed attachments (including early caregiving relationships), then any genuine solution to said addiction must be currently grounded in healthy relational attachments.

According to Khantzian (1999) for addicts to develop a healthy and stable sense of self, they need to be in a supportive and empathically attuned social environment. He believes that only through this maintenance of solid connection with reliable others can the disorders of the self be repaired, which, from this relational (or attachment) point of view, lie at the root of addiction. That is why many believe that 12-step programs provide the ideal environment for addicts to heal. For example,

> Ernst Kurtz views the mutuality of AA – one alcoholic needing and helping another – as the cornerstone of the recovery process and the main reason why Twelve-Step programs are so successful. Isolation of one's self from the rest of humanity is one consequence of shame and the driving force behind addiction, since the use of chemicals enhances the denial, fuels the grandiose defenses, and keeps one isolated (in Flores, 1997, p. 245).

The various 12-step fellowships (Alcoholics Anonymous, Narcotics Anonymous, etc.) provide easily accessible and well-established recovering communities. A 12-step program infrastructure and community provide a space and culture where "[g]radually, alcoholics or addicts are able to give up the grandiose defenses (narcissism) and false-self persona for a discovery of self (true self) as they really are" (Flores, 1997, p. 293).

According to William White (1996, p. xxvii) participation in 12-step fellowships helps the transition from the culture of addiction into the culture of recovery, an essential element for sustainable recovery. In addressing the need for a cultural transition as part of a recovery process he states that:

> Addiction and recovery are more than something that happens inside someone. Each involves deep human needs in interaction with a social environment. For addicts, addiction provides a valued cocoon where these needs can be, and historically have been, met [even if self-destructively]. No treatment can be successful if it doesn't offer an [alternate] pathway to meet those same needs and provide an alternative social world that has perceived value and meaning.

From the above discussion, it is clear that the quality of our relationships is imperative for sustained recovery. The Requirements we have for others can greatly influence the quality of our relationships. One of the biggest hindrances to forming healthy relationships is our Requirements for others. These "shoulds" or "musts" we hold for others often lead to disappointment and resentment and may eventually erode even our most valued relationships. Consequently, to maintain healthy relationships, which are imperative for sustained and successful recovery, we need to become aware of the Requirements we have for others, as they unfold in real time. Otherwise, our relationships, which are meant to be supportive, can become a significant trigger or high-risk situation for relapse.

Use the following **sample dialogue** to guide clients in completing Exercise 5.4 which will help them identify high-risk situations related to their relationships that have or could cause their I-Systems to become overactive:

> In the following exercise, we are going to look at situations or triggers related to your relationships (romantic partner, family, or friends) that have the potential to activate your I-System and possibly lead to an addicted mode.
>
> Using the template provided list some of the situations or triggers related to your relationships that could activate your I-System. Then write down how you typically act when encountering the situation or trigger. Refer to the examples provided.

EXAMPLE 5.4

Completed example of Exercise 5.4

High-risk situation/Trigger	How do I act
Arguing with partner	Isolate
Jealousy	Pester partner with questions
Lack of intimacy	Pout

Completed example of Exercise 5.5

Situation Map (Example)

My partner doesn't listen

My partner always brings up my past

We don't communicate

We never resolve anything

Arguing with my partner

My partner gives me the silent treatment

We say hurtful things

My partner doesn't care about me

My partner pushes my buttons

My partner doesn't try to see it from my perspective

Description of body tension? My stomach hurts and my face feels hot

EXAMPLE 5.6

Completed example of Exercise 5.6

Requirements for Others
My partner should not push my buttons
My partner should not give me the silent treatment
My partner should not bring up the past

Use the following **sample dialogue** to guide clients in completing Exercise 5.5 which has them "Map out" a high-risk situation related to their relationships:

> Choose one of the high-risk situations or triggers from Exercise 5.4 that is the most distressing (i.e., has the most body tension and mind clutter associated with it). Write it inside the oval on the Map provided. Then take a couple of minutes to scatter your thoughts and feelings about that situation around the outside of the oval. Don't edit or second-guess, just write down whatever thoughts come to mind. Describe your body tension in the space provided at the bottom of the page.

Use the following **sample dialogue** to help clients complete Exercise 5.6 which has them recognize Requirements they have that are connected to a high-risk situation involving their relationships:

> In the next exercise see if you can recognize on the Map you just completed any Requirements ("shoulds" or "musts") you have for **others** in connection to the high-risk situation. List them in the template provided. A few examples connected to the example map above are provided.

Use the following **sample dialogue** to conclude this batch of exercises:

Now that you have recognized some of the Requirements you have for others, you can defuse them in real time as they arise in your daily activities.

Requirements for the World

Use the following **sample dialogue** to assist clients in completing Exercise 5.7 which will help them identify high-risk situations related to their environments ("the world") that have or could cause their I-Systems to become overactive:

> In the following exercise, we are going to look at situations or triggers related to your environment (for example, your financial situation, political events, social and cultural events, world events, existential beliefs, etc.) that have the potential to activate your I-System possibly leading to an addicted mode.
>
> In the template provided list some of the situations and/or triggers related to your environment that could activate your I-System. Then write down how you typically act when encountering the situation or trigger.

Use the following **sample dialogue** to assist clients in completing Exercise 5.8 which has them "map out" a high-risk situation related to their environments:

> Choose one of the high-risk situations or triggers from Exercise 5.7 that is the most distressing (i.e., has the most body tension and mind clutter associated with it). Write it inside the oval on the Map provided. Then take a couple of minutes to scatter your thoughts and feelings about that situation around the outside of the oval. Don't edit or second-guess, just write down whatever thoughts come to mind. Describe your body tension in the space provided at the bottom of the page.

Use the following **sample dialogue** to guide clients in completing Exercise 5.9 which has them recognize Requirements they have that are connected to a high-risk situation involving their environments:

Completed example of Exercise 5.7

High-risk situation/Trigger	How do I act
Need more money	Isolate
Holidays	Over spend
Elections	Doom scroll on social media

> In the next exercise see if you can recognize on the Map you just completed any Requirements ("shoulds" or "musts") you have for **the world** in connection to the high-risk situation. List them in the box provided.

Use the following **sample dialogue** to conclude this batch of exercises:

> Now that you have recognized some of the Requirements you have for "the world," you can defuse them in real time as they arise in your daily activities.

Practice I-System Map

Use the following **sample dialogue** to help clients complete Exercise 5.10 which has them complete an I-System Map that incorporates all components of their Recovery Resilience Practice. This is an important exercise as this will be the Map that clients will practice going forward.

> Now that we have introduced all the components of a Recovery Resilience Practice, you will have the opportunity to incorporate them all in doing a Map of a distressing situation. We want to emphasize that the primary focus of your Recovery Resilience Practice is your activities of daily living (i.e., recognizing I-System interference in your day-to-day

Completed example of Exercise 5.8

Situation Map (Example)

Co-workers should not play politics

The boss should not play favorites

Promotions should go to those who are most qualified

People are fake

Problems at work

Frustrated with company I work for

Quit and tell them all how I feel

Policies are unfair

I can't deal with the politics

Request a transfer

Description of body tension? Tight chest. Clenched teeth

Completed example of Exercise 5.9

Requirements for the World
Policies should be fair
I should not be frustrated about things I can't control
Promotions should go to those who deserve them

life, moment by moment) but Mapping regularly is also very helpful because it helps you "see" your I-System in action.

We will outline a Mapping process which combines all the components of a Recovery Resilience Practice and represents a comprehensive way of doing a Map.

Your Recovery Resilience Practice is:

(1) Mapping
(2) Recognize I-System Activity
(3) Sensory Awareness
(4) Recognize and Defuse Requirements
(5) Defuse Depressor Storylines Depressor
(6) Defuse Fixer Storylines
(7) Experience the Shift.

Follow the instructions provided with the template for Exercise 5.10 to complete your own Map. Each component of your Recovery Resilience Practice is indicated in **bold text**.

Use the **sample dialogue** below to explain to clients how to complete all aspects of the Map. Remind clients that the way the Map is presented here is the suggestions for their ongoing Mapping Practice.

For Exercise 5.10 choose a distressing situation that you are currently facing and write it inside the oval on the Map (Mapping). Take a couple of minutes to scatter your thoughts and feelings about that situation around the outside of the oval. Don't edit or second-guess, just write down whatever thoughts come to mind. When you've finished writing down your thoughts, write a description of your body tension in the allocated space below the Map (i.e., How much body tension am I experiencing? Where in my body do I notice any tension? How do I describe it?) (**Recognize I-System Activity**).

Identify (using the letter R) the Requirements you have about the situation (**Recognize Requirements**). (Remember that you can only defuse a Requirement when it pops up in the moment. Mapping helps you to be able to recognize a Requirement so that you can defuse it in real time.)

Identify (using the letter D) negative thoughts on your Map that have accompanied Depressor Storylines and identify (using the letter F) any thoughts on your Map that have accompanied Fixer Storylines. Refer to the example provided.

In Exercise 5.11 list the Requirements you identified on your Map using the template provided and also write down the Depressor and Fixer Storylines associated with the thoughts on your Map. Now that you have written down your Depressor Storylines you can defuse them by labeling them. This can be done by saying: "I'm having a thought that ______" (**Defuse Depressor Storylines**). Refer to the examples provided.

In the same way you can defuse your Fixer Storylines by labeling them. This can be done by saying: "I'm having a thought that ______" (**Defuse Fixer Storylines**).

Becoming aware that your I-System is overactive due to a violated Requirement, and Defusing Depressor and Fixer Storylines allows you to befriend it, to use it as a compass that guides a shift to Natural Functioning. Focusing on your senses (**Sensory Awareness**) will also help facilitate this shift.

Completed example of Exercise 5.10

EXAMPLE 5.10

Mind–Body Map (Troubling Situation)

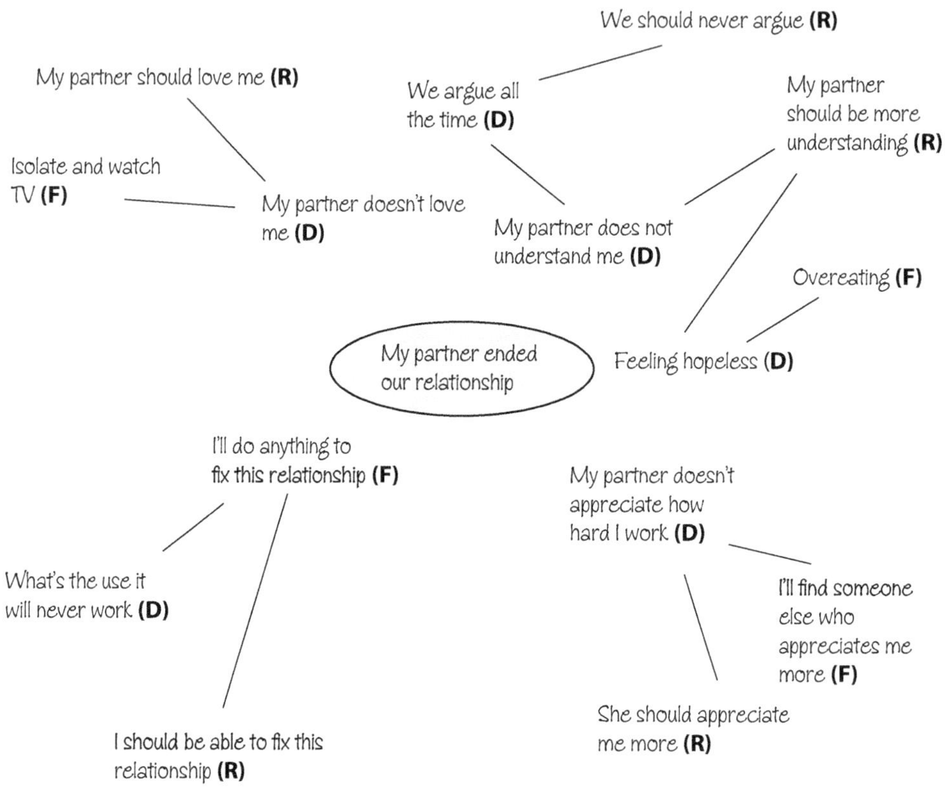

Description of body tension: <u>My chest is tight and heavy</u>

Completed example of Exercise 5.11

Requirement	Depressor Storyline(s)	Fixer Storyline(s)
My partner should appreciate me	My partner doesn't appreciate how hard I work	I'll find someone else who appreciates me
I should be able to fix this relationship	What's the use it will never work	I'll do anything to fix this relationship
My partner should be more understanding	My partner does not understand me; feeling hopeless	Eating (overeating) will help me feel better

As you completed the Map and became more intimate with the dynamics of your I-System you likely experienced the **Shift** as you start inhabiting a Natural Functioning mode of being. You are now able to contemplate the situation or deal with it in a mode that allows for more flexibility, resilience, creativity, and a broader range of responses. You will recognize that the situation you are dealing with is the same – but the "**who**" that is dealing with it has shifted.

Recovery Resilience Journal

Use the following sample dialogue to instruct clients to incorporate all components of a Recovery Resilience Practice into their daily journaling (Exercise 5.12):

> Now that we have introduced all the components of your Recovery Resilience Practice, you can now incorporate them in your Recovery Resilience journal.

Completed example of Exercise 5.12

Recovery Resilience Journal

	Addicted Mode Relapse Signs	Requirements	Depressor/ Fixer Activity	Recovery Resilience Practice
Self	Thinking about and regretting bad decisions made in the past	I should not make bad decisions	Replaying storylines about bad decisions made and how you might fix the damage they caused	Sensory Awareness. Became aware of storylines Recognized and Defused my Requirement. Felt the shift Returned my focus to the tasks at hand
Others	Was angry at my co-worker most of the day for sucking-up to the boss	My co-worker should not play politics	Was distracted most of the day with thoughts about co-worker (how he is wrong and how I can change his behavior), was not productive	Recognized and Defused my Requirement Sensory Awareness Shifted to Natural Functioning Able to focus on work
The World	Argued with my boss about an unfair company policy, stewed about it all day	Policies should be fair	Spent time arguing instead of doing what needed to be done (Fixer). Spent time stewing about unfair policy (Depressor)	Defused Depressor and Fixer Storylines Recognized the Requirement that triggered my I-System

Concluding Session 5

Conclude Session 5 by providing clients with exercise templates for any homework that is required before the next session. Provide the Homework for Session 5 handout which provides a summary of the Recovery Resilience Practices introduced in Session 5 as well as instructions for the Flourishing Scale, Recovery Resilience Practice Scale, and Addicted Mode Warning Signs template.

Session 6

Recovery Resilience Practice

SESSION OBJECTIVE

1. Discuss the aim of this session.
2. Discuss the notions of freedom and powerlessness.
3. Introduce the Recovery Resilience Analysis.
4. Introduce the Recovery Resilience Analysis Synopsis.
5. Discuss how to integrate Recovery Resilience Practice as part of Step Eleven.
6. Discuss how to integrate a Recovery Resilience Practice as part of an existing recovery program.
7. Conclude this session and program.

SESSION DESCRIPTION

The focus of this final Session of the program is to help clients consolidate their Recovery Resilience Practice and learn how to use it to support their existing recovery program and pathway. As mentioned throughout the manual a Recovery Resilience Practice is designed to augment existing recovery practices and relapse prevention skills and increase a client's capacity to apply all aspects of their recovery capital.

Use the following **sample dialogue** to provide an overview of the session:

> In the previous session we provided an overview of all aspects of a Recovery Resilience Practice that will contribute toward a sustainable recovery lifestyle. In this session, you will consolidate your Recovery Resilience Practice and see how to use it to support any recovery program and pathway you choose. As highlighted throughout the program, the central aim of your Recovery Resilience Practice is to remove the hindrance that obstructs your capacity to access your recovery capital and apply recovery skills as well as provide a practice that can help you moment by moment to deal with stress, high-risk situations, triggers, or any troubling situations. In short, your Recovery Resilience Practice removes the hindrance to your innate resilience and capacity for flourishing and assists you in achieving your recovery and life goals. With continued practice, your self-efficacy will grow, and this is important because higher levels of self-efficacy are predictive of improved substance use disorder treatment outcomes (Greenfield et al., 2000).
>
> One of the central aims of any adequate addiction recovery process is to not only gain freedom from addiction but also to live up to our potential, to flourish. As we have highlighted in this workbook, having this freedom also requires us to understand and manage our I-Systems, which when overactive can lead to a relapse as well as to a limited state of being and an impaired way of relating to ourselves, others, and the world (i.e., addicted mode).

Freedom and Powerlessness

Discuss the following information with clients which highlights the relationship between freedom and powerlessness.

> The concepts of "freedom" and "powerlessness" are frequently used in addiction treatment and recovery communities. South African philosopher and statesman, Jan Smuts (1926, p. 321), asserted "[to] be a free personality represents the highest achievement of which any human being is capable." Addiction can be understood as a

lifestyle that severely constricts our capacity for freedom, whereas a recovery lifestyle allows for a fuller expression of freedom and wholeness. Existential psychiatrist Medard Boss (1983, p. 283) asserts that: "[a]ddiction, whatever its form, has always been a desperate search, on a false and hopeless path, for the fulfillment of human freedom." Recall how we earlier examined the etymology of the word "addiction," discovering it to be *addictus* (from the original Latin). *Addictus*, in the ancient Roman world, connoted being a bondservant, that is, someone bound in servitude to a master. If we explore the analogy to addictions, we can readily see how freedom is lost, as with a bondservant, in active addiction. And whatever recovery implies, it surely has as its primary foundation a return to freedom and choice.

Even though a person might have an addiction problem that limits their free will in relation to the use of substances, known as "powerlessness" in 12-step programs, it does not make them "powerless" over the choices they can make to get the right support and to follow practices that will prevent them from regressing into this "powerless" condition. A person has the free will to make choices that support either a recovery lifestyle or an addictive lifestyle. The choice and the responsibility are theirs alone. Accepting our powerlessness over our addiction has the paradoxical consequence of resulting in more freedom because true freedom entails functioning within limitations. Philip Flores (1997, p. 273) argues that "[p]owerlessness over alcohol and the acceptance of one's limitation in relation to alcohol serves as a prototype for the alcoholic facing and accepting other limitations of the human condition."

Addiction can be understood as an attempt to bypass certain of our inherent limitations and basic human needs (recall our discussion of Max-Neef and how substance use can be a destructive means of having basic needs met). While in active addiction, individuals try to control the uncontrollable to avoid and self-medicate the natural human experiences of pain, disappointment, loss, and boredom. Certain aspects of life are within our capacity to control and manipulate, but some aspects are simply given and cannot be avoided or controlled. Existential philosophers sometimes refer to these as "existential givens" (Du Plessis, 2019b). At the core of addiction dynamics, there is a fantasy of having an unrealistic sense of control of oneself, others, and these "existential givens" where an individual becomes a "captive of these addictive fantasies and then becomes an addict, lost in a wonderland" (Ulman & Paul, 2006, p. 6).

Through a recovery practice, we not only aim to find freedom from our addiction but also to find freedom and meaning within the limitations of our human condition. In a lifestyle that resonates with Natural Functioning, we step out of this "wonderland" and we gain more freedom while not trying to control the uncontrollable or striving to meet impossible-to-attain and perfectionistic demands that are imposed on us by our I-System. We simply see things more realistically and deal with life as it is, not with how we think it ought to be.

Recovery Resilience Analysis

Use the following **sample dialogue** to introduce clients to the Recovery Resilience Analysis exercises. Highlight to clients that a Recovery Resilience Analysis is akin to Step Four of the 12-step program where one conducts a "moral inventory." In a Recovery Resilience Analysis, instead of focusing on the moral component and identifying character defects, the focus is on I-System activity.

The Recovery Resilience Program is based on the premise (like 12-step philosophy) that addiction is a dysfunctional way of being and stopping the use of drugs is only one aspect of a sustainable recovery process. In short, one needs a complete lifestyle change – a change from a lifestyle dominated by an addicted mode to a lifestyle that resonates with Natural Functioning. Without a shift in lifestyle and access to recovery capital, the individual may eventually gravitate back to his or her habitual mode of being-in-the-world, that is, substance use. The Recovery Resilience Program, like 12-step programs, views recovery as a "way of life" and "not a plan for recovery that can be finished and done with" and an approach to "living that allows for limitless expansion" (Wilson, 1976, p. 311).

We have seen that any activity is carried out in either the I-System or Natural Functioning mode. What is of primary importance is not only what you are doing, but who is doing it. That is, are your daily activities and goals driven by your I-System in an attempt to "fix" yourself or are they inspired by Natural Functioning? When your activities and goals are driven by your I-System, you will view yourself against the backdrop of unattainable and perfectionistic Requirements. Instead of improving your well-being, this adds to your distress and feelings of inadequacy and shame. Your Fixer will drive you relentlessly to fix these unpleasant and painful thoughts, feelings, and body sensations caused by the Depressor. And when your goals are achieved your Depressor will let you know that whatever you did was not good enough.

The Recovery Resilience Program is based on the premise that the more your daily activities are done in Natural Functioning the greater your recovery resilience will be – and that activities that are Fixer-driven make you more prone to lapse and relapse. However, it is not always obvious or easy to know when your activities are I-System driven and this is acting as a hindrance to your innate resilience.

To assist you in gaining awareness of how your I-System can hinder your recovery lifestyle and keep you from achieving your goals, Exercise 6.1 will engage you in what we call a Recovery Resilience Analysis. A Recovery Resilience Analysis is a systematic and comprehensive exploration of how your I-System acts as a hindrance in your daily life. It involves exploring your relationship with yourself, others, and the world (environment), as well as how plans and goals may be influenced by your I-System. In short, the focus here is on how I-System activity manifests in your daily life and how it influences your activities and goals. The attention here is on the hindrance, not only on the practices, as our approach is based on the notion that your resilience naturally flourishes when the hindrance is removed. So, in one way your recovery resilience depends not only on what you do but also on the extent to which the I-System is not interfering with what you do. That is to say, your recovery resilience is proportionately tied to your Recovery Resilience Practice (those moment-by-moment practices that quiet your I-System).

> Performing a Recovery Resilience Analysis can help you see how your I-System is influencing your daily activities, relationships, and worldview. Through the insight gained you can alter your worldview, improve your relationships, and adjust plans and goals so that they are more congruent with the life you actually desire and want to live, rather than a life driven by the I-System where nothing is ever good enough and you feel perpetually unfulfilled. When your life is I-System driven you are like a "hungry ghost" (using a phrase from addiction expert Gabor Maté, 2011) where, like a ghost, it does not matter how much you "eat," it falls right through you and never satisfies your hunger. In Natural Functioning you are more likely to use appropriate methods to meet your needs and feel satisfied.

A Recovery Resilience Analysis is akin to Step Four of the 12-step program where one conducts a "moral inventory." In a Recovery Resilience Analysis, instead of focusing on the moral component and highlighting character defects, the focus is on I-System activity. A Recovery Resilience Analysis is in no way meant to replace a Step Four process as the focus of that process is different. However, making "a searching and fearless" inventory of I-System activity can be a good adjunct to a Step Four process for those in 12-step programs. A Recovery Resilience Analysis provides you with an opportunity to take a "bird's-eye view" of your total being-in-the-world.

To perform a **Recovery Resilience Analysis,** follow these instructions:

Exercises 6.1, 6.3, 6.5

1. Using the templates provided complete a Map for each of these life domains: (1) self, (2) others, and (3) the world and your environment. Write any thoughts related to each domain that come to mind. Feel free to include thoughts about your various recovery practices (for example, *I am lazy when it comes to Step Work, I am bored in meetings*). Write whatever comes to mind without editing. *Refer to the examples provided.*

Exercises 6.2, 6.4, 6.6

2. Once you have completed the Maps list the I-System activity related to the Map. Write down your Requirements and Depressor and Fixer Storylines using the template provided. *Refer to the examples provided.*

Completed example of Exercise 6.1

Recovery Resilience Analysis Map for Self

I should never feel down

I should not need to smoke weed

I'm broken

I'll never accept myself as I am

Smoke weed to find temporary relief

Isolate and watch TV

Self

I've never been able to focus on the positive, and never will

I am grumpy

I am going to start memorizing affirmations right now

I should be able to simply count my blessings, rather than complain all the time

Force myself to smile at people even though I often don't feel like it

I should be nicer to everybody

Completed example of Exercise 6.2

Requirements	I should never feel down
Depressor	I'll never accept myself as I am
Fixer	Smoke weed to find temporary relief

Completed example of Exercise 6.3

Recovery Resilience Analysis Map for Others

My partner shouldn't argue with me

My partner should love me

My partner should be more understanding

We argue all the time

Isolate and watch TV

My partner does not understand me

Overeating

My partner doesn't love me

Others

People are mean

I'll tell my boss off

I'll find someone else who appreciates me more

My boss doesn't appreciate how hard I work

I'll just quit my job

People shouldn't judge me

People are two-faced

Completed example of Exercise 6.4

Requirements	My partner shouldn't argue with me
Depressor	My boss doesn't appreciate how hard I work
Fixer	I'll just quit my job

EXAMPLE 6.5

Completed example of Exercise 6.5

Recovery Resilience Analysis Map for the World

The world is broken

Life should be fair

Trust nobody

My 12-step program isn't run right

I'll look for another program

World

My community should do more to support recovery

This town is boring

I need to move

My car shouldn't break down

My employer should care more about its employees

EXAMPLE 6.6

Completed example of Exercise 6.6

Requirements	Life should be fair
Depressor	The world is broken
Fixer	*I'll look for another program*

Use the following **sample dialogue** to conclude the Recovery Resilience Analysis exercises:

> Completing a Recovery Resilience Analysis will provide you with an insight of how I-System activity is interfering in the various domains of your life and with your recovery practices. Consequently, we recommend that you do this routinely as part of your Recovery Resilience Practice. Keep in mind that completing a Recovery Resilience Analysis will do you very little good unless you apply what you learn about your I-System in your daily life and continue to apply your Recovery Resilience Practice.

Recovery Resilience Analysis Synopsis

Use the following **sample dialogue** to guide clients in completing a **Recovery Resilience Analysis Synopsis** (Exercise 6.7):

> In the next exercise, you are going to complete a **Recovery Resilience Analysis Synopsis**. This provides a summary and integration of your Recovery Resilience Analysis.
>
> Using the template provided, list the Requirements and Depressor/Fixer thoughts from your Recovery Resilience Analysis that pose the biggest threat to your recovery lifestyle. Refer to the examples provided.
>
> You may notice that there is some commonality between the Requirements, Depressors, and Fixers you have for self, others, and the world/environment.
>
> Notice and write down any patterns you may find and consider how you can apply your Recovery Resilience Practice in your activities of daily living when you next encounter these same situations.

Use the following **sample dialogue** to help clients process Exercise 6.7.

> Once you have completed the Recovery Resilience Analysis and Synopsis, you will be more aware of how your I-System manifests in

Completed example of Exercise 6.7

	Requirements	Depressor	Fixer
Self	I should never feel down	I'll never accept myself as I am	Smoke weed to find temporary relief
Others	My partner shouldn't argue with me	My partner should be more understanding	Isolate and watch TV
World	Life should be fair	The world is broken	Trust nobody

your life as well as how it may potentially hijack your various recovery practices. A Recovery Resilience Analysis can help you identify the aspects of your life that can benefit from using your Recovery Resilience Practices to remove what hinders (I-System overactivity) your innate resilience (for example, Defusing Requirements you have for your partner, Recognizing Depressor thoughts about your job, or Recognizing your Fixer thoughts about your finances).

As has been pointed out, any practice, even your recovery practices can be hijacked by your I-System. One of the major strengths of the recovery resilience approach is that it does not only focus on "what" you are doing but also on "who" is doing it (you in I-System mode or you in Natural Functioning mode). So even if the healthiest of activities is I-System driven it can have the opposite effect that it is designed to achieve or simply cause you to feel disappointment and shame.

For example, a central feature of 12-step programs is the application of spiritual principles in our daily lives. This can be seen to be a similar approach to Aristotle's virtue ethics. Virtue ethics is a philosophy developed by the ancient Greek philosopher Aristotle. It is the quest to live a life of moral character.[1] This character-based approach to morality assumes that we acquire virtue through practice (Peterson & Seligman, 2004). By practicing being honest, brave, just, generous, and so on, a person develops an honorable and moral character. According to Aristotle, by honing virtuous habits, people will likely make the right choice when faced with ethical challenges. So, virtue ethics helps us understand what it means to be a virtuous human being. And it gives us a guide for living life without giving us specific rules for resolving ethical dilemmas.

Now the problem is that if our practice of virtues or spiritual principles is I-System driven we will be held hostage by Requirements, and no matter how hard we try the Depressor will be there to tell us that we are not good enough. Failing to live up to these ideals will result in shame. Moreover, we could hold others accountable to unrealistic and perfectionistic virtuous or spiritual ideals, which can only lead to resentment and disappointment. A Recovery Resilience Analysis can thus help us to see from a more objective distance the degree to which our I-Systems are interfering with our ethical life and recovery practices and life goals.

In the same way that those who practice a 12-step program incorporate a shortened version of Step Four as part of their Step Ten practice when completing a daily journal, a shortened version of a Recovery Resilience Analysis can be incorporated as part of your daily journal practice. The value of doing a daily journal as part of a recovery process is well documented. Reflecting on the “who” (I-System or Natural Functioning) as well as the “what” (your daily activities) can greatly add to the benefit of this foundational recovery practice. As you become more aware of how your I-System interferes with your activities of daily living you become better able to recognize it as it happens, and simply being aware of your I-System’s activities is often enough to get you back on track.

1 See Hursthouse (2001).

Step Eleven

Discuss the following information with clients regarding meditation and its role in the Recovery Resilience Program:

> The practice of meditation is central in Step Eleven of the 12-step program where the suggestion is made to use "meditation to improve our conscious contact" (Wilson, 1976, p. 45) with a power greater than oneself. The focus of the suggestions made in Step Eleven is on gaining acceptance of things as they are and the capacity to deal with reality as it is. Step Eleven has congruence with the Stoic-influenced notion of "amor fati" as advocated by Friedrich Nietzsche. He states:
>
>> I want to learn more and more to see as beautiful what is necessary in things; then I shall be one of those who makes things beautiful. *Amor fati*: let that be my love henceforth! I do not want to wage war against what is ugly. I do not want to accuse; I do not even want to accuse those who accuse. Looking away shall be my only negation. And all in all and on the whole: someday I wish to be only a Yes-sayer (Nietzsche, 2003, p. 157).
>
> Nietzsche clearly takes poetic license in his description of "amor fati," and it may be an unattainable goal, but we can learn from his suggestion, as a pure practice of virtuous or spiritual principles is ultimately unattainable. That is, we never attain an attitude of unconditional acceptance but instead strive toward it. We can never be free from expectations and Requirements but instead strive toward minimizing their potentially destructive effects. It is our I-System's Fixer that demands perfection. In short, a practice like Step Eleven aims to assist us in becoming more accepting of things that are beyond our control and not to try and "fix what isn't broken." The French philosopher Simone de Beauvoir (1948) shares a similar notion in her expression of "ambiguity," which is that we are free but at the same time powerless over many things; that we are not totally free nor are we totally at the mercy of things. Our nature is ambiguous – as a central feature of our existence – and this ambiguity or tension is not to be regarded as a flaw that should be eliminated. Instead, she suggests that if "we do not succeed in fleeing it, let us, therefore, try to

look the truth in the face. Let us try to assume our fundamental ambiguity. It is in the knowledge of the genuine conditions of our life that we must draw our strength of life and our reason for acting" (De Beauvoir 1948, p. 22).

Step Eleven is more closely related to Western traditions and techniques of philosophical contemplation[2] than typical Eastern meditation practices, in that we seek to "improve our conscious contact." The aim is not detached awareness as is the case in most meditation practices, but insight. This aligns with a Recovery Resilience Practice where we become familiar with the workings of our minds. The aim is to gain familiarity with and recognize your I-System Storylines. Recall that the premise of this workbook is that in a state of Natural Functioning we unleash our innate resilience, inner wisdom, and resourcefulness. Thus, the goal here is not to gain decentered awareness of thoughts but rather to gain what the Greek philosophers called *phronesis* or practical wisdom. In short, the aim is to access your inner wisdom, which is found in Natural Functioning, which guides you on how to act and meet the imperative of the moment. Phronesis is concerned with particulars because it is concerned with how to act in particular situations. In a Natural Functioning state, we connect to a source of wisdom that is greater and deeper than our usual thinking patterns (and depending on your belief it may be that your source of inner wisdom is your True or Inner Self, Higher Power, or God). This is congruent with Step Eleven where the aim is to "improve our conscious contact." So, we suggest your Step Eleven practice include an awareness and befriending of your I-System activity. The philosopher Bertrand Russell describes philosophical contemplation that resonates with our view of a Natural Functioning orientation toward existence – where we are not caught up in the self-centered vicissitudes of the I-System:

> The mind that has become accustomed to the freedom and impartiality of philosophic contemplation will preserve something of the same freedom and impartiality in the world of action and emotion. It will view its purposes and desires as parts of the whole, with the absence of insistence that results from seeing them as

2 See Butler (2003).

> infinitesimal fragments in a world in which all the rest is unaffected by any one man's deeds. The impartiality which, in contemplation, is the unalloyed desire for truth, is the very same quality of mind which, in action, is justice, and in emotion is that universal love which can be given to all, and not only to those who are judged useful or admirable. Thus, contemplation enlarges not only the objects of our thoughts but also the objects of our actions and our affections: it makes us citizens of the universe, not only of one walled city at war with all the rest. In this citizenship of the universe consists man's true freedom, and his liberation from the thralldom of narrow hopes and fears (Russell, 1912, pp. 248–249).

A Recovery Resilience Practice may, quoting Russell, enlarge "not only the objects of our thoughts but also the objects of our actions and our affections" (expanded mode of Natural Functioning) and "with the absence of insistence" (Defusing Requirements) liberate us from our "narrow hopes and fears" (contracted mode of I-System Functioning and addicted mode).

Integrating a Recovery Resilience Practice into a Client's Existing Recovery Program

Use the following **sample dialogue** to explain to clients how to incorporate a Recovery Resilience Practice within their existing recovery programs. As stressed throughout the manual, the RRP aims to lessen the load on both the client and counsellor, therefore it is best to integrate the various practices outlined in this manual as part of existing practices.

> We reiterate that the Recovery Resilience Program outlined in this program is not in any way designed to replace your existing recovery practices or be a self-standing approach to treating your addiction. A Recovery Resilience Practice is not designed to address all aspects of developing a sustainable recovery lifestyle. It primarily focuses on strengthening your inner resources and helping you take full advantage of your recovery capital. We believe that it is imperative that apart from strengthening your inner resources you also need external support and

structure, such as being part of a support group such as 12-step fellowships or SMART Recovery or therapy support groups that consistently reinforce your intentions and various recovery skills and practices. In short, a Recovery Resilience Practice is an adjunct to your overall recovery process, whether that is facilitated primarily through self-help groups or psycho-educational support groups.

There are two aspects to having a Recovery Resilience Practice:

(1) The application of a Recovery Resilience Practice in **activities of daily living** as the need arises in the moment: for example, dealing with high-risk situations, triggers, or stressful situations.

The seven components of your Recovery Resilience Practice are:

- Mapping
- Recognize I-System Activity
- Sensory Awareness
- Recognize and Defuse Your Requirements
- Defuse Depressor Storylines
- Defuse Fixer Storylines
- Experience the Shift

(2) The incorporation of your Recovery Resilience Practice as part of your **daily recovery-oriented routine** in a structured way: this aspect provides structure to your practice. this is especially important in the early stages of developing a Recovery Resilience Practice.

As with any newly acquired practice, it takes repetition to achieve mastery. There is much evidence that supports the value of having a daily routine as part of a recovery process. You may already have a daily recovery routine as this is a common part of most recovery processes, and if you do we suggest that you incorporate your Recovery Resilience Practice into this daily routine.

We suggest the following routine (if you are working a 12-step program add this to your existing routine):

Morning Routine:

- Do a Map as part of your morning routine.
- Incorporate your Recovery Resilience Practice as part of Step Eleven.

Evening Routine:

- Incorporate your Recovery Resilience Practice as part of Step Eleven.
- Keep a Recovery Resilience Practice Journal where you write down your experience of the day through the lens of a Recovery Resilience Practice. At times it helps to do a Map about the day before writing in your journal. (Note moments of I-System activity – Requirements, Depressor and Fixer Storylines, and addicted mode, moments when you experienced the Shift.) Include this if you are already doing a daily journal as part of your Step Ten practice.

Weekly Routine:

- One day a week, preferably at the end of the week, complete the scales that are included in this Workbook. These are especially helpful in the early stages of your practice. And once you are comfortable with your Recovery Resilience Practice, they can fall away, and you can just continue with your daily journaling – something we suggest that you keep on doing regardless of your clean time.

Progress Not Perfection

Use the following **sample dialogue** to discuss the value of having a "progress, not perfection" mindset towards their Recovery Resilience Practice and highlight how even a client's recovery program can be hijacked by I-System Activity.

> Now that we have presented all the features of a Recovery Resilience Practice, we want to highlight that one of the perils of any personal development process is that we can have Requirements about the outcome of such a process. Requirements can lead us to continuously measure ourselves against unattainable and perfectionist ideals. Instead of improving our well-being, this adds to our distress and feelings of inadequacy. Individuals working an addiction recovery program run the risk of succumbing to this common problem. As we have discussed, addicts are often known to have perfectionistic tendencies with

overdeveloped inner critics, fueled by low self-esteem and internalized shame. Their shame often drives them relentlessly to prove to themselves and others that they are good enough – keeping them stuck in a Sisyphean struggle.

Most recovery programs focus primarily on the "doing" or "what" of recovery, the tangible practice components of a recovery lifestyle. We have referred to these skills and tools as recovery capital. Certainly, this is a crucial component of any sustainable recovery process. But as we have shown in this workbook, another equally important component of recovery is "being" (as opposed to only "doing"), or in other words, paying close attention to "who" is doing these recovery practices – you in an I-System Functioning or addicted mode or you in Natural Functioning mode. In short, each recovery practice can be understood as having two qualities: the "doing" or "what" of the practice, and the "being" or "who" of the practice. A recovery lifestyle may consist of ostensibly healthy practices, but if these practices are Fixer-driven, they may seriously compromise or even have a long-term destructive effect on your well-being. For example, you could be going to the gym five times a week, but if this is influenced by the Storylines of your Depressor and Fixer (e.g., perfectionism and over-criticalness), it could result in negative outcomes such as over-training and burnout. Another example is participating in a 12-step meeting with an attitude of arrogance and closed-mindedness or with an open attitude of humility, gratitude, and willingness. The attitude of your participation – "who" is at the helm – will profoundly affect the value you get from the practice. You must maintain a healthy balance between "doing" and "being" (i.e., the what and the who). Your recovery program ought not to become another Fixer-driven and ultimately futile attempt (like your addictive behavior) to "fix what ain't broke."

For recovery to be sustainable you must work hard – not to fix yourself – but to realize that essentially you are good enough. A Recovery Resilience Practice is not about fixing yourself, but rather the slow process of realizing that there is indeed nothing to fix.

In Conclusion

Use the following **sample dialogue** to conclude the final Session of the program.

> Now that we have come to the end of the workbook, we would like to reiterate the Charlie Parker quote mentioned in the Introduction: "If you don't live it, it won't come out of your horn" – which is to say that your Recovery Resilience Practice and your recovery will be sustainable only if you "live it," that is, through ongoing daily practice. With an ongoing Recovery Resilience Practice, you will become more intimately familiar with the workings of your I-System. Armed with this awareness, you can simply use your I-System as a compass to warn you that you are drifting off your recovery pathway and use your Recovery Resilience Practice to get back on track. As we have stressed throughout the workbook, your Recovery Resilience Practice aims to deal with situations and to live your life in Natural Functioning. In this state, you are innately resilient and have more access to your recovery capital – and with continued practice, this leads to flourishing and enhances your capacity to achieve your recovery and life goals.
>
> In conclusion and reiterating the central premise of the Recovery Resilience Program, recovery is not just about abstaining from alcohol and other drugs, but also about gaining "liberation from the [I-System's] thralldom of narrow hopes and fears" (Russell, 1912, p. 249), and discovering a life and way of being that is joyful and meaningful, and has true freedom.

Concluding Session Six

Conclude Session 6 by providing clients with exercise templates for any homework that is required before the next session. Provide the Homework for Session 6 handout which includes a summary of the Recovery Resilience Practices introduced in Session 6, as well as instructions for the Flourishing Scale, Recovery Resilience Practice Scale, and Addicted Mode Warning Signs template.

Appendix

Client Session Handouts

Session 1 Client Handouts

EXERCISE 1.1

Map 1

Description of body tension: ____________________

EXERCISE 1.2

Map 2

Description of body tension: ______________________________

EXERCISE 1.3

Map 1	Map 2

Difference Between Maps:

EXERCISE 1.5

How I Would Like Certain People to Act Map

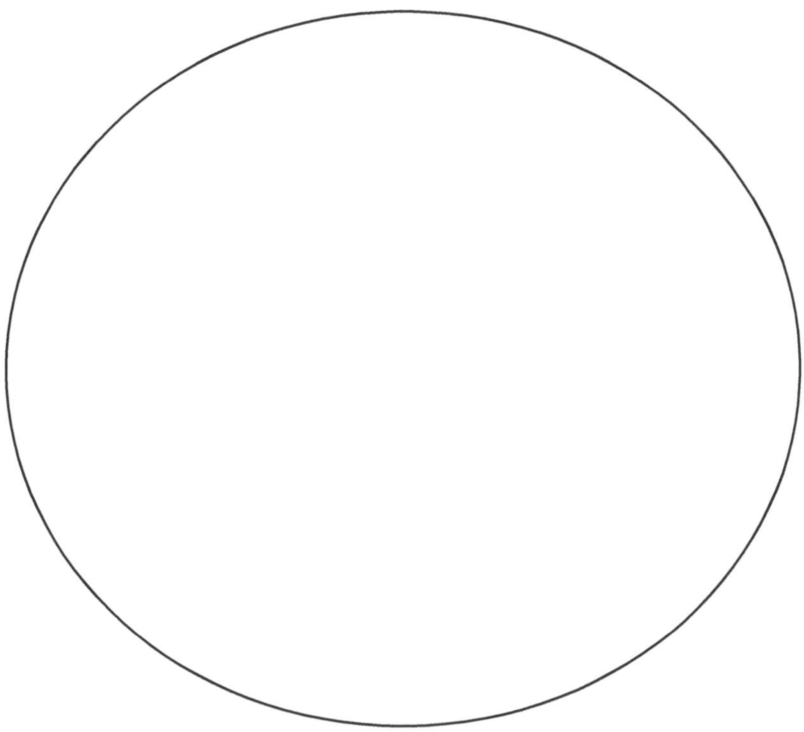

EXERCISE 1.6

How I Would Like to Be Map

EXERCISE 1.7

High-Risk Situations		
Intrapersonal (self)	**Interpersonal (others)**	**Environmental (the world)**

EXERCISE 1.8

High-Risk Situation Map 1

Description of body tension: ______________________________

EXERCISE 1.9

High-Risk Situation Map 2

Description of body tension: ______________________________

EXERCISE 1.10

Map 1	Map 2

Difference between Maps:

Flourishing Scale

Date: _____________

Below are 8 statements with which you may agree or disagree. Using the 1–7 scale below, indicate your agreement with each item by indicating that response for each statement.

- 7 – Strongly agree
- 6 – Agree
- 5 – Slightly agree
- 4 – Neither agree nor disagree
- 3 – Slightly disagree
- 2 – Disagree
- 1 – Strongly disagree

Indicate your agreement with each item	**(1–7)**
I lead a purposeful and meaningful life	
My social relationships are supportive and rewarding	
I am engaged and interested in my daily activities	
I actively contribute to the happiness and well-being of others	
I am competent and capable in the activities that are important to me	
I am a good person and live a good life	
I am optimistic about my future	
People respect me	
Total Score:	_____

The *Flourishing Scale* was developed by Diener, E., Wirtz, D., Tov, W., Kim-Prieto, C., Choi, D., Oishi, S., & Biswas-Diener, R. (2010). New measures of well-being: Flourishing and positive and negative feelings. *Social Indicators Research, 39*, 247–266.

Recovery Resilience Practice Scale

Date: ______________

Over the past week indicate the frequency of your Recovery Resilience Practice. Check the description that most closely reflects your practice: Never, Hardly Ever, Occasionally, or Regularly

Frequency of Recovery Resilience Practice	Never	Hardly Ever	Occasionally	Regularly
Recognize I-System Activity				
Mapping				
Recognize Requirements				
Sensory Awareness				
Experience the Shift				

Homework for Session One

Recovery Resilience Practice

- Do **Mapping** related to any high-risk situation or troubling experience.
- **Recognize I-System Activity** by being aware of body tension and mental clutter.
- Practice **Sensory Awareness.**
- **Recognize Requirements** when performing daily activities.
- **Experience the Shift** as you move from I-System Functioning to Natural Functioning.

Complete the following at the end of each week:

> **Flourishing Scale:** Complete the scale and calculate your score, from 1 to 7, for each question over the past week or two. The Flourishing Scale will provide a measure to help you track your progress as you work through this workbook and develop a Recovery Resilience Practice. The Flourishing Scale is designed to measure your subjective happiness, well-being and quality of life.
>
> **Recovery Resilience Practice Scale:** Complete the scale and calculate and write down the frequency of your Recovery Resilience Practice. Indicate whether it was never, hardly ever, occasionally, or regularly.

As you incorporate your Recovery Resilience Practice into your life it will feel more natural and instinctive. And remember "progress not perfection."

Session 2 Client Handouts

EXERCISE 2.1

Intrapersonal (self)	Interpersonal (others)	Environmental (the world)

EXERCISE 2.2

Trigger Map 1

Description of body tension: ______________________________

EXERCISE 2.3

Trigger Map 2

Description of body tension: ______________________________

EXERCISE 2.4

Map 1	Map 2

Difference between Maps:

EXERCISE 2.6

	Addicted Mode Warning Signs
Self	
Others	
The World	

EXERCISE 2.7

Recovery Resilience Journal

	Addicted Mode Warning Signs	Recovery Resilience Practice
Self		
Others		
The World		

Homework for Session Two

Recovery Resilience Practice

- Do **Mapping** related to any high-risk situation, trigger or troubling experience.
- **Recognize I-System Activity** by being aware of body tension and mental clutter.
- Practice **Sensory Awareness.**
- **Recognize Requirements** when performing daily activities.
- **Experience the Shift.**

Complete the following:

Addicted Mode Warning Signs: Use the template and write down, in the space provided your addicted mode warning signs for the past week. Try and be as comprehensive as possible.

Flourishing Scale: Complete the scale and calculate your score, from 1 to 7, for each question over the past week or two.

Recovery Resilience Practice Scale: Complete the scale and calculate and write down the frequency of your Recovery Resilience Practice. Indicate whether it was never, hardly ever, occasionally, or regularly.

Addicted Mode Warning Signs

Date: ______________

Over the past week write down any addicted mode warning signs you noticed in each of your life dimensions

	Addicted Mode Warning Signs
Self	
Others	
The World	

Flourishing Scale

Date: ____________

Below are 8 statements with which you may agree or disagree. Using the 1–7 scale below, indicate your agreement with each item by indicating that response for each statement.

- 7 – Strongly agree
- 6 – Agree
- 5 – Slightly agree
- 4 – Neither agree nor disagree
- 3 – Slightly disagree
- 2 – Disagree
- 1 – Strongly disagree

Indicate your agreement with each item	**(1–7)**
I lead a purposeful and meaningful life	
My social relationships are supportive and rewarding	
I am engaged and interested in my daily activities	
I actively contribute to the happiness and well-being of others	
I am competent and capable in the activities that are important to me	
I am a good person and live a good life	
I am optimistic about my future	
People respect me	
Total score:	_____

The *Flourishing Scale* was developed by Diener, E., Wirtz, D., Tov, W., Kim-Prieto, C., Choi, D., Oishi, S., & Biswas-Diener, R. (2010). New measures of well-being: Flourishing and positive and negative feelings. *Social Indicators Research*, *39*, 247–266.

Recovery Resilience Practice Scale

Date: ____________

Over the past week indicate the frequency of your Recovery Resilience Practice. Check the description that most closely reflects your practice: never, hardly ever, occasionally, or regularly.

Frequency of Recovery Resilience Practice	Never	Hardly Ever	Occasionally	Regularly
Recognize I-System Activity				
Mapping				
Sensory Awareness				
Recognize Requirements				
Experience the Shift				

Session 3 Client Handouts

EXERCISE 3.1

Depressor Map

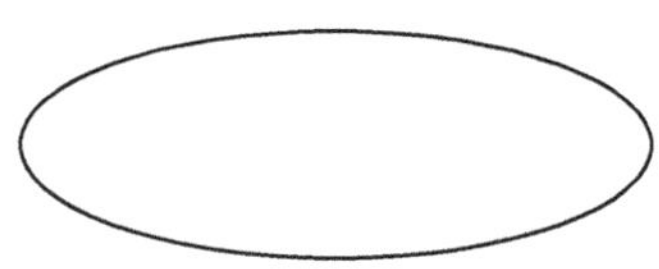

EXERCISE 3.2

Thought:

Story:

EXERCISE 3.3

Requirement	What Violates the Requirement?	Depressor Thought/ Storyline

EXERCISE 3.4

Situation:

Story:

EXERCISE 3.5

EXERCISE 3.6

Depressor Storyline:

Thought Label:

EXERCISE 3.7

How I Am Going to Improve My Life Map

How I am Going to Improve My Life

EXERCISE 3.8

Depressor/Fixer Map

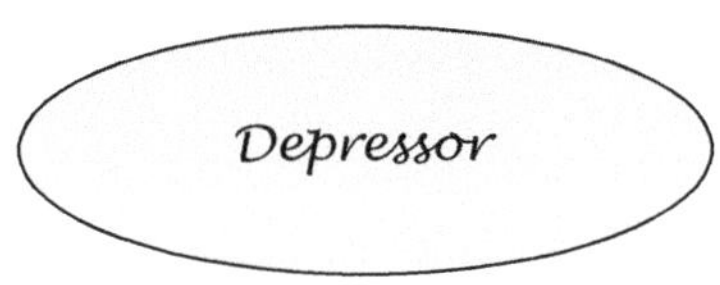

EXERCISE 3.9

Depressor Storyline:

Fixer Storyline:

EXERCISE 3.10

High-Risk/ Trigger	Requirement	What Violates the Requirement?	Depressor Thought/ Storyline	What Do I Feel Driven to Do About It? (Fixer)

EXERCISE 3.11

Fixer Storyline:

Thought Label:

EXERCISE 3.12

Recovery Resilience Journal

	Addicted Mode Warning Signs	Requirements	Depressor/ Fixer Activity	Recovery Resilience Practice
Self				
Others				
The World				

Homework for Session Three

Recovery Resilience Practice

- Do **Mapping** related to any high-risk situation or troubling experience.
- **Recognize I-System** Activity.
- Practice **Sensory Awareness.**
- **Recognize Requirements** when performing daily activities.
- **Defuse Depressor Storylines.**
- **Defuse Fixer Storylines.**
- **Experience the Shift.**
- Complete your **Recovery Resilience Journal** daily.

Complete the following:

Addicted Mode Warning Signs: Use the template and write down, in the space provided your addicted mode warning signs for the past week. Try and be as comprehensive as possible.

Flourishing Scale: Complete the scale and calculate your score, from 1 to 7, for each question over the past week or two.

Recovery Resilience Practice Scale: Complete the scale and calculate and write down the frequency of your Recovery Resilience Skills practice. Indicate whether it was never, hardly ever, occasionally, or regularly.

Addicted Mode Warning Signs

Date: ______________

Over the past week write down any addicted mode warning signs you noticed in each of your life dimensions

	Addicted Mode Warning Signs
Self	
Others	
The World	

Flourishing Scale

Date: ___________

Below are 8 statements with which you may agree or disagree. Using the 1–7 scale below, indicate your agreement with each item by indicating that response for each statement.

- 7 – Strongly agree
- 6 – Agree
- 5 – Slightly agree
- 4 – Neither agree nor disagree
- 3 – Slightly disagree
- 2 – Disagree
- 1 – Strongly disagree

Indicate your agreement with each item	**(1–7)**
I lead a purposeful and meaningful life	
My social relationships are supportive and rewarding	
I am engaged and interested in my daily activities	
I actively contribute to the happiness and well-being of others	
I am competent and capable in the activities that are important to me	
I am a good person and live a good life	
I am optimistic about my future	
People respect me	
Total score:	_____

The Flourishing Scale was developed by Diener, E., Wirtz, D., Tov, W., Kim-Prieto, C., Choi, D., Oishi, S., & Biswas-Diener, R. (2010). New measures of well-being: Flourishing and positive and negative feelings. *Social Indicators Research*, *39*, 247–266.

Recovery Resilience Practice Scale

Date: ______________

Over the past week indicate the frequency of your Recovery Resilience Practice. Check the description that most closely reflects your practice: never, hardly ever, occasionally, or regularly.

Frequency of Recovery Resilience Practice	Never	Hardly Ever	Occasionally	Regularly
Recognize I-System Activity				
Mapping				
Sensory Awareness				
Recognize Requirements				
Defuse Depressor Storylines				
Defuse Fixer Storylines				
Experience the Shift				

Session 4 Client Handouts

EXERCISE 4.1

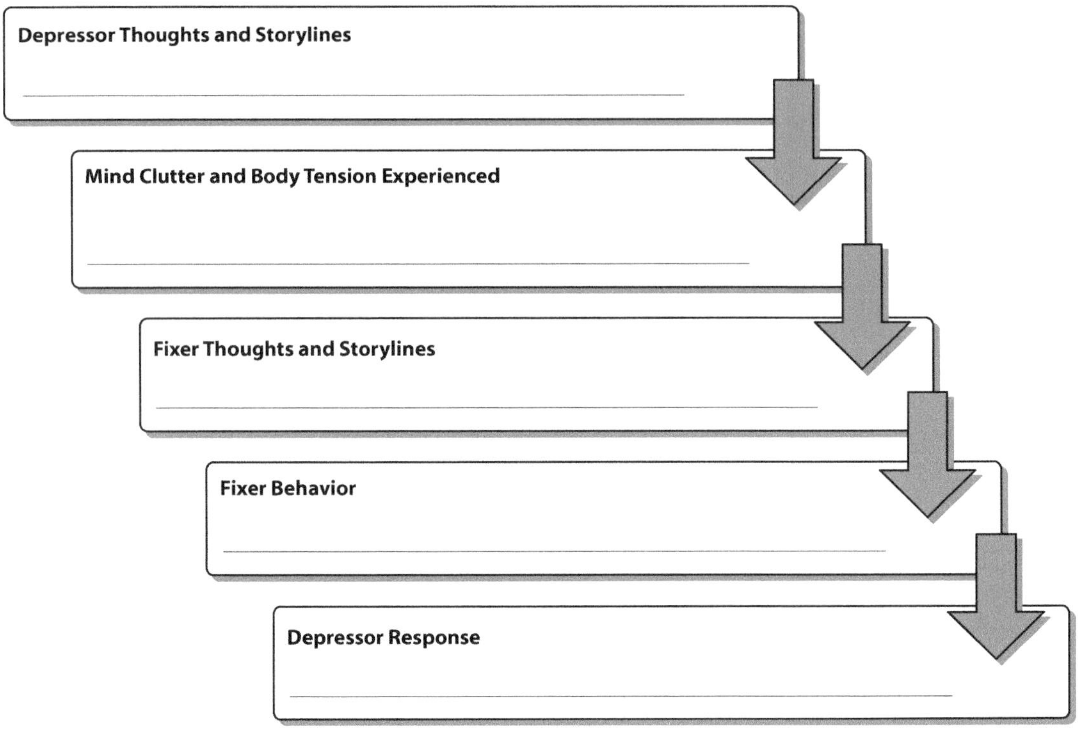

EXERCISE 4.2

Write down in the space below how your Depressor–Fixer Cycle has interfered with your life. Try to write down specific examples.

EXERCISE 4.3

Write down in the space below the role the Depressor–Fixer Cycle has played in your addiction.

EXERCISE 4.4

Goal	Requirements	Depressor Storylines	Fixer Storylines

EXERCISE 4.5

Recovery Resilience Journal

	Addicted Mode Warning Signs	Requirements	Depressor/ Fixer Activity	Recovery Resilience Practice
Self				
Others				
The World				

Homework for Session Four

Recovery Resilience Practice

- Do **Mapping** related to any high-risk situation or troubling experience.
- **Recognize I-System** Activity**.**
- Practice **Sensory Awareness.**
- **Recognize Requirements**.
- **Defuse Depressor Storylines.**
- **Defuse Fixer Storylines.**
- **Experience the Shift.**
- Recognize your **Depressor–Fixer Cycle** in activities of daily living
- Complete your Recovery Resilience Journal daily.

Complete the following:

Addicted Mode Warning Signs: Use the template and write down, in the space provided, your addicted mode warning signs for the past week. Try and be as comprehensive as possible.

Flourishing Scale: Complete the scale calculate your score, from 1 to 7, for each question over the past week or two.

Recovery Resilience Practice Scale: Complete the scale and calculate and write down the frequency of your Recovery Resilience Skills practice. Indicate whether it was never, hardly ever, occasionally, or regularly.

Addicted Mode Warning Signs

Date: ______________

Over the past week write down any addicted mode warning signs you noticed in each of your life dimensions

	Addicted Mode Warning Signs
Self	
Others	
The World	

Flourishing Scale

Date: ____________

Below are 8 statements with which you may agree or disagree. Using the 1–7 scale below, indicate your agreement with each item by indicating that response for each statement.

- 7 – Strongly agree
- 6 – Agree
- 5 – Slightly agree
- 4 – Neither agree nor disagree
- 3 – Slightly disagree
- 2 – Disagree
- 1 – Strongly disagree

Indicate your agreement with each item	**(1–7)**
I lead a purposeful and meaningful life	
My social relationships are supportive and rewarding	
I am engaged and interested in my daily activities	
I actively contribute to the happiness and well-being of others	
I am competent and capable in the activities that are important to me	
I am a good person and live a good life	
I am optimistic about my future	
People respect me	
Total score:	_____

The Flourishing Scale was developed by Diener, E., Wirtz, D., Tov, W., Kim-Prieto, C., Choi, D., Oishi, S., & Biswas-Diener, R. (2010). New measures of well-being: Flourishing and positive and negative feelings. *Social Indicators Research*, *39*, 247–266.

Recovery Resilience Practice Scale

Date: ____________

Over the past week indicate the frequency of your Recovery Resilience Practice. Check the description that most closely reflects your practice: never, hardly ever, occasionally, or regularly.

Frequency of Recovery Resilience Practice	Never	Hardly Ever	Occasionally	Regularly
Recognize I-System Activity				
Mapping				
Sensory Awareness				
Recognize Requirements				
Defuse Depressor Storylines				
Defuse Fixer Storylines				
Experience the Shift				

Session 5 Client Handouts

EXERCISE 5.1

High-Risk Situation/Trigger	How do I Act

EXERCISE 5.2

Situation Map

Description of body tension: ______________________________

EXERCISE 5.3

Requirements for Self

EXERCISE 5.4

Situation/Trigger	How do I act

EXERCISE 5.5

Situation Map

Description of body tension: ______________________________

EXERCISE 5.6

Requirements for Others

EXERCISE 5.7

Situation/Trigger	How do I act

EXERCISE 5.8

Situation Map

Description of body tension: ______________________________

EXERCISE 5.9

Requirements for the World

EXERCISE 5.10

Mind–Body Map (Troubling Situation)

Description of body tension: ______________________________

EXERCISE 5.11

Requirement	Depressor Storyline(s)	Fixer Storyline(s)

EXERCISE 5.12

	Addicted Mode Warning Signs	Requirements	Depressor/Fixer Activity	Recovery Resilience Practice
Self				
Others				
The World				

Homework for Session Five

Recovery Resilience Practice

- Do **Mapping** related to any high-risk situation or troubling experience.
- **Recognize I-System** Activity.
- Practice **Sensory Awareness.**
- **Recognize Requirements.**
- **Defuse Depressor Storylines.**
- **Defuse Fixer Storylines.**
- **Experience the Shift.**
- Recognize your **Depressor–Fixer Cycle** in activities of daily living.
- Complete your Recovery Resilience Journal daily.

Complete the following:

Addicted Mode Warning Signs: Use the template and write down, in the space provided, your addicted mode warning signs for the past week. Try and be as comprehensive as possible.

Flourishing Scale: Complete the scale and calculate your score, from 1 to 7, for each question over the past week or two.

Recovery Resilience Practice Scale: Complete the scale and calculate and write down the frequency of your Recovery Resilience Skills practice. Indicate whether it was never, hardly ever, occasionally, or regularly.

Addicted Mode Warning Signs

Date: ____________

Over the past week write down any addicted mode warning signs you noticed in each of your life dimensions

	Addicted Mode Warning Signs
Self	
Others	
The World	

Flourishing Scale

Date: ____________

Below are 8 statements with which you may agree or disagree. Using the 1–7 scale below, indicate your agreement with each item by indicating that response for each statement.

- 7 – Strongly agree
- 6 – Agree
- 5 – Slightly agree
- 4 – Neither agree nor disagree
- 3 – Slightly disagree
- 2 – Disagree
- 1 – Strongly disagree

Indicate your agreement with each item	**(1–7)**
I lead a purposeful and meaningful life	
My social relationships are supportive and rewarding	
I am engaged and interested in my daily activities	
I actively contribute to the happiness and well-being of others	
I am competent and capable in the activities that are important to me	
I am a good person and live a good life	
I am optimistic about my future	
People respect me	
Total score:	______

The *Flourishing Scale* was developed by Diener, E., Wirtz, D., Tov, W., Et al. (2010). New measures of well-being: Flourishing and positive and negative feelings. *Social Indicators Research*, *39*, 247–266.

Recovery Resilience Practice Scale

Date: ______________

Over the past week indicate the frequency of your Recovery Resilience Practice. Check the description that most closely reflects your practice: never, hardly ever, occasionally, or regularly.

Frequency of Recovery Resilience Practice	**Never**	**Hardly Ever**	**Occasionally**	**Regularly**
Recognize I-System Activity				
Mapping				
Sensory Awareness				
Recognize Requirements				
Defuse Depressor Storylines				
Defuse Fixer Storylines				
Defuse Requirements				
Experience the Shift				

Session 6 Client Handouts

EXERCISE 6.1

Recovery Resilience Analysis Map for Self

Self

EXERCISE 6.2

I-System Activity for Self

Requirements	
Depressor	
Fixer	

EXERCISE 6.3

Recovery Resilience Analysis Map for Others

Others

EXERCISE 6.4

I-System Activity for Others

Requirements	
Depressor	
Fixer	

EXERCISE 6.5

Recovery Resilience Analysis Map for the World

World

EXERCISE 6.6

I-System Activity for the World

Requirements	
Depressor	
Fixer	

EXERCISE 6.7

Recovery Resilience Analysis Synopsis

	Requirements	Depressor	Fixer
Self			
Others			
World			

Homework for Session Six

Recovery Resilience Practice

- Do **Mapping** related to any high-risk situation or troubling experience.
- **Recognize I-System** Activity.
- Practice **Sensory Awareness.**
- **Recognize Requirements.**
- **Defuse Depressor Storylines.**
- **Defuse Fixer Storylines.**
- **Experience the Shift.**
- Recognize your **Depressor–Fixer Cycle** in activities of daily living.
- Complete your Recovery Resilience Journal daily.

Complete the following:

Addicted Mode Warning Signs: Use the template and write down, in the space provided, your addicted mode warning signs for the past week. Try and be as comprehensive as possible.

Flourishing Scale: Complete the scale and calculate your score, from 1 to 7, for each question over the past week or two.

Recovery Resilience Practice Scale: Complete the scale and calculate and write down the frequency of your Recovery Resilience Skills practice. Indicate whether it was never, hardly ever, occasionally, or regularly.

Addicted Mode Warning Signs

Date: ______________

Over the past week write down any addicted mode warning signs you noticed in each of your life dimensions

	Addicted Mode Warning Signs
Self	
Others	
The World	

Flourishing Scale

Date: _____________

Below are 8 statements with which you may agree or disagree. Using the 1–7 scale below, indicate your agreement with each item by indicating that response for each statement.

- 7 – Strongly agree
- 6 – Agree
- 5 – Slightly agree
- 4 – Neither agree nor disagree
- 3 – Slightly disagree
- 2 – Disagree
- 1 – Strongly disagree

Indicate your agreement with each item	**(1–7)**
I lead a purposeful and meaningful life	
My social relationships are supportive and rewarding	
I am engaged and interested in my daily activities	
I actively contribute to the happiness and well-being of others	
I am competent and capable in the activities that are important to me	
I am a good person and live a good life	
I am optimistic about my future	
People respect me	
Total score:	______

The *Flourishing Scale* was developed by Diener, E., Wirtz, D., Tov, W., Kim-Prieto, C., Choi, D., Oishi, S., & Biswas-Diener, R. (2010). New measures of well-being: Flourishing and positive and negative feelings. *Social Indicators Research*, *39*, 247–266.

Recovery Resilience Practice Scale

Date: ____________

Over the past week indicate the frequency of your Recovery Resilience Practice. Check the description that most closely reflects your practice: never, hardly ever, occasionally, or regularly.

Frequency of Recovery Resilience Practice	Never	Hardly Ever	Occasionally	Regularly
Recognize I-System Activity				
Mapping				
Sensory Awareness				
Recognize Requirements				
Defuse Depressor Storylines				
Defuse Fixer Storylines				
Defuse Requirements				
Experience the Shift				

References

Ahmed. S. H., & Pickards, H. (Eds.) (2019). *The Routledge Handbook of the Philosophy and Science of Addiction*. Routledge.

American Psychiatric Association. (2013). *Diagnostic and Statistical Manual of Mental Disorders*. 5th ed. American Psychiatric Association.

Andersen, S. M., & Chen, S. (2002). The relational self: An interpersonal social-cognitive theory. *Psychological Review, 109*, 619–645.

Andreu, M., Balcells-Olivero, M., Alcaraz, N., Marco, O., Bueno, L., Gual, A., & Barrio, P. (2024). Destination matters more: relapse following hospital-based treatment of substance use disorders with and without co-occurring disorders. *Journal of Dual Diagnosis, 20*(2), 111–121. https://doi.org/10.1080/15504263.2024.2311634.

Arp, R., Smith, B., & Spear, A. (2015). *Building Ontologies with Basic Formal Ontology*. MIT Press.

Austin, J.L. (1975). *How To Do Things With Words*. 2nd ed. Harvard University Press.

Badenoch, B. (2017). *The Heart of Trauma: Healing the Embodied Brain in the Context of Relationships*. Norton.

Baer, R. A. (2003). Mindfulness training as a clinical intervention: A conceptual and empirical review. *Clinical Psychology: Science and Practice, 10*, 125–143.

Baker, T. B., Piper, M. E., McCarthy, D. E., Majeskie, M. R., & Fiore, M. C. (2003). Addiction motivation reformulated: An affective processing model of negative reinforcement. *Psychological Review, 111*, 33–51.

Barber, J. G., & Crisp, B. R. (1995). Social support and prevention of relapse following treatment for alcohol abuse. *Research on Social Work Practice, 5*(3), 283–296.

Baumeister, R. F. (2001). Ego depletion and self-control failure: An energy model of the self's executive function. *Self and Identity, 1*, 129–136.

Bayne, T., & Montague, M. (Eds.) (2011). *Cognitive Phenomenology*. Oxford University Press.

Beaulieu, M., Tremblay, J., Baudry, C., Pearson, J., & Bertrand, K. (2021). A systematic review and meta-analysis of the efficacy of the long-term treatment and support of substance use disorders. *Social Science & Medicine, 285,* 114289.

Beck, A. T. (1976). *Cognitive Therapy and the Emotional Disorders.* International Universities Press.

Bell, S., Carter, A., Mathews, R., et al. (2014). Views of addiction neuroscientists and clinicians on the clinical impact of a "Brain Disease Model of Addiction." *Neuroethics, 7,* 19–27. http://doi.org/10.1007/s12152-013-9177-9.

Block, S. H. (1987). Psychotherapy of the individual with brain injury. *Brain Injury, 1*(2), 203–206. https://doi.org/10.3109/02699058709034459.

Block, S. H., & Block, C. B. (2002). *Bridging the I-System: Unifying Spirituality and Behavior.* White Cloud Press.

Block, S. H., & Block, C. B. (2007). *Come to Your Senses: Demystifying the Mind–Body Connection.* 2nd ed. Atria Books/Beyond Words Publishing.

Block, S. H., & Du Plessis, G. (2018). *The Mind–Body Bridging Substance Abuse Program Training Manual.* I-Systems Inc. [unpublished training manual].

Block, S. H., Block, C., & Du Plessis, G. (2016). *Mind–Body Workbook for Addiction: Effective Tools for Relapse Prevention and Recovery.* New Harbinger.

Block, S. H., Block, C. B., Tollefson, D., & Du Plessis, G. (2020). *Social Unrest: Resolving the Dichotomies of You/Me and Us/Them.* Utah State University.

Boss, M. (1983). *The Existential Foundations of Medicine and Psychology.* Jason Aronson.

Bowen, S., Chawla, N., & Marlatt, G. A. (2011). *Mindfulness-Based Relapse Prevention for Addictive Behaviors: A Clinician's Guide.* Guilford Press.

Bowen, S., Chawla, N., Grow, J., & Marlatt, G. A. (2021). *Mindfulness-based Relapse Prevention for Addictive Behaviors.* 2nd ed. Guilford Press.

Bowen, S., Witkiewitz, K., Clifasefi, S. L., Grow, J., Chawla, N., Hsu, S. H., ... & Larimer, M. E. (2014). Relative efficacy of mindfulness-based relapse prevention, standard relapse prevention, and treatment as usual for substance use disorders: a randomized clinical trial. *JAMA Psychiatry, 71*(5), 547–556.

Bradizza, C. M., Stasiewicz, P. R., & Paas, N. D. (2006). Relapse to alcohol and drug use among individuals diagnosed with co-occurring mental health and substance use disorders: a review. *Clinical Psychology Review, 26*(2), 162–178.

Bradshaw, J. (2005). *Healing the Shame that Binds You.* Health Communications Inc.

Breslin, F. C., Zack, M., & McMain, S. (2002). An information-processing analysis of mindfulness: Implications for relapse prevention in the treatment of substance abuse. *Clinical Psychology: Science and Practice*, *9*(3), 275.

Brewer, D. D., Catalano, R. F., Haggerty, K., Gainey, R. R., & Fleming, C. B. (1998). A meta-analysis of predictors of continued drug use during and after treatment for opiate addiction. *Addiction, 93*, 73–92.

Brewer, J. (2017). *The Craving Mind: From Cigarettes to Smartphones to Love – Why We Get Hooked and How We Can Break Bad Habits*. Yale University Press.

Brewin C. R., Gregory J. D., Lipton M., & Burgess N. (2010). Intrusive images in psychological disorders: Characteristics, neural mechanisms, and treatment implications. *Psychology Review, 117*(1), 210–232.

Brown, S. A., Goldman, M. S., & Christiansen, B. A. (1985). Do alcohol expectancies mediate drinking patterns of adults? *Journal of Consulting and Clinical Psychology, 53*, 512–519.

Brown, T. G., Seraganian, P., Tremblay, J., & Annis, H. (2002). Process and outcome changes with relapse prevention versus 12-Step aftercare programs for substance abusers. *Addiction, 97*(6), 677–689.

Butler, D. C. (2003). *Western Mysticism: Augustine, Gregory and Bernard on Contemplation and the Contemplative Life*. Dover.

Carnes, P. (2008). *Recovery Start Kit: The First 130 Days* (Bundle). Gentle Path Press.

Carroll, H., & Lustyk, M. K. B. (2018). Mindfulness-based relapse prevention for substance use disorders: effects on cardiac vagal control and craving under stress. *Mindfulness*, *9*(2), 488–499.

Chalmers, D. J. (Ed.) (2002). *Philosophy of Mind: Classical and Contemporary Readings*. Oxford University Press

Chaney, E. R., O'Leary, M. R., & Marlatt, G. A. (1978). Skill training with alcoholics. *Journal of Consulting and Clinical Psychology, 46*, 1092–1104.

Clark, A. (2014). *Mindware: An Introduction to the Philosophy of Cognitive Science*. Oxford University Press.

Clarke, P. B., Lewis, T. F., Myers, J. E., Henson, R. A., & Hill, B. (2020). Wellness, emotion regulation, and relapse during substance use disorder treatment. *Journal of Counseling & Development, 98*(1), 17–28.

Cloud, W., & Granfield, R. (2004). *A life course perspective on exiting addiction: The relevance of recovery capital in treatment.* NAD Publication (Nordic Council for Alcohol and Drug Research) *44*, 185–202.

Cohen, E. (2021). *Cognitive Behavior Interventions for Self-Defeating Thoughts: Helping Clients to Overcome the Tyranny of "I Can't"*. Routledge.

Colvin, C. R., Block, J., & Funder, D. C. (1995). Overly positive self-evaluations and personality: Negative implications for mental health. *Journal of Personality and Social Psychology, 68*(6), 1152–1162

Connors, G. J., Maisto, S. A., & Zywiak, W. H. (1996). Extensions of relapse predictors beyond high-risk situations: Understanding relapse in the broader context of post-treatment functioning. *Addiction, 91*(Suppl.), 173–189.

Connors, G. J., Tarbox, A. R., & Faillace, L. A. (1993). Changes in alcohol expectancies and drinking behavior among treated problem drinkers. *Journal of Studies on Alcohol, 54*, 676–683.

Cowdrey, F. A., Lomax, C., Gregory, J. D., & Barnard, P. J. (2017). Could a unified theory of cognition and emotion further the transdiagnostic perspective? A critical analysis using interacting cognitive subsystems as a case example. *Psychopathology Review, 4*(3), 377–399.

Creswell, J. D., Way, B. M., Eisenberger, N. I., & Lieberman, M. D. (2007). Neural correlates of dispositional mindfulness during affect labeling. *Psychosomatic Medicine, 69*(6), 560–565. https://doi.org/10.1097/PSY.0b013e3180f6171f.

Crocker, J., & Wolfe, T. (2001). Contingencies of self-worth. *Psychological Review, 108*, 593–623

Csiernick, R. C., & Troller, J. (2002). Evaluating the effectiveness of a relapse prevention group. *Journal of Social Work Practice in the Addictions, 2*(2), 29–37.

Curry, S., Marlatt, G. A., & Gordon, J. R. (1987). Abstinence violation effect: Validation of an attributional construct with smoking cessation. *Journal of Consulting and Clinical Psychology, 55*, 145–149.

Daley, D. C., & Marlatt, G. A. (2006). *Overcoming Your Alcohol or Drug Problem: Effective Recovery Strategies*. 2nd ed. Oxford University Press.

Danielian, J., & Gianotti, P. (2012). *Listening with Purpose: Entry Points into Shame and Narcissistic Vulnerability*. Jason Aronson.

Danielian, J., & Gianotti, P. (2017). *Uncovering the Resilient Core: A Workbook on the Treatment of Narcissistic Defenses, Shame, and Emerging Authenticity*. Routledge.

De Beauvoir, S. (1948). *The Ethics of Ambiguity*, trans. B. Frechtman. Philosophical Library.

Dennett, D. C. (1991). *Consciousness Explained*. Little Brown.

Dennett, D. C. (1996). *Kinds of Mind*. Norton.

Dennett, D. C., (2005). *Sweet Dreams: Philosophical Obstacles to a Science of Consciousness*. MIT Press.

Dennis, M. L., Scott, C.K., Funk, R., & Foss, M.A. (2005). The duration and correlates of addiction treatment careers. *Journal of Substance Abuse Treatment, 28*, S51–S62.

DiClemente, C. C., Holmgren, M. A., & Rounsaville, D. (2011). Relapse prevention and recycling in addiction. In B. Johnson (Ed.) *Addiction Medicine: Science and Practice* (pp. 765–782). Springer.

Diener, E., Wirtz, D., Tov, W., Kim-Prieto, C., Choi, D., Oishi, S., & Biswas-Diener, R. (2010). New measures of well-being: Flourishing and positive and negative feelings. *Social Indicators Research, 39*, 247–266.

Donovan, D. M. (1996). Assessment issues and domains in the prediction of relapse. *Addiction 91*, S29–S36.

Douaihy, A., Stowell, K. R., Park, T. W., & Daley, D. C. (2007). Relapse prevention: Clinical strategies for substance use disorders. In K. A. Witkiewitz & G. A. Marlatt (Eds.) *Therapist's Guide to Evidence-based Relapse Prevention* (pp. 37–71). Elsevier Academic Press.

Du Plessis, G. (2014). An integral ontology of addiction: A multiple object existing as a continuum of ontological complexity. *Journal of Integral Theory and Practice, 9*(1), 38–54.

Du Plessis, G. (2018). *An Integral Foundation for Addiction Treatment: Beyond the Biopsychosocial Model*. Integral Publishers.

Du Plessis, G. (2019a). "Incompatible knots" in harm reduction: A philosophical analysis. In T. Waetjen (Ed.) *Opioids in South Africa: Towards a Policy of Harm Reduction*. Human Sciences Research Council Press.

Du Plessis, G. (2019b). An existential perspective on addiction treatment: A logic-based therapy case study. *International Journal of Philosophical Practice, 5*(1), 1–32.

Du Plessis, G. (2022). Philosophy as a way of life for addiction recovery: A logic-based therapy case study. *International Journal of Applied Philosophy, 35*(1), 68–87.

Du Plessis, G. (2023). The integrated metatheoretical model of addiction. In E. Ermagan (Ed.) *Current Trends in Addiction Psychology*. Cambridge Scholars Publishing.

Du Plessis, G. (2024). The utility of Friedrich Nietzsche's philosophy for philosophical counseling. *International Journal of Philosophical Practice, 10*(1), 141–157.

Du Plessis, G., Webb, K., & Tollefson, D. (2021). *Resilient Mind Skills Workbook.* Utah State University.

Du Plessis, G., Tollefson, D. R., Weathers, R., & Webb, K. G. (2024). *Building Recovery Resilience: Addiction Recovery and Relapse Prevention Workbook – An I-System Model Application.* Cambridge University Press.

Earley, P. C. (1994). Self or group? Cultural effects of training on self-efficacy and performance. *Administrative Science Quarterly, 39*, 89–117.

Edwards, G. (1987). Book review of Relapse Prevention, edited by G. Alan Marlatt and J.R. Gordon. *British Journal of Addiction, 82*, 319–323.

Ehlers, C. L. (1992). The new physics of chaos: Can it help us understand the effects of alcohol? *Alcohol Health & Research World, 16*, 169–176.

Ehring T., & Watkins E. R. (2008). Repetitive negative thinking as a transdiagnostic process. *International Journal of Cognitive Therapy, 1*(3), 192–205.

Einstein, S. (1994). Relapse revisited: Failure by whom and what? *International Journal of Addictions 29*, 409–413.

Ellis, A. (1962). *Reason and Emotion in Psychotherapy.* Citadel Press.

Feder, A., Nestler, E. J., Westphal, M., & Charney, D. S. (2010). Psychobiological mechanisms of resilience to stress. In J. W. Reich, A. J. Zautra & J. S. Hall (Eds.) *Handbook of Adult Resilience* (pp. 35–54). Springer.

Fletcher, L., & Hayes, S. (2005). Relational frame theory, acceptance and commitment therapy, and a functional analytic definition of mindfulness. *Journal of Rational-Emotive and Cognitive-Behavior Therapy, 23*, 315–336.

Fleury, M. J., Djouini, A., Huỳnh, C., Tremblay, J., Ferland, F., Ménard, J. M., & Belleville, G. (2016). Remission from substance use disorders: A systematic review and meta-analysis. *Drug and Alcohol Dependence, 168*, 293–306.

Flores, P. J. (1997). *Group Psychotherapy with Addicted Populations: An Integration of Twelve-step and Psychodynamic Theory.* The Haworth Press.

Fodor, J. A. (1975). *The Language of Thought.* Crowell.

Fodor, J. A. (1998). *Concepts: Where Cognitive Science Went Wrong.* Oxford University Press.

Fodor, J. A. (2008). *LOT 2: The Language of Thought Revisited.* Oxford University Press.

Foote, J., Wilkens, C., & Kosanke, N. (2014). *Beyond Addiction: A Guide for Families.* Scribner.

Frankl, V. (1953). *Man's Search for Meaning.* Pocket Books.

Frankl, V. (1969). *The Will to Meaning: Foundations and Applications of Logotherapy*. New American Library.

Gallagher, S. (2011). Embodiment and phenomenal qualities: An enactive interpretation. *Philosophical Topics, 39*(1), 1–14.

Gire, J. T. (2002). A cross-national study of motives for drinking alcohol. *Substance Use and Misuse, 37*, 215–223.

Gorski, T. (1995). *Relapse Prevention Therapy Workbook: Managing Core Personality and Lifestyle Issues*. Herald House.

Gorski, T. T. (2009). *Passages Through Recovery: An Action Plan for Preventing Relapse*. Simon and Schuster.

Gossop, M., Green, L., Phillips, G., & Bradley, B. P. (1989). Lapse, relapse, and survival among opiate addicts after treatment: A prospective follow-up study. *British Journal of Psychiatry, 154*, 348–353.

Greenfield, S., Hufford, M., Vagge, L., et al. (2000). The relationship of self-efficacy expectancies to relapse among alcohol dependent men and women: A prospective study. *Journal of Studies on Alcohol, 61*, 345–351.

Greeson, J., Garland, E. L., & Black, D. (2014). Mindfulness: A transtherapeutic approach for transdiagnostic mental processes. In A. Ie, C. T. Ngnoumen & E. J. Langer (Eds.) *The Wiley-Blackwell Handbook of Mindfulness*. Wiley-Blackwell.

Grella, C. E. (2003). Effects of gender and diagnosis on addiction history, treatment utilization, and psychosocial functioning among a dually-diagnosed sample in drug treatment. *Journal of Psychoactive Drugs, 35*(Suppl. 1), 169–179.

Groves, P., & Farmer, R. (1994). Buddhism and addictions. *Addictions Research, 2*, 183–194.

Gwaltney, C. J., Shiffman, S., Balabanis, M. H., & Paty, J. A. (2005). Dynamic self-efficacy and outcome expectancies: Prediction of smoking lapse and relapse. *Journal of Abnormal Psychology, 114*(4):, 661–675.

Hadot, P. (1992). Reflections on the notion of the 'cultivation of the self'. In *Michel Foucault, Philosopher*, trans. Timothy Armstrong. Harvester.

Hadot, P. (1995). *Philosophy as a Way of Life: Spiritual Exercises from Socrates to Foucault*, trans. Michael Chase. Blackwell.

Hadot, P. (2002). *What is Ancient Philosophy?*, trans. Michael Chase. Harvard University Press.

Hastings, J., Cox, S., West, R., & Notley, C. (2020). Addiction ontology: Applying basic formal ontology in the addiction domain. *Qeios*. https://doi.org/10.32388/HZHJIP.

Havermans, R. C., & Jansen, A. T. (2003). Increasing the efficacy of cue exposure treatment in preventing relapse of addictive behavior. *Addictive Behaviors, 28*(5), 989–994.

Hayes, S. C. (2003). Buddhism and acceptance and commitment therapy. *Cognitive and Behavioral Practice, 9*(1), 58–66.

Hayes, S. C., Strosahl K., & Wilson, K. G. (1999). *Acceptance and Commitment Therapy: An Experiential Approach to Behavior Change.* Guilford Press.

Hayes, S. C., Strosahl, K. D., & Wilson, K. G. (2012). *Acceptance and Commitment Therapy: The Process and Practice of Mindful Change*. 2nd ed. Guilford Press.

Heather, N. (1998). A conceptual framework for explaining drug addiction. *Journal of Psychopharmacology, 12*(1), 3–7. https://doi.org/10.1177/026988119801200101.

Heather, N. (2017). Addiction as a form of akrasia. In N. Heather & G. Segal (Eds.) *Addiction and Choice: Rethinking the Relationship* (pp. 133–150). Oxford University Press.

Heather, N. (2020). The concept of akrasia as the foundation for a dual systems theory of addiction. *Behavioural Brain Research, 390*, 112666. https://doi.org/10.1016/j.bbr.2020.112666.

Heaton, K., Merlo, L. J., Roche, B. T., & Puga, F. (2023). Relapse prevention and prediction strategies in substance use disorder: A scoping review. *Journal of Addictions Nursing, 34*(2), 146–157.

Hill, K. (2008). A strengths-based framework for social policy: Barriers and possibilities. *Journal of Policy Practice, 7*(2–3), 106–121.

Ho, S. S., & Nakamura, Y. (2017). Healing dysfunctional identity: Bridging mind-body intervention to brain systems. *Journal of Behavioral and Brain Science, 7*, 137–164.

Horney, K. (1950). *Neurosis and Human Growth.* Norton.

Hser, Y. I., Anglin, M. D., Grella, C., Longshore, D., & Prendergast, M. L. (1997). Drug treatment careers: A conceptual framework and existing research findings. *Journal of Substance Abuse Treatment, 14*, 543–558.

Hser, Y., Hoffman, V., Grella, C. E., & Anglin, M. D. (2001). A 33-year follow-up of narcotics addicts. *Archives of General Psychiatry, 58*, 503–508.

Hursthouse, R. (2001). *On Virtue Ethics.* Oxford University Press.

Irvin, J. E., Bowers, C. A., Dunn, M. E., & Wang, M. C. (1999). Efficacy of relapse prevention: A meta-analytic review. *Journal of Consulting and Clinical Psychology, 67*, 563–570.

Jones, B. T., & McMahon, J. (1996). A comparison of positive and negative alcohol expectancy value and their multiplicative composite as predictors of post-treatment abstinence survivorship. *Addiction, 91*, 89–99.

Jones, B. T., Corbin, W., & Fromme, K. (2001). A review of expectancy theory and alcohol consumption. *Addiction, 96*, 57–72.

Kabat-Zinn, J. (2003). Mindfulness-based interventions in context: Past, present, and future. *Clinical Psychology: Science and Practice, 10*(2), 144–156.

Kabisa, E., Biracyaza, E., Habagusenga, J. D. A., & Umubyeyi, A. (2021). Determinants and prevalence of relapse among patients with substance use disorders: case of Icyizere Psychotherapeutic Centre. *Substance Abuse Treatment, Prevention, and Policy, 16*, 1–12.

Kadden, R.M. (1996). Commentary on replications of Marlatt's taxonomy: Is Marlatt's relapse taxonomy reliable or valid? *Addiction, 91*, S139–S145.

Kargin, M., & Hicdurmaz, D. (2020). Psychoeducation program for substance use disorder: Effect on relapse rate, social functioning, perceived wellness, and coping. *Journal of Psychosocial Nursing and Mental Health Services, 58*(8), 39–47.

Kashdan, T. B., & Rottenberg, J. (2010). Psychological flexibility as a fundamental aspect of health. *Clinical Psychology Review, 30*(11), 865–878.

Kaufman, W. (Ed.) (1997). *Marcus Aurelius Meditations.* Dover Publications.

Kelly, J. F., Humphreys, K., & Ferri, M. (2020) Alcoholics Anonymous and other 12-step programs for alcohol use disorder. *Cochrane Database of Systematic Reviews, 3*, CD012880. https://doi.org/10.1002/14651858.CD012880.pub2.

Kendler, K. S. (2009). An historical framework for psychiatric nosology. *Psychological Medicine, 39*(12), 1935–1941. https://doi.org/10.1017/S0033291709005753.

Kenny, A. (1978). *The Aristotelian Ethics: A Study of the Relationship Between the Eudemian and the Nicomachean Ethics of Aristotle.* Clarendon Press.

Khantzian, E. J. (1997). The self-medication hypothesis of substance use disorders: A reconsideration and recent applications. *Harvard Review of Psychiatry, 4*(5), 231–244. https://doi.org/10.3109/10673229709030550.

Khantzian, E. J. (1999). *Treating Addiction as a Human Process.* Jason Aronson.

Kohut, H. (1971). *The Analysis of the Self: A Systematic Approach to the Psychoanalytic Treatment of Narcissistic Personality Disorders.* International University Press.

Kohut, H. (1977). *The Restoration of Self.* International University Press.

Kowalski, J., & Dragan, M. (2019). Cognitive-attentional syndrome: The psychometric properties of the CAS-1 and multi-measure CAS-based clinical diagnosis. *Comprehensive Psychiatry, 91*, 13–21.

Kramer, R. (1995). The birth of client-centered therapy: Carl Rogers, Otto Rank, and "The Beyond". *Journal of Humanistic Psychology, 35*, 54–110.

Kurtz, E., & Ketcham, K. (2002). *The Spirituality of Imperfection: Storytelling and the Search for Meaning.* Bantam Books.

Larimer, M. E., Palmer, R. S., & Marlatt, G. (1999). Relapse prevention: An overview of Marlatt's cognitive-behavioral model. *Alcohol Research & Health, 23*(2),151–160.

Lazarus, R. S., & Folkman, S. (1984). *Stress, Appraisal, and Coping.* Springer.

Leary, M. R., Terry, M. L., Allen, A. B., & Tate, E. B. (2009). The concept of ego threat in social and personality psychology: Is ego threat a viable scientific construct? *Personality and Social Psychology Review, 13*, 151–164.

Levin, J. D. (1995). Psychodynamic treatment of alcohol abuse. In J. P. Barber & P. Crits-Christoph (Eds.) *Dynamic Therapies for Psychiatric Disorders (Axis 293).* Basic Books.

Lewis, M. (2015). *The Biology of Desire: Why Addiction is Not a Disease.* Public Affairs.

Liese, B. S., & Beck, A. T. (2022). *Cognitive-behavioral Therapy of Addictive Disorders.* Guilford Press.

Linehan, M. M., & Kehrer, C. A. (1993). Borderline personality disorder. In D. H. Barlow (Ed.) *Clinical Handbook of Psychological Disorders: A Step-by-Step Treatment Manual.* 2nd ed. (pp. 396–441). Guilford Press.

Linville, P. W. (1985). Self-complexity and affective extremity: Don't put all of your eggs in one cognitive basket. *Social Cognition, 3*(1), 94–120.

Linville, P. W. (1987). Self-complexity as a cognitive buffer against stress-related depression and illness. *Journal of Personality and Social Psychology, 52*, 663–676.

Lipiansky, E. (2008). Critical analysis of assumptions of cognitivism. *Connexions, 89*, 47–61.

Lipschitz, D. L., Kuhn, R., Kinney, A. Y., Donaldson, G. W., & Nakamura, Y. (2013). Reduction in salivary α-amylase levels following a mind-body intervention in cancer survivors: An exploratory study. *Psychoneuroendocrinology, 38*(9), 1521–1531.

Lipschitz, D. L., Kuhn, R., Kinney, A. Y., et al. (2015). An exploratory study of the effects of mind-body interventions targeting sleep on salivary oxytocin levels in cancer survivors. *Integrated Cancer Therapies, 14(*4), 366–380.

Lipschitz, D. L., Olin, J. A., & Nakamura, Y. (2016). A randomized controlled pilot study of a mind-body intervention compared with treatment as usual in the management of insomnia among active-duty military personnel. *European Journal of Integrative Medicine, 8*(5), 769–780.

Litman, G. K., Stapleton, J., Oppenheim, A. N., Peleg, M., & Jackson, P. (1983). Situations related to alcoholism relapse. *British Journal of Addiction, 78*, 381–389.

Litt, M. D., Kadden, R. M., Cooney, N. L., & Kabela, E. (2003). Coping skills and treatment outcomes in cognitive-behavioral and interactional group therapy for alcoholism. *Journal of Consulting and Clinical Psychology, 71*(1), 118–128.

Lutovac, S., Kaasila, R., Petäjäniemi, M., et al. (2024) How does mind–body bridging support professional identity development? *International Journal for Educational and Vocational Guidance, 24*, 151–172. https://doi.org/10.1007/s10775-022-09552-0.

Macaro, A. (2002). Weakness of will, addiction and self-control: Using relapse prevention methods in philosophical counselling. *Practical Philosophy*, 55–63. Corpus ID: 166221034.

Maisto, S. A., Connors, G. J., & Zywiak, W. H. (1996). Section IIA. Replication and extension of Marlatt's taxonomy: Construct validation analyses on the Marlatt typology of relapse precipitants. *Addiction, 91*, 89–97.

Maisto, S. A., Zywiak, W. H., & Connors, G. J. (2006). Course of functioning 1 year following admission for treatment of alcohol use disorders. *Addictive Behaviors, 31*(1), 69–79.

Mansell, W., Harvey, A., Watkins, E. R., & Shafran, R. (2008). Cognitive behavioral processes across psychological disorders: A review of the utility and validity of the transdiagnostic approach. *International Journal of Cognitive Therapy, 1*(3), 181–191.

Markus, H., & Wurf, E. (1987). The dynamic self-concept: A social psychological perspective. *Annual Review of Psychology, 38*, 299–337.

Marlatt, G. A. (1985a). Relapse prevention: Theoretical rationale and overview of the model. In G. A. Marlatt & J. R. Gordon (Eds.) *Relapse Prevention: Maintenance Strategies in the Treatment of Addictive Behaviors.* Guilford Press.

Marlatt, G. A. (1985b). Lifestyle modification. In G. A. Marlatt & J. R. Gordon (Eds.) *Relapse Prevention: Maintenance Strategies in the Treatment of Addictive Behaviors* (pp. 280–348). Guilford Press.

Marlatt, G. A. (1988). Research on behavioral strategies for the prevention of alcohol problems. *Contemporary Drug Problems, 15*, 31–45.

Marlatt, G. A. (1996a). Lest taxonomy become taxidermy: A comment on the relapse replication and extension project. *Addiction, 91*, 147–153.

Marlatt, G. A. (1996b). Taxonomy of high-risk situations for alcohol relapse: Evolution and development of a cognitive-behavioral model of relapse. *Addiction, 91*, 37–50.

Marlatt, G. A., & Donovan, D. M. (Eds.) (2005). *Relapse Prevention: Maintenance Strategies in the Treatment of Addictive Behaviors*. 2nd ed. Guilford Press,

Marlatt, G. A., & George, W. H. (1984). Relapse prevention: Introduction and overview of the model. *British Journal of Addiction, 79*, 261–273.

Marlatt, G. A., & Gordon, J. R. (1980). Determinants of relapse: Implications for the maintenance of behavior change. In P. O. Davidson & S. M. Davidson (Eds.) *Behavior Medicine: Changing Health Lifestyles* (pp. 410–452). Brunner/Mazel.

Marlatt, G. A., & Gordon, J. R. (Eds.) (1985). *Relapse Prevention: Maintenance Strategies in the Treatment of Addictive Behaviors*. Guilford Press.

Marlatt, G. A., & Witkiewitz, K. (2002). Harm reduction approaches to alcohol use: Health promotion, prevention, and treatment. *Addictive Behaviors, 901*, 1–20.

Marlatt, G. A., & Witkiewitz, K. (2005). Relapse prevention for alcohol and drug problems. In *Relapse Prevention: Maintenance Strategies in the Treatment of Addictive Behaviors*. 2nd ed. (pp. 1–44). Guilford Press.

Marlatt, G. A., Baer, J. S., & Quigley, L. A. (1995). Self-efficacy and addictive behaviour. In A. Bandura (Ed.) *Self-Efficacy in Changing Societies* (pp. 289–315). Cambridge University Press.

Maté, G. (2011). *In the Realm of Hungry Ghosts: Closer Encounters with Addiction.* North Atlantic Books.

Max-Neef, M. A. (with Antonio, E., & Hopenhayn, M.) (1991). *Human Scale Development: Conception, Application and Further Reflections.* Apex.

McCarthy, D. E., Curtin, J. J., Piper, M. E., & Baker, T. B. (2010). Negative reinforcement: Possible clinical implications of an integrative model. In J. D. Kassel (Ed.) *Substance Abuse and Emotion* (pp. 15–42). American Psychological Association. https://doi.org/10.1037/12067-001.

McConnell, A. R. (2011). The multiple self- aspects framework: Self-concept representation and its implications. *Personality and Social Psychology Review, 15*, 3–27.

McEvoy, P. M., Nathan, P., & Norton, P. J. (2009). Efficacy of transdiagnostic treatments: A review of published outcome studies and future research directions. *Journal of Cognitive Psychotherapy, 23*(1), 20–33. https://doi.org/10.1891/0889-8391.23.1.20.

McGuire, W. J., & McGuire, C. V. (1980). Salience of handedness in the spontaneous self-concept. *Perceptual and Motor Skills, 50*(1), 3–7.

McGuire, W. J., McGuire, C. V., & Winton, W. (1979). Effects of household sex composition on the salience of one's gender in the spontaneous self-concept. *Journal of Experimental Social Psychology, 15*, 77–90.

McPeak, J. D., Kennedy, B. P., & Gordon, S. M. (1991). Altered states of consciousness therapy: A missing component in alcohol and drug rehabilitation treatment. *Journal of Substance Abuse Treatment, 8*, 75–82.

Melemis, S. M. (2015). Relapse prevention and the five rules of recovery. *The Yale Journal of Biology and Medicine, 88*(3), 325.

Mellinger, J. L., Winder, G. S., Fernandez, A. C., Asefah, H., & Zikmund-Fisher, B. J. (2024). Critical misconceptions and knowledge gaps regarding alcohol cessation and risk of relapse in alcohol-related liver disease patients: A qualitative mental models study. *Journal of Substance Use and Addiction Treatment, 161*, 209292.

Menon, J., & Kandasamy, A. (2018). Relapse prevention. *Indian Journal of Psychiatry, 60* (Suppl. 4), S473–S478.

Mhaidat, I., Taherian, M. R., Nazari, S. S. H., Mosavi-Jarrahi, A., Yeganeh, H., Al-Yateem, N., … & Rahman, S. A. (2023). Effect of cognitive–behavioural therapy on resilience and relapse in adult patients with substance use disorder: a systematic review protocol. *BMJ Open, 13*(5), e067115.

Milby, J. B., Schumacher, J. E., Vuchinich, R. E., Wallace, D., Plant, M. A., Freedman, M. J., et al. (2004). Transitions during effective treatment for cocaine-abusing homeless persons: Establishing abstinence, lapse, and relapse, and reestablishing abstinence. *Psychology of Addictive Behaviors, 18*, 250–256.

Milkman, H. B., & Sunderworth, S. G. (2010). *Craving for Ecstasy and Natural Highs: A Positive Approach to Mood Alteration*. Sage.

Miller, W.R. (1996). What is a relapse? Fifty ways to leave the wagon. *Addiction, 9*, S15–S27.

Miller, W. R., Westerberg, V. S., Harris, R. J., & Tonigan, J. S. (1996). What predicts relapse? Prospective testing of antecedent models. *Addiction, 91*, 155–171.

Mischel, W., & Shoda, Y. (2008). Toward a unifying theory of personality: Integrating dispositions and processing dynamics within the cognitive–affective processing system (CAPS). In O. P. John, R. W. Robins, & L. A. Pervin (Eds.) *Handbook of Personality*. 3rd ed. (pp. 208–241). Guilford Press.

Moe, F. D., Moltu, C., McKay, J. R., Nesvåg, S., & Bjornestad, J. (2022). Is the relapse concept in studies of substance use disorders a 'one size fits all' concept? A systematic review of relapse operationalisations. *Drug and Alcohol Review, 41*(4), 743–758.

Monti, P. M., Rohsenow, D. J., Swift, R. M., Gulliver, S. B., Colby, S. M., Mueller, T. I., ... & Asher, M. K. (2001). Naltrexone and cue exposure with coping and communication skills training for alcoholics: treatment process and 1-year outcomes. *Alcoholism: Clinical and Experimental Research, 25*(11), 1634–1647.

Moos, R. H., & Moos, B. S. (2005). Paths of entry into Alcoholics Anonymous: Consequences for participation and remission. *Alcoholism: Clinical and Experimental Research, 29*(10), 1858–1868.

Moos, R. H., & Moos, B. S. (2006). Rates and predictors of relapse after natural and treated remission from alcohol use disorders. *Addiction, 101*(2), 212–222.

Morf, C. C., & Horvath, S. (2007). Connectionism as metaphor: Toward an integrated, unified conception of self-system and individual differences. *Psychological Inquiry, 18*, 108–113.

Morf, C. C., & Mischel, W. (2012). The self as a psycho-social dynamic processing system: Toward a converging science of selfhood. In M. R. Leary & J. P. Tangney (Eds.) *Handbook of Self and Identity*. 2nd ed. (pp. 21–49). Guilford Press.

Morf, C. C., Torchetti, L., & Schürch, E. (2011). Narcissism from the perspective of the dynamic self-regulatory processing model. In W. K. Campbell & J. D. Miller (Eds.) *The Handbook of Narcissism and Narcissistic Personality Disorder: Theoretical Approaches, Empirical Findings, and Treatment* (pp. 56–70). Wiley.

Mueller, S. E., Petitjean, S., Boening, J., & Wiesbeck, G. A. (2007). The impact of self-help group attendance on relapse rates after alcohol detoxification in a controlled study. *Alcohol and Alcoholism, 42*(2), 108–112.

Nakamura, Y., Lipschitz, D. L., Donaldson, G. W., et al. (2017). Investigating clinical benefits of a novel sleep-focused mind-body program on Gulf War illness symptoms: A randomized controlled trial. *Psychosomatic Medicine, 79*(6), 706–718.

Nakamura, Y., Lipschitz, D. L., Kanarowski, E., et al. (2015). Investigating impacts of incorporating an adjuvant mind-body intervention method into treatment as usual at a community-based substance abuse treatment facility: A pilot randomized controlled study. *SAGE Open, 5*(1), 492–512.

Nakamura, Y., Lipschitz, D. L., Landward, R., Kuhn, R., & West, G. (2011). Two sessions of sleep-focused mind–body bridging improve self-reported symptoms of sleep and PTSD in veterans: A pilot randomized controlled trial. *Journal of Psychosomatic Research, 70*, 335–345.

Narcotics Anonymous World Services, Inc. (1983). *It Works How and Why: The Twelve Steps and Twelve Traditions*. Narcotics Anonymous World Services, Inc.

Nattala, P., Leung, K. S., Nagarajaiah, & Murthy, P. (2010). Family member involvement in relapse prevention improves alcohol dependence outcomes: a prospective study at an addiction treatment facility in India. *Journal of Studies on Alcohol and Drugs, 71*(4), 581–587.

Nietzsche, F. (1974). *The Gay Science*, trans. W. Kaufmann. (p. 270). Vintage Books.

Nietzsche, F. (1992). *Ecce Homo*, trans. R. Hollingdale. Penguin Books. (Original work published 1908).

Nietzsche, F. (2003). *The Joyful Science: With a Prelude in German Rhymes and an Appendix of Songs*, B. Williams (Ed.) Cambridge University Press.

Normann, N., & Morina, N. (2018). The efficacy of metacognitive therapy: a systematic review and meta-analysis. *Frontiers in Psychology, 9*, 2211.

Perls, F. (1969). *In and Out the Garbage Pail.* Real People Press.

Peterson, C., & Seligman, M. E. P. (2004). *Character Strengths and Virtues: A Handbook of Classification.* Oxford University Press.

Pickard, H., & Ahmed, S. (Eds.) (2019). *The Routledge Handbook of Philosophy and Science of Addiction*. Routledge.

Rahbarian, M., & Doosti, P. (2016). Effect of training the communication skills with cognitive-behavioral model to drug dependent couples on communication patterns and recurrent relapse. *Journal of Inflammatory Diseases, 20*(5), e155991.

Reginster, B. (2006). *The Affirmation of Life: Nietzsche on Overcoming Nihilism.* Harvard University Press.

Renaud, J., & McConnell, A. R. (2002). Organization of the self-concept and the suppression of self-relevant thoughts. *Journal of Experimental Social Psychology, 38*(1), 79–86.

Rhodewalt, F., & Agustsdottir, S. (1986). Effects of self-presentation on the phenomenal self. *Journal of Personality and Social Psychology, 50*(1), 47–55.

Rumelhart, D. E., & McClelland, J. L. (1986). *Parallel Distributed Processing: Explorations in the Microstructure of Cognition: Vol. 1. Foundations.* MIT Press.

Russell, B. (1912). *The Problems of Philosophy.* Oxford University Press.

Russell, B. (1918). The philosophy of logical atomism, Lectures 1–2. *The Monist, 28*(4), 495–527.

Ryan, R. M., & Deci, E. L. (2017). *Self-determination Theory: Basic Psychological Needs in Motivation, Development, and Wellness.* Guilford Press.

Scott, C. K., Foss, M. A., & Dennis, M. L. (2005). Pathways in the relapse–treatment–recovery cycle over 3 years. *Journal of Substance Abuse Treatment, 28,* S63–S72.

Segal, Z. V., Williams, J. M. G., & Teasdale, J. D. (2002). *Mindfulness-based Cognitive Therapy for Depression: A New Approach to Preventing Relapse.* Guilford Press.

Shoda, Y., & Mischel, W. (1998). Personality as a stable cognitive–affective activation network: Characteristic patterns of behavior variation emerge from a stable personality structure. In S. Read & L. C. Miller (Eds.) *Connectionist Models of Social Reasoning and Social Behavior* (pp. 175–208). Lawrence Erlbaum.

Showers, C. J., & Zeigler-Hill, V. (2012). Organization of self-knowledge: Features, functions, and flexibility. In M. R. Leary & J. P. Tangney (Eds.) *Handbook of Self and Identity*. 2nd ed. (pp. 105–123). Guilford Press.

Smith, B., & Ceusters, W. (2010). Ontological realism: A methodology for coordinated evolution of scientific ontologies. *Applied Ontology, 5*(3–4), 139–188.

Smolkin, N. (2018). *The Relationship Between Boredom and Relapse in Substance Use Disorder Recovery.* The Wright Institute.

Smuts, J. C. (1926). *Holism and Evolution.* Macmillan.

Solomon, S., Greenberg, J., & Pyszczynski, T. (1991). Terror management theory of self-esteem. In C. R. Snyder & D. R. Forsyth (Eds.) *Handbook of Social and Clinical Psychology: The Health Perspective* (pp. 21–40). Pergamon Press.

Sripada, C. (2022). Impaired control in addiction involves cognitive distortions and unreliable self-control, not compulsive desires and overwhelmed self-control. *Behavioural Brain Research, 418*, 113639.

Steele, C. M. (1988). The psychology of self-affirmation: Sustaining the integrity of the self. In L. Berkowitz (Ed.) *Advances in Experimental Social Psychology* (Vol. 21, pp. 261–302). Academic Press.

Taylor, J. (2021). *Change Your Life's Direction: Break Free from Your Past Inertia and Chart a Better Future.* Rowman & Littlefield Publishers.

Teasdale, J. D. (1993). Emotion and two kinds of meaning: cognitive therapy and applied cognitive science. *Behavior Research and Therapy, 31*(4), 339–354.

Teasdale, J. D. (1999). Emotional processing, three modes of mind and the prevention of relapse in depression. *Behavior Research and Therapy , 37* (Suppl. 1), S53–S77.

Teasdale, J. D., & Barnard, P. J. (1993). *Affect, Cognition and Change: Re-modelling Depressive Thought.* Lawrence Erlbaum Associates.

Teyber, E., McClure, F., & Weathers, R. (2011). Shame and the family: Transmission across generations. In R. Dearing & J. Tangney (Eds.) *Shame in the Therapy Hour.* American Psychological Association Press.

Tollefson, D. R., & Phillips, I. (2015). A mind-body bridging treatment program for domestic violence offenders: Program overview and evaluation results. *Journal of Family Violence, 30*(6), 783–794.

Tollefson, D. R., Webb, K., Shumway, D., Block, H., & Nakamura, Y. (2009). A mind–body approach to domestic violence perpetrator treatment: Program overview and preliminary outcomes. *Journal of Aggression, Maltreatment, and Trauma, 18*(1), 17–45.

Ulman, R. B., & Paul, H. (2006). *The Self Psychology of Addiction and Its Treatment: Narcissus in Wonderland.* Routledge.

VanderWeele, T. J. (2017). On the promotion of human flourishing. *Proceedings of the National Academy of Sciences USA, 31*, 8148–8156.

Vernon, A., & Doyle, K. A. (2017). *Cognitive Behavior Therapies: A Guidebook for Practitioners.* Wiley.

Volkow, N. D., Fowler, J. S., Wang, G. J., & Goldstein, R. Z. (2002). Role of dopamine, the frontal cortex and memory circuits in drug addiction: insight from imaging studies. *Neurobiology of Learning andMemory, 78*(3), 610–624.

Walsh, R. (2011). Lifestyle and mental health. *American Psychologist, 66*(7), 579.

Walton, G. M., Paunesku, D., & Dweck, C. S. (2012). Expandable selves. In M. R. Leary & J. P. Tangney (Eds.) *Handbook of Self and Identity*. 2nd ed. (pp. 141–154). Guilford Press.

Warren, K., Hawkins, R. C., & Sprott, J. C. (2003). Substance abuse as a dynamical disease: Evidence and clinical implications of nonlinearity in a time series of daily alcohol consumption. *Addictive Behaviors, 28*(2):369–374.

Wells, A. (1995). Meta-cognition and worry: A cognitive model of generalised anxiety disorder. *Behavioural and Cognitive Psychotherapy, 23*, 301–320.

Wells, A. (2005). The metacognitive model of GAD: Assessment of meta-worry and relationship with DSM-IV generalized anxiety disorder. *Cognitive Therapy and Research, 29*, 107–121.

Wells, A. (2006). Cognitive therapy case formulation in anxiety disorders. In N. Tarrier (Ed.) *Case Formulation in Cognitive Behaviour Therapy: The Treatment of Challenging and Complex Cases* (pp. 52–80). Routledge.

Wells, A., & Matthews, G. (1994). *Attention and Emotion: A Clinical Perspective.* Erlbaum.

Wells, A., & Matthews, G. (1996). Modelling cognition in emotional disorder: The S-REF model. *Behaviour Research and Therapy, 32*, 867–870.

West, R. (2005). *Theory of Addiction*. Blackwell.

West, R. (2017). *100 Key Facts about Addiction*. Silverback Publishing.

West, R., Christmas, S., Hastings, J., & Michie, S. (2019a). Developing general models and theories of addiction. In S. H. Ahmed & H. Pickards (Eds.) *The Routledge Handbook of the Philosophy and Science of Addiction* (pp. 160–172). Routledge.

West, R., Cox, S., Nortley, C., Du Plessis, G., & Hasting, J. (2024). Achieving consensus, coherence, clarity, and consistency when talking about 'addiction'. *Addiction, 119*(5), 796–798.

West, R., Marsden, J., & Hastings J. (2019b). Addiction theories and constructs: A new series. *Addiction, 114* (6), 955–956. https://doi.org/10.1111/add.14554.

White, W. L. (1996). *Pathways: From the Culture of Addiction to the Culture of Recovery*. Hazelden.

White, W., & Cloud, W. (2008). Recovery Capital: A Primer for Addictions Professionals. *Counselor, 9*(5), 22–27.

Wiers, R. W., Stacy, A. W., Ames, S. L., Noll, J. A., Sayette, M. A., Zack, M., et al. (2002). Implicit and explicit alcohol-related cognitions. *Alcoholism: Clinical and Experimental Research, 26*(1), 129–137.

Wilber, K. (2000). *Integral Psychology: Consciousness, Spirit, Psychology, Therapy.* Shambhala.

Wills, T. A., & Shiffman, S. (1985). Coping and substance use: A conceptual framework. In S. Shiffman & T. A. Wills (Eds.) *Coping and Substance Use.* Academic Press.

Wilson, B. (1976). *Alcoholics Anonymous: The Story of How Many Thousands of Men and Women Have Recovered from Alcoholism.* Alcoholics Anonymous World Services.

Wilson, B. (1987). *Twelve Steps and Twelve Traditions.* Alcoholics Anonymous World Services.

Winhall, J. (2021). *Treating Trauma and Addiction with the Felt Sense Polyvagal Model.* Routledge.

Winkelman, M. (2001). Alternative and traditional medicine approaches for substance abuse programs: A shamanic perspective. *International Journal of Drug Policy, 12,* 337–351.

Winner, N. A. (2021). Bridging the gap: The compatibility of CBT-based approaches with twelve-step programs in the treatment of substance use disorders. *Substance Use & Misuse, 56*(11), 1662–1669.

Witkiewitz, K., & Marlatt, G. A. (2007). Overview of relapse prevention. In *Therapist's Guide to Evidence-Based Relapse Prevention* (pp. 3–17). Academic Press.

Witkiewitz, K., Bowen, S., Douglas, H., & Hsu, S. H. (2013a). Mindfulness-based relapse prevention for substance craving. *Addictive Behaviors, 38*(2), 1563–1571.

Witkiewitz, K., Lustyk, M. K. B., & Bowen, S. (2013b). Retraining the addicted brain: a review of hypothesized neurobiological mechanisms of mindfulness-based relapse prevention. *Psychology of Addictive Behaviors, 27*(2), 351.

Witkiewitz, K., Marlatt, G. A., & Walker, D. (2005). Mindfulness-based relapse prevention for alcohol and substance use disorders. *Journal of Cognitive Psychotherapy, 19*(3), 211–228.

Witkiewitz, K., Warner, K., Sully, B., Barricks, A., Stauffer, C., Thompson, B. L., & Luoma, J. B. (2014). Randomized trial comparing mindfulness-based relapse prevention with relapse prevention for women offenders at a residential addiction treatment center. *Substance Use & Misuse, 49*(5), 536–546.

Xie, H., McHugo G. J., Fox, M. B., & Drake, R. E. (2005). Substance abuse relapse in a ten-year prospective follow-up of clients with mental and substance use disorders. *Psychiatry Services, 56,* 1282–1287.

Yazıcı, A. B., & Bardakçı, M. R. (2023). Factors associated with relapses in alcohol and substance use disorder. *Eurasian Journal of Medicine, 55*, 75–81.

Zaidi, U. (2020). Role of social support in relapse prevention for drug addicts. *International Journal of Innovation, Creativity and Change, 13*(1), 915–924.

Zoja, L. (1989). *Drugs, Addiction and Initiation: The Modern Search for Ritual.* Sigo.

Zywiak, W. H., Connors, G. J., Maisto, S. A., & Westerberg, V. S. (1996). Relapse research and the reasons for drinking questionnaire: A factor analysis of Marlatt's relapse taxonomy. *Addiction, 91*, 121–130.

Index

Printed by Integrated Books International,
United States of America